EVERYMAN, I will go with thee,
and be thy guide,
In thy most need to go by thy side

Note on The Salamander Oasis Trust

POEMS OF THE SECOND WORLD WAR

The Oasis Selection

Editor-in-Chief
Victor Selwyn

Editors
Erik de Mauny, Ian Fletcher, Norman Morris

Advisers
Field Marshal Lord Carver, General Sir John Hackett
Hamish Henderson, William E. Morris

Dent: London and Melbourne
EVERYMAN'S LIBRARY
in association with
THE SALAMANDER OASIS TRUST

First published in Great Britain 1985.
© Selection, introductory material and notes,
The Salamander Oasis Trust 1985

This book is set in 10 on 11 VIP Bembo by
D. P. Media Limited, Hitchin, Hertfordshire.
Printed in Great Britain by
Richard Clay (The Chaucer Press) Ltd,|for
J.M. Dent & Sons Ltd
Aldine House, 33 Welbeck Street, London W1M 8LX.

British Library Cataloguing in Publication Data

Poems of the Second World War : the Oasis
    selection
    I. Selwyn, Victor
    821'.914'08   PR6069.E382/

    ISBN 0-460-10432-2
    ISBN 0-460-01432-3 Pbk

The compilation of this Anthology is the copyright of The
Salamander Oasis Trust. Every endeavour has been made by the Trust
to contact poets, who have been previously published, and their
publishers. Where the Trust has established the holder of copyright of
a specific poem, this has been indicated in Acknowledgements,
together with permission to publish. The Trust retains copyright of
poems first published in its books, *RETURN TO OASIS* (1980) and
FROM OASIS INTO ITALY (1983), and the poems not previously
published in this anthology, except where the poet has written
otherwise. This is also indicated in the Acknowledgements.

Contents

The Poems

Dedication

From earliest times the poet has been war's reporter. In our anthology we have over two hundred named reporters, some with no names, who took part in war and saw and wrote with a poet's eye. They wrote mainly of people. For war is about people, those who survive and those who do not.

Many who did not return were the poets.

This then is their memorial, to live on with their fellows, speaking to generations to come of what men and women did, thought and felt in the War of Nineteen Thirty Nine to Forty Five.

V.S.

In Memory

ALLISON, John Drummond: Lieutenant, East Surrey Regiment *Italy, 2 December 1943*

ALLWOOD, John Brian: Leading Aircraftman, RAFVR *Italy, 30 June 1944*

BOURNE, David: Pilot Officer, 43 Squadron RAFVR *United Kingdom, 5 September 1941*

BRANSON, Clive A.C.: Sergeant, 25th Dragoons *Burma, 25 February 1944*

BURT, William H.: Lieutenant, Highland Light Infantry *Germany, 10 April 1945*

CHAVE, O.C.: Flight Lieutenant, 15 Squadron RAF *Over Europe, 14 February 1943*

DUNKERLEY, William Donald: Lieutenant-Commander RN, HM Submarine *Thames At Sea, 23 July 1940*

DOUGLAS, Keith C.: Captain, Derbyshire Yeomanry★ *Normandy, 9 June 1944*

FOOTTIT, Keith Alan Murray: Flying Officer, 77 Squadron RAFVR *Germany, 21 January 1944*

GOLDSMITH, Anthony M.: Lieutenant, Royal Artillery *North Africa, 24 April 1943*

JARMAIN, William John F.: Major, Royal Artillery *Normandy, 26 June 1944*

KEYES, Sidney A.K.: Lieutenant, Royal West Kent Regiment *North Africa, 29 April 1943*

LEWIS, Alun: Lieutenant, South Wales Borderers *Burma, 5 March 1944*

SPENDER, Richard W.O.: Lieutenant, Parachute Regiment *North Africa, 28 March 1943*

STEWART, Gervase Leslie: Sub-Lieutenant RNVR, Fleet Air Arm, HMS *Goshawk West Indies, 25 August 1941*

STRICK, John Richard: Captain, Royal Ulster Rifles *Italy, 18 February 1944*

THOMPSON, William Frank: Major, Royal Artillery *Bulgaria, 10 June 1944*

WHITE, Alan V.H.: Lieutenant, Royal Artillery *Italy, 12 May 1944*

★ Served with Sherwood Rangers

A Preliminary Note

by General Sir John Hackett

The exercise of choice over what to include in an anthology of war poetry demands prior enquiry into what war poetry *is*.

It would almost certainly not be sensible to seek a tightly exclusive definition, but choice would be impossible without some sort of criterion. The poetry we look for need not be concerned only with experience in battle. It should, however, be such as would be unlikely to be written except in wartime. It is the product of the pressures and tensions, the pangs and passions, the fears and frenzy, the loneliness, excitement, boredom and despair, the disgust, the compassion and the weariness, and all the other stimuli to self-expression which, though they are not uniquely found in wartime, react then upon the human condition with special force. Poetry that could as easily have been written in peace tells us little about the explosive creative urge which develops so strongly in men and women under wartime stress. It is the cry from the heart which is wrung from quite ordinary people by what happens to them in war that we look for, a cry that probably would never have been heard at all in peace. The response to a general invitation to show us work of this sort has been enormous. The question of adjudication upon literary merit and aptness has added hugely to the burden upon editors. Whatever choices are made, however, they must stand up against the general criterion, set out above, that what we put in here must be seen to be the product of experience and emotions which are found at a unique level and in unique combination in wartime.

The Second Word War: an Historical Review

by Field Marshal Lord Carver

The 1939–45 war was more truly a world war than the 1914–18 conflict, known as The Great War until the second one competed for the title. Both started as European conflicts, and were extended to regions beyond Europe and over all the oceans; but the entry of Japan, which was already at war with China, into the arena in 1941, directly involving the USA, which was already indirectly involved through Lend/Lease, made it truly a world war, affecting all continents and oceans. Neither Hitler, when he invaded Poland in September 1939, nor Britain and France when they delivered an ultimatum to him to withdraw, imagined that it would spread to a global conflict. Both sides, as in 1914, thought that, although aerial operations might wreak horrific destruction on cities, hostilities on land and at sea were not likely to last long nor to extend beyond Europe and the shores of the Mediterranean.

The origin of the war was the growing insistence of the British and French people that the extension of Germany's power by force over the smaller countries of Eastern Europe could no longer be tolerated. Austria had succumbed in 1938 and Czechoslovakia in 1939. Attempts to restrain Hitler's ambition by diplomatic means had failed ignominiously, and the situation had gravely turned for the worse when the Soviet-German non-aggression pact was signed on 23 August, 1939. The British Chiefs of Staff had warned the Prime Minister, Neville Chamberlain, that on no account should Britain be involved simultaneously in war with Germany, Italy and Japan, who, since 1936, had been loosely allied in two separate pacts, one between Germany and Italy, the other between Germany and Japan. Germany invaded Poland on 1 September, 1939. When Germany refused to accept the British and French ultimatum to withdraw from Poland and war was declared on 3 September, neither Italy nor Japan joined in. Poland was speedily overrun and the bombing of Warsaw set a pattern for similar attacks in the world war that followed.

The so-called 'phoney war' that followed, in which there were no hostilities between the two sides, not even in the air, was broken when British and French intervention in Norway in April 1940 was forestalled by the German invasion of that country and Denmark. The result was disastrous for the British forces which took part in that ill-fated and ill-organized expedition. They had just succeeded in capturing Narvik when Germany launched its offensive in France and the Low Countries. The British army there saw little fighting before it was withdrawn from Dunkirk and Cherbourg in June, leaving all its equipment and nearly 40,000 prisoners of war behind. It had been forced back initially by the withdrawal of the French on its right and the Belgians on the left.

Britain now stood alone, its people led by Winston Churchill, determined to resist. The German-planned invasion of Britain with the assembly of barges in Continental ports did not materialize, as the would-be invaders could not gain command of the skies. In the great air battles of September 1940, the RAF inflicted sufficient losses on the Luftwaffe to stop any moves across the Channel and North Sea. The Luftwaffe, however, continued its bombing of British cities whilst in return Britain's Bomber Command mounted a prolonged offensive against German towns and industry, to which Fighter Command made an essential contribution. While the 'few' of the RAF fought over South East England, Britain began its operation in the Middle East, the only place where its forces faced those of Mussolini's Italy. This campaign, which was to last until 1943, with the final defeat of the Axis powers in North Africa, proved to be the last major campaign which Britain, with its Commonwealth partners, would direct on its own. In this historical review we accordingly deal with the Middle East at length, for, aside from its historical interest, it also accounts for a great deal of the poetry in this book and, incidentally, for the origins of the Trust that has produced this collection.

As British forces left France and the French collapsed, Mussolini's Italy joined the fray. The only places where his forces faced those of Britain were on the frontier between Libya and Egypt and on those of Ethiopia, in the Sudan, Kenya and Somaliland. Despite an overwhelming superiority in numbers in both areas, the Italians made no immediate move, but in August they attacked and ejected the tiny British Force in British Somaliland. In September they advanced ponderously 60 miles into Egypt's

Western Desert to Sidi Barrani, where they settled down. By the end of the year Wavell had planned his counterstroke. In December O'Connor attacked at Sidi Barrani and, in a brilliant campaign, routed the Italians, the remnants of whom were finally cut off and defeated south of Benghazi in February 1941. Meanwhile Wavell's forces had attacked the Italians in Ethiopia from north and south, defeated them and forced their surrender in May.

By that time the Germans had come to the rescue of their Italian ally in North Africa and in Greece, which Italy had invaded from Albania without consulting Hitler in October 1940. British forces had been sent to Greece in March 1941, weakening those in Libya facing the newly arrived Rommel, who drove them back to the Egyptian frontier, isolating the Australian garrison of Tobruk. The Germans declared war on Yugoslavia and Greece on 6 April 1941, and were soon forcing the Allies (mostly New Zealanders and Australians) out of Greece in a campaign reminiscent of that in France a year earlier. Again the troops saw little fighting, being forced, by the withdrawal of their Greek allies on their left, to retreat, under constant air attack. The New Zealanders and many of the British were transferred to Crete, which fell to German airborne attack at the end of May. This severe setback was followed by an unsuccessful attempt to relieve Tobruk in June. In this disastrous short campaign in Greece and Crete the navy, which had previously trounced the Italian navy at Cape Matapan and Taranto, suffered heavy losses at the hands of the German Air Force, which was to remain its principal opponent in the Mediterranean throughout the war, the whole course of which was transformed by Germany's invasion of Russia in June 1941.

In that month Auchinleck replaced Wavell in the Middle East, under pressure from Churchill to launch an offensive into Libya to relieve Tobruk, where a British and Polish garrison had replaced the Australians, and secure the airfields of Cyrenaica in order to give air cover to ships carrying supplies to beleaguered Malta. That offensive was launched in November 1941 and, after many vicissitudes, succeeded in its aim, driving Rommel and his Italian allies back to where O'Connor had driven the latter a year before.

By that time the course of the war had once more been transformed by the entry of Japan into the lists in December 1941. Still at war with China, her forces occupied French Indo-China when France fell in 1940. She was not so much concerned to help Germany as to extend her empire to absorb the colonial posses-sions of France, Britain and Holland in the Far East, while they and the Soviet Union were distracted by the war against Ger-many. On 8 December, 1941, as her naval aircraft struck at the American fleet in Pearl Harbor, leading to the American declara-tion of war against her, her forces attacked Hong Kong and invaded Malaya. The British and Canadian garrison of the former fought gallantly against overwhelming odds, but all was over by Christmas. In Malaya the British forces, the army's divisions being Indian and Australian, were ill-prepared and badly deployed to face the battle-experienced Japanese. They were immediately forced to withdraw, as the RAF abandoned its airfields, the navy suffering a severe blow with the loss of the battleships *Prince of Wales* and *Repulse* to Japanese air attack. The culmination of this disastrous campaign was the fall of Singapore on 15 February, 1942, 130,000 British, Indian and Australian troops entering the grim compounds of Japanese prisoner-of-war camps. By then the Japanese had already invaded Burma, where the Malayan pattern was repeated. By the middle of May, led by Alexander and Slim, the British forces, almost all of the Indian Army, had struggled back through the mountains into India as the monsoon rains fell, and all of Burma was in Japanese hands.

The diversion of troops and aircraft from the Middle East had done little to affect these sombre events, but had weakened Auchinleck's ability to withstand Rommel's counter-strokes in Libya. In February he had attacked and forced Ritchie's Eighth Army back to the Gazala Line, covering Tobruk. Auchinleck again came under pressure to launch an offensive from there to secure the airfields from which convoys to Malta, then in dire straits, could be given air cover; but Rommel pre-empted him at the end of May 1942, and, after fierce tank battles round Tobruk, defeated Ritchie's army and drove it all the way back to El Alamein, only fifty miles from Alexandria.

This was the low ebb of the war, Russia's armies also being flung back to the Volga at Stalingrad and to the Caucasus Moun-tains. But the tide was turning as the United States mobilized and deployed its strength, the first signs of this being seen in major naval battles against the Japanese in the Pacific. Montgomery's

victory at El Alamein, coinciding with the Anglo-American landings under Eisenhower in French North Africa in November, the
British contribution to which was Anderson's 1st Army, was
followed by a massive Russian counter-offensive which encircled
the German Sixth Army facing Stalingrad. From then on, the
anti-Axis alliance, which styled itself The United Nations, of
which Britain, the United States and the Soviet Union were the
principal powers, was set on the·path to victory. It was not to be
an easy one and they were to see many setbacks, but progress
towards victory was inexorable.

In May 1943 the German and Italian forces in North Africa
surrendered at Tunis to the Anglo-American forces under
Eisenhower, directed by Alexander, which Montgomery's
Eighth Army had joined when it entered Tunisia in February
after its long trek from the Nile. The successful invasion of
Sicily in July was followed by landings in Italy in September. It
was hoped that Italy's surrender, which accompanied them,
would lead to the rapid occupation of at least southern Italy,
which would provide airfields from which southern Germany
and her oil supplies from Romania could be bombed; but Hitler,
who had originally decided to withdraw to the north, had second
thoughts and decided to fight for every inch of Italy's rugged
terrain. As a result the American, French and British forces, the
latter including New Zealand, Indian, South African and Polish
troops, were faced with fighting battles as fierce, and enduring
hardships as great, as those experienced by their forbears in the
First World War. The fiercest were those involved in trying to
break into the Liri valley around Cassino, to which the landing at
Anzio was intended to be a contribution, in the early months of
1944. The deadlock was broken in May, as Juin's French, in Mark
Clark's US Fifth Army, broke through the Aurunci Mountains,
and Anders's Poles, in Leese's British Eighth Army, at last cleared
Monte Cassino.

Meanwhile, as Russia's huge armies struck blow after blow
against the German armies and drove them back, British, Canadian and American forces gathered in Britain ready to cross the
Channel. Two days after Mark Clark's Fifth Army, under Alexander, entered Rome, Eisenhower's armies, under Montgomery,
landed on the beaches of Normandy on 6 June 1944; but it was
nearly a year later, on 8 May 1945, a week after British troops had

joined hands with the Russians on the Baltic coast, before the German armies finally surrendered, those in Italy having done so three days earlier. In the Far East, Slim's Fourteenth Army, after beating off Japanese attacks in the Arakan and Manipur in the spring of 1944, had reconquered Burma and entered Rangoon on 2 May, 1945; but the war against Japan did not come to an end until after two atomic bombs had been dropped on Hiroshima and Nagasaki on 6 and 9 August. On 12 September the Japanese surrendered to Admiral Mountbatten at Singapore, and four days later to Admiral Harcourt at Hong Kong.

While these movements of armies and fleets had been taking place, two other campaigns of great significance had been in train: the Battle of the Atlantic, the anti–submarine war to keep the lifelines to Britain open, and the war in the air. The former, combined with escorting convoys of supplies to Russia, was the navy's principal campaign, in which RAF Coastal Command played a vital part. Sir Arthur Harris's Bomber Command, supported by Fighter Command, had continued its relentless attacks on targets in Germany, while the RAF's support of its sister services in all theatres of war was as important as its efforts in these fields.

The Second World War, like the First, saw the whole nation in arms. Civilians at home were at times as much in the front line as those in uniform, London and the South East being subjected to bombardment by V1 and V2 rockets until Montgomery's forces had cleared their launching sites in France and the Low Countries. The whole life of the nation was devoted to its war effort. As also in the First, the contribution of the British Commonwealth must not be forgotten, nor that of our allies. It was the war in Russia which bled the German armies to death. Without that, the British and Americans could not have prevailed on their own. The fact that it is now inconceivable that the nations of Western Europe could go to war against each other is proof that that effort was not in vain. In the balance against that must be set the fate of the countries of Eastern Europe which have exchanged one tyranny for another. The cost of the war to its participants was high, although, in terms of human casualties, in Britain's case, much less than that of the First World War – 326,000 in uniform and 62,000 civilians dead, compared with 950,000 in the First.

Requiescant in Pace.

Introduction

'An eye witness account of Waterloo is more permanent than a biography of Wellington.'

C.B.H. Wightman, *British Book News*

Forty years after the victory in Europe, this anthology of Second World War poetry provides a new, full and vivid reflection of the events of the wartime years and the emotions they stirred. This record of the time is expressed in the poetry written there and then by those who served. Thus this book becomes more than a collection of poems. It is history, too, seen with the poet's perceptive eye.

There have been other collections of poetry from the Second World War. In what way, then, does our new anthology differ? We can only say, at the end of reading 140 books published both during the war and since – many in private editions – and having worked carefully through the anthologies we are expected to supersede, including the finest of them all, *The Terrible Rain*, edited by Brian Gardner, that *Ours smells of war. We were there and wrote then, and this is how it was*. In that respect we are unique.

The Salamander Oasis Trust has already compiled two anthologies, *Return to Oasis*, from the Middle East, and *From Oasis into Italy*, from Africa and Italy.[1] Although this is our third published collection, strictly speaking it is Book Four, as our first effort was the *Oasis Anthology of Poetry from the Forces in the Middle East*, published in Cairo in 1943 by the Salamander Society (from which the Trust takes its name). So we could truly say that our new book started from a chance meeting between three of us in 1942,[2] in a services club in Cairo, where the *Oasis* project was conceived. Although more than forty years have passed since that day, the spirit of those times has remained very much alive in the minds of the editors. It is that spirit, we believe, that informs this

---

[1] Published by Shepheard-Walwyn, London, 1980 and 1983.

[2] Denis Saunders, the South African poet who wrote under the name 'Almendro', David Burk, pre-war with the *Daily Mirror*, and myself (Victor Selwyn). The full story is written in *Return to Oasis*. *Oasis* was essentially a grass-roots project in a grass-roots war.

book. For the Oasis approach to war poetry has always differed from other anthologies in a most important respect. Whereas, for example, Ian Hamilton in the introduction to his anthology of World War Two poetry, says that he looked for what the poets wrote when they went to war, our concern has been the converse, to seek the writings of those who *became* poets as a result of going to war. Naturally we select from the established poets, too. But to get the feel of war we have deliberately sought unpublished manuscripts, the verses written by unknowns from the airfields of Britain to the POW camps of South-East Asia – many of which have lain hidden in desks and drawers for forty years, or were left to widows and children along with the medals.

These poems are the product of a literate, aware and compassionate generation belonging to a less materialistic world than the one we live in today. Perhaps, in retrospect, the poets were naive in their belief that from the war an ideal world would emerge. But then it was the Army Council itself that promoted the discussion of the issues of the war and the caring world that would emerge at the end of it. Adhering to the Cromwellian dictum that a soldier should know why he fights and love what he knows, the troops were told of the Beveridge Plan on the welfare of society, and the Butler Education Act with its universal concept, and a United Nations to preserve the alliance of the war and keep the peace. All this was to form part of the stimulation of ideas. Instructors sent out were themselves enjoined, 'Never force your opinions on the group. An intelligent instructor will avoid ramming his ideas down men's throats. It is one of the cardinal sins.' Men had to reach conclusions from their own thoughts and from interchange with others, backed up by information – no better tribute to the intelligence of the men who served. It was this atmosphere of free circulation of thoughts that fostered the creativity of writers and poets. There was more to the war than just defeating Hitler.

Yet if men became starry-eyed about the future that would follow the war, they began the conflict with few illusions about the nature of the war itself.

For the generation of the Second World War had been born to the generation of the First World War. It knew what war was like from those who had survived, from their parents and teachers, from plays and novels like *Journey's End* and *All Quiet on the Western Front*, from the poetry of the time, and from the annual remembrance of the Armistice of 11 November, when children assembled in school halls and for two silent minutes the traffic stopped and the world stood still. Yet within twenty-one years of the end of that First War, this new generation went to war again. They felt they had no choice. Hitler had to be stopped. So an essentially unwarlike people were now committed to a new war – not with the waving of flags (no one spoke of King and Country this time) but with the quiet determination of a job to be done. They enlisted at two shillings a day (ten new pence), and when it was all over, no less a figure than the Chief of the Imperial General Staff, Field Marshal Viscount Alanbrooke, was obliged to sell his prized collection of books on retirement.

The men of the Second World War were a modest lot. They did not boast: it was called 'shooting a line'. They did not get on to TV: there was no TV to get on to. Instead, they thought about things, and discussed things, and above all they *read*. Penguin Books had just begun, and for a few pence one could buy a reprint of the classics. The tanks going into Alamein were well stocked with Penguin paperbacks, and twenty-four hours before the battle, when the then Lieutenant-Colonel Michael Carver, GSO1 7th Armoured Div., was asked by his commander, General John Harding, for a book to while away the time, he handed over his copy of Tolstoy's *Anna Karenina*. He could have lent the general *War and Peace*, but maybe that would have delayed the battle! The insatiable appetite of the troops for reading is recalled by Lawrence Durrell in his introduction to *Return to Oasis*, where he describes New Zealanders combing the book shops of Cairo for the written word. They even bought a multi-volume collection of sermons by an eighteenth-century parson – no doubt to the profound relief of the bookseller, who had received them in error from London.

As they read so did they write: more, we should point out, in the Middle East than in any other theatre of war. Many factors contributed. The men there were far from home, the journey out took three months or more by sea, and once in the Middle East, they could face a stay of four years or more. So they created their own world. For here was the desert and its limitless space, inspirer of saints and prophets; here was Cairo – and a welcome absence of domestic trivia. The War Office, in its wisdom, had picked literary talent to staff the many intelligence agencies in the

Middle East and it was these writers who founded magazines and clubs. Printers and publishers were available in Cairo, and many publications appeared, a lot of which never even reached home.

This background and the élan of those days shape this book. We have given due space to the contributions to war poetry from the Commonwealth forces in that war, from New Zealand, Australia, South Africa and Canada, as well as to Gaelic poetry from the Scottish regiments. The poets all shared a common cultural tradition which, in those days, still derived from the durable inheritance of the Renaissance. They built on the best of the past, and created the new, but with learning, skill, talent and application. They were neither haunted by the fear of being labelled old-fashioned, nor obsessed by the belief that yesterday is already dated. True recognition did not depend on having an astute PR, or on a fleeting appearance on the 'box'. So those who made it were a little older, more mature and not so rich.

From this background came the poetry, of which there were two streams: the established poets who had already published and the unknowns, moved to write for the first time.

Whereas it is a subjective exercise, so much a matter of opinion, to compare one poet with another, say Keith Douglas of the Second World War with Wilfred Owen of the First – for on what scale do we measure? – an objective comparison of the poetry of the two World Wars proves a useful and indeed a necessary task, somewhat overdue. For in its absence we are left with the myth in which the First World War produced the poets whilst little worthwhile was written in the Second. The myth has been repeated so often as to become accepted fact, chiefly by those who have not read the poetry of the Second World War – and, we suspect, not even the *anthologies* of the First War – with an editorial eye, viz. assessing the collection of poetry for content, quality and range of emotion and experience. So how do they judge? No doubt on what the advertising men call 'image', supported by such observations as that of Robert Graves who once asked where were the poets of the 8th Army – a question easily answered in the books of poetry from that theatre of war, including those produced by the Trust. Reality, though, does not always destroy the myth. As in so many situations in life prejudice takes precedence over fact.

Furthermore, this prejudice has been reinforced by the absence of Second World War poetry from most university and school curricula, unlike that of the First World War. Generally there has been a playing-down of the Second World War compared with the First, extending even to the teaching of its history in schools. Maybe not enough men were killed – though the Russians may think otherwise. From a literary viewpoint, too, the change in what is regarded as poetry has been much greater since the 1940s than it was between the two wars, and so the poetry of the Second World War has tended to be overlooked. Yet as it happens, some of today's leading poets – Roy Fuller, Gavin Ewart, Vernon Scannell, Bernard Gutteridge and Alan Ross, among others – began writing during the war and their poems are in this collection. Many of the established poets of the Second World War, however, did not return. It is one of the tragedies of that war that they did not survive to write more and, who knows, even better poetry. They might have transformed the post-war literary scene. We list their names at the beginning of this book.

It is not difficult to see how the more renowned poets of the First World War gained their reputations. They brought back tidings from hell. The Second World War poets could not repeat the impact of their predecessors a generation before. For, in newspaper terms, the First World War poets 'got the story first'. They shattered a system of beliefs that had been deeply and emotionally held. Until then, war had been greeted with the waving of the flag. War meant glory. Then came the shock of the trenches, of tens of thousands of men killed in the first hour of battle for a few yards of mud, causing Owen to cry out. . .

> What passing-bells for these who die as cattle?
> Only the monstrous anger of the guns.
> Only the stuttering rifles' rapid rattle. . . .

And Sassoon to remember,

> The rank stench of those bodies haunts me still.

And Rosenberg to write,

> The wheels lurched over sprawled dead
> But pained them not, though their bones crunched,
> Their shut mouths made no moan. . . .

These are powerful lines deservedly famous. But they would not be repeated in the Second World War, not because men were not wounded and killed – the 8th Army suffered 13,500 casualties at Alamein[1] – but because the poets had changed. They were not only now aware of war before they joined up but they saw it more in terms of the fate of individuals. Whereas in the First World War, huge masses of men were directed from afar, in the Second World War more men felt personally involved. It was their war. But then followed a question of conscience. One kills because one has to; that is war. But it forces a compassionate man to reflect.

So Keith Douglas, for all his professional commitment to soldiering, as a Tank Captain at Alamein, observes in his poem 'How to Kill',

> How easy it is to make a ghost.

'Almendro' is tortured with the thought,

> Today I killed a man. God forgive me!
> Tomorrow I shall sow another political corpse.
> Or be dead myself. . . .

And Melville Hardiment, an infantry sergeant and the last survivor of his unit in the costly fighting from the Normandy beaches to east of Caen, writes of a man *on the other side*.

> Poor dead Panzer!
> It must have cost you some
> to crawl through this wheat
> . . .
> . . .
> where swollen flies
> buzz round the stiff upturned legs
> of a Uccello cart-horse:
> And you must have hated the stench
> of which you now stink too. . . .

It is the same stench of war, but this time war is seen as man to man – not as the anonymous 'bodies' of Sassoon.

---

[1] They had learned to bury the dead quickly to support morale, see Nigel Hamilton's biography of Montgomery. The forward medical services performed miracles unknown in the First War. One did not see, after the Second World War, ex-servicemen with only one leg playing a barrel organ in the streets.

Other Second World War poets show compassion for the man in uniform on the other side, who also has to stand up and be shot at. Thus, C.P.S. Denholm-Young (a Lt-Col.), laments, in 'Dead German Youth',

> For I would rather hear your youthful mirth
> At stories which I have often loved to tell
> Than stand here looking down at you
> So terrible, so quiet and so still.

Brian Gallie, a Captain in the Royal Navy and holder of the DSC, pays tribute to a German airman who flew slowly through the British Fleet to his death . . .

> That something in you, like a bird,
> Knowing no cage's bars,
> Courage supreme – an instant dream
> Of mind beneath the stars. . .

(This admiration for the *professional* enemy was so prevalent in the desert that Monty had to remind his army that the legendary Rommel was not a romantic hero, but a ruthless enemy.)

In short, we have the sharing of a common experience in which the individual recognises his own responsibility. No one pleads: 'I am only carrying out orders.' There is never a word of this. Interestingly, so many of the actions recounted in the poetry are by men *on their own account*.[1] So their poetry often goes deeper than that of the First World War, and thus any collection of poetry from the First World War will be found to be narrow in experience, range of feeling and emotion, compared with that of the Second World War. For the former covers only one sector of war and was written mainly from the viewpoint of a group of subalterns of similar social background, some of whose writing in relation to the troops we find condescending, and that includes Owen and Sassoon. Jon Silkin in his comprehensive sixty-page introduction to the *Penguin Book of First World War Poetry* – it has a

---

[1] For example, Keith Douglas, officially posted to base, made his own way to El Alamein to take a tank into action. Melville Hardiment and another sergeant took charge when their officers were killed on the Normandy beach and operated their own war for the next month, just advancing towards the sound of the guns, fighting pockets of German resistance as they found them. Instructions were not needed. This dedication of our war-poets is reflected in the casualty list on the 'In Memory' page.

great deal to say about poets from Coleridge and Wordsworth to Whitman but less about war – talks of the compassion of the First World War poets. We see pity and anger in their words. True compassion belongs more to the poets in *this* book. Where the Second World War poets undoubtedly excel is in the art of the close-up, of relating the experiences of the many through that of the individual. In this way the reader is brought close to the varied aspects of the war – from tragic death to the ability of men and women to cope.

The poetry of the Second World War not only covers a far wider range of experience than that of the First; the subjects, as the reader will find, are far more diverse. The poems also come from writers of all ranks, in contrast to the generation before. The social scene had radically changed between the wars, and now the products of the grammar schools and universities were to be found in the ranks, and many others whose education was limited also blossomed in the services.

To show the diversity of Second World War poetry – and the poets – let us first take a poem by Jim Barker, a sapper in the Engineers, who wrote under the name of J.G. Meddemmen. This is how he ends his poem on the LRDG, the Long Range Desert Group, whose task was to raid far behind the enemy lines and minefields:

> It's the lucky ones get dead:
> He's still alive. I wonder if his wife understands
> How you can't even shoot yourself without your hands.

Then there is E.F. Gosling, a Yeomanry Lieutenant Colonel, unhappy with the transition from horses to armoured cars:

> No more, alas, the head-tossed foam, the fretful foot that pawed:
> Oh glory that was Tetrarch's might, oh drabness that is Ford!

A delicious last line!

Then there is Les Cleveland, a Staff Sergeant with the 2nd New Zealand Division at Cassino (and today a Reader in Political Science at Victoria University, Wellington, New Zealand), writing from Italy:

> At the face of the smoking crag
> a horde of screeching machines
> labour at this season's assignment:

> spurts of furious dust rise and fall,
> curtaining flesh ripped and thwacked
> by fanged rods of shrapnel. . . .
>
> Steel tracks rage over pulverised streets
> as enemy armour-piercing, self-propelled artillery
> lashes pointblank at our newborn organism scuttling,
> limbs entangled, heads devoutly flattened to earth,
> huddling together under the barrage.

The Italian campaign came nearest to that of the Western Front in the earlier war. Les Cleveland's lines are those of the man involved. In comparison, the writers of a generation before often seem more like observers than participants.

In Cairo, Brigadier Ropes, after serving in the desert, wrote for the entertainment of the troops on leave:

> So if you ever want some ping-pong, some billiards or a bath
> Without military policemen and a nasty aftermath
> We'll try to keep your footsteps on the straight and narrow path.
> We're the voluntary ladies of the town.

And here is a subject which surely some cynic must have written about in the First World War, but which we fail to find in any of the anthologies: yet after all it was Napoleon who said that an army marches on its stomach. Norman Morris writes a poem, 'It's always mealtime', which evokes memories:

> There is porridge made from biscuits. There's soya for the fry.
> There is tea that tastes of onions: there is bread that's rather dry . . .
> So the cooks are looking browned off, slightly woebegone and worn,
> The look that comes from cards all night, and lighting fires at dawn.

We also get the cynical views of the squaddie in the anonymous ballads, from the 'D' Day Dodgers, dedicated to Lady Astor, to the Australian 'bloody' protest at Tobruk. We have poems, too, from the POW camps in Europe and South-East Asia.

Finally, in one undisputed way, the Second World War produced a group of poets hardly known in the First World War: women poets. Their verse has an especially keen perception of human relationships, and we only wish we could publish some of the letters that came in with the poetry. An extract from one tells its own story. It is a letter from an ex-Wren accompanying her verse to a man in the services whom she feared would not return and it ends simply with the words '. . . hence I sign myself "Miss".' Need anything more be said?

Ian Fletcher observed in *Return to Oasis* that the poems really selected themselves. But problems always arise over one central fact of publishing life: space. We are limited even with the pages the publisher has given us. Because this anthology comes from all fronts, commands and services in the Second World War, it covers a very wide territory indeed. We began with more than a thousand potential contributors. In the end this number was reduced to just over two hundred.

The problems of compiling this anthology demanded first the drawing up of suitable definitions. The criteria we have adopted are these. As in previous *Oasis* collections, the poetry is written by British and Commonwealth forces serving in the Second World War, and it was written *during* that War, for such poetry enjoys an immediacy, a quality, that cannot be recreated in later years.

These guidelines entailed a great deal of back-checking and judgment including looking through service records and biographies. Yet having made our rules, confining our choices to those who served in the forces, which gives the book its unity, we have – as regards the Middle East – added poems by Terence Tiller, Bernard Spencer and Lawrence Durrell, who were there, though not in uniform, during the campaign. This enabled us to include some very good poems relevant to that theatre of war. And we have bent our rules completely for one other civilian, Elsie Cawser, who sent in an irresistible piece, the last lines of which read:

> So now, when I hear on the wireless
> Of Hurricanes showing their mettle,
> I see, in a vision before me,
> A Dornier chased by my kettle.

The poem chose itself. Here was an aspect of the war, which we felt we had to represent, the surrender by housewives of their pots and kettles and hardware to make guns and planes for the common cause. The poem also exudes humour, on which we regret we are otherwise a little short. Without humour – or tea – neither British Forces nor civilians would have coped. So Elsie finds her place alongside the poets from the services.

We had to select, too, from the published *Oasis* collections, a difficult task as these anthologies were already selections from the wealth of material that we acquired.

So in this limited space, we added rule three; if we had to choose between the known and unknown, then we normally chose the unknown, since known poems had already appeared in other collections. We wanted to give this anthology the freshness of hitherto unheard voices. And it is, of course, their inclusion that differentiates this book from others, bringing it nearer to the war.

Many poems spoiled themselves by being badly put together and by being infected with pretentiousness and false sentiment. What serving men really felt is best summed up in a verse by Dennis McHarrie, a Wing Commander in the RAF:

> "He died who loved to live," they'll say,
> "Unselfishly so we might have today."
> Like Hell! He fought because he had to fight;
> He died that's all. It was his unlucky night.

and that is why we have led the anthology with this poem, since it says it all. In the First World War, they used to say as the shells came over, 'If your number's not on it, you're all right'. In all wars, it is this sense of fatalism that helps to pull a man through.

In our view, therefore, a poem had to be well written, it had to have a point to make, an original twist often on a worn theme, it had to be honest and true to itself, it had to *sound* right to our ears, and above all, it had to show that indefinable spark we call inspiration. We had to ask ourselves: would it have mattered had it not been written?

We had somehow to achieve a balance between the purely literary merit of a poem and its value as a record of an historic event. The reassuring factor was the measure of common agreement between us as editors, for we too had shared the same experience as our contributors: we were there. In the end, too, we faced a problem that confronts any anthologist. We could not have too many poems on the same theme. For example, in the poems on the Western Desert, only a limited number could deal with sand and flies and Tobruk. So, sadly, some good poems had to be dropped.

It was a lengthy selection process, but on the way we were

helped by many kind people we had never met. They wrote to draw attention to the poems of one writer or another; they sent us books and manuscripts that might otherwise have gone unnoticed; they resurrected pages from service magazines and personal diaries that had long slumbered in a bottom drawer. To all of them we say 'thank you'. The reward is here, in this anthology from those who served and wrote in the Second World War.

V.S.

Note on Arrangement of The Poems

We have arranged the poems by eight different theatres of war. Two sections, AIR and SEA, cover the operations of the RAF and the Navy where they were acting mainly on their own – the RAF in its Bomber and Coastal Commands and the Navy in its convoys. Clearly there was bound to be some overlapping, as there was in the war itself, because of the joint operations of the services. For instance, in the case of the RAF in the Middle East, where it became the Desert Air Force, such poems have been included with these of the Middle East Forces.

Generally within each area the poems are arranged alphabetically by names of the writers. This has been our practice in our previous anthologies. However, we have, in the 1939–40 section, put the two poems about Dunkirk at the end together with Douglas Street's poems on Britain preparing for invasion, just as we have led this section with Bernard Gutteridge's 'September 1939'. And we have put Douglas Street's ' "Commando Briefing", Dec 1941' as a prelude to the section NORMANDY to BERLIN, covering the period June 1944–August 1945.

The HOME FRONT poems cover the Blitz and the units serving at home from 1941 onwards. Most of the women's services and poems will be in this group.

Martin Bell's poem 'Three Days', which deals with the end of the war, is printed at the end of the SEAC and PACIFIC section; though it was written on his return to Britain and not actually in the theatre of war, we feel this is chronologically correct.

Finally, we have singled out two poems with which to 'frame' the entire anthology: Dennis McHarrie's 'Luck', which expresses the philosophy of the man and woman in war, appears at the front of the book, and Edward Lowbury's poem 'August 10th 1945 – The Day After', on the dropping of the atomic bomb, clearly belongs at the end.

Writing Poetry in War

Service away from home, especially overseas, turned men – and women – into letter-writers. Within the limits of censorship, they had new experiences and places to write home about. They were concerned, too, for those at home.

This exercise in self-expression proved for many the first step to the writing of diaries, short stories and poetry. For the letter home often became a self-educator. Men and women found they had something to say and the facility to do so. Letters home became more descriptive, had the odd illustration – especially airgraphs – and often contained poems. People wrote poetry, too, for the unit's entertainment and to go on notice boards, the latter especially in POW Camps.

On leave in Cairo or Naples the aspiring poet would buy an exercise book and the collection of his work began. (Service message pads came in handy for the first draft and for diaries, often the final version, too, together with RAF log books.) He also had the chance on leave to compare notes with others at service clubs which performed a vital role. But poems sent home had a hurdle to cross – the unit censor – and verse could disappear that way. Norman Morris is sure that his censoring officer – also a poet – consigned his efforts to the waste-paper basket. However, for more serious reasons the BEF discouraged poets in the early days of the war. They felt that poems with a cynical touch falling into enemy hands might be used for adverse propaganda. The Navy, one suspects, was the most security-conscious service. Naval poetry is limited, as is that, for obvious reasons, from the Fighter Command of the RAF.

In previous *Oasis* anthologies we have noted the problems faced by the infantry in having to carry their kit and keep on the move. Hence we get more poetry from the artillery and tanks and units on the line of communication and from base, together with the medical services. However, as an example of the problem of the war poet, let us cite the experience of John Rimington, whose 'Danse Grotesque' is one of the most polished pieces in this collection. He drove a tank transporter in the desert – a long low-loaded vehicle ferrying tanks to the front. One day the front pulled back and he became a prisoner for forty-eight hours, before escaping. In that time he lost two years' writing. All his filled exercise books were gone. Here, incidentally, is the justification for the official dicta on security.

However, as editors, we have been interested to note the numbers who obviously had access to the unit typewriter - witness the unmistakable type-face on manuscripts we have received of the service Oliver, a machine that could withstand the heaviest hammering. These original manuscripts are of special joy to the Imperial War Museum, to which we hand over our archives of all poetry, published or not – with the senders' assent. They form a record of the times.

So far we have noted the operation mostly of those who wrote poetry for the first time, learning as they went along and adapting to the life in the services. But equally the established poets had to adapt. One talks of reflective poetry in this context: their first inspiration, too, came from the events. Of course, they had the experience and discipline to put their work away for a time and then go back to rewrite and polish it. A Keith Douglas would revise and revise and still not always be satisfied. Incidentally the version of his poems in *this* anthology are his *own* text and not a revision a generation later: before he went to Normandy to be killed – after being repatriated from the Middle East – he handed over his manuscripts, having worked on them as if he knew he would not see them again, to Tambimuttu, from whom we have taken them. From the service records of so many of the established poets who were killed the writing had to be close to the action. They could not have gone back to a country house or college cloister to contemplate and write. There was neither the time nor opportunity.

How I Wrote My First Poem

Spike Milligan

It was January, 1944, Italy – a small group of Gunners had come forward to a small decimated wood outside the village of Lauro – overlooking the Garigliano plain. We were to dig gun positions for our Battery to occupy (19 Bty 56 Heavy Artillery) for the forthcoming attack across the Garigliano river to coincide with the attack on Cassino, we being the left flank – owing to our close proximity to the enemy, work had to be done (digging gun pits, command post etc) with great stealth – mostly at night, it was bitter cold weather – a mixture of icy rain and hoar frost in the mornings – one night when we had completed the work I was in my dug-out, it was a quiet night – occasional harassing fire – and sporadic small arms fire from various sentries – or patrols meeting in some area between the lines, I could hear digging – nearby – and thought it was a similar operation to ours – I remember saying to my trench-mate 'Thank Christ we've finished ours' – but the digging I could hear was a much grimmer affair. It was the London Scottish (or The Scabs Fusaliers) burying their dead – suddenly to the sound of rain a lone piper struck up 'Over the Sea to Skye', the words of the song come to mind 'Carry the boy who's born to be king' – it was a haunting experience. Then 10 days later – by which time our guns had moved in – came a midnight disaster – a German gun found our range and a direct hit on Sgt. Wilson's gun position – the camouflage net caught fire – the charges started to explode – all were killed – or burnt to death except 2. Next day we buried them – we had no piper – just the sound of the guns around us – and I felt moved to write what was in fact my first poem – I offer it to Oasis for what it's worth.

Dennis McHarrie

Luck

I suppose they'll say his last thoughts were of simple things,
Of April back at home, and the late sun on his wings;
Or that he murmured someone's name
As earth reclaimed him sheathed in flame.
Oh God! Let's have no more of empty words,
Lip service ornamenting death!
The worms don't spare the hero;
Nor can children feed upon resounding praises of his deed.
'He died who loved to live,' they'll say,
'Unselfishly so we might have today!'
Like hell! He fought because he had to fight;
He died that's all. It was his unlucky night.

The Poems

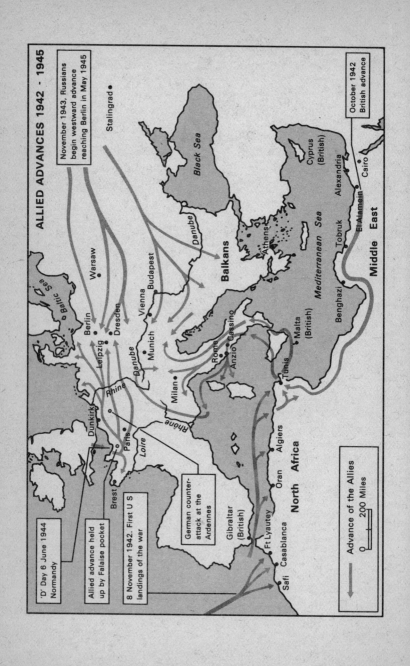

ALLIED ADVANCES 1942 - 1945

November 1943, Russians begin westward advance reaching Berlin in May 1945

October 1942 British advance

'D' Day 6 June 1944 Normandy

Allied advance held up by Falaise pocket

8 November 1942. First U S landings of the war

German counter-attack at the Ardennes

Stalingrad

Black Sea

Cyprus (British)

Alexandria

Cairo

El Alamein

Tobruk

Mediterranean Sea

Benghazi

Middle East

Athens

Balkans

Danube

Warsaw

Vienna

Budapest

Berlin

Dresden

Leipzig

Munich

Danube

Rome

Cassino

Anzio

Malta (British)

Tunis

Rhine

Milan

Rhône

Dunkirk

Paris

Brest

Loire

Baltic Sea

North Africa

Algiers

Oran

Gibraltar (British)

Ft Lyautey

Casablanca

Safi

Advance of the Allies

0   200 Miles

The Contents

1939–40

The Middle East

The Home Front

The Mediterranean, North Africa, Italy and the Balkans

Air

Sea

Normandy to Berlin

South East Asia and the Pacific

1939–40

Bernard Gutteridge

In September 1939

The last war was my favourite picture story.
Illustrated London News bound in the study;
The German bayonet we believed still bloody

But was just rusty. Privacy of death.
My uncle's uniform meant more than glory;
Surprise that grief should be so transitory . . .

All the predictions of adolescence had
Disposed of glory in their realist path:
There'd be no need to duck and hold your breath.

Now, looking as useless and as beautiful
As dragonflies, the plump silver balloons
Hang over London also like zany moons.

Yet from the blacked-out window death still seems
Private, not an affair that's shared by all
The distant people, the flats, the Town Hall.

But some remember Spain and the black spots
They shouted 'Bombers' at. That memory screams
That we know as a film or in bad dreams.

Fear will alight on each like a dunce's cap
Or an unguessed disease unless death drops
Quicker than the sirens or the traffic stops.

Brian Allwood

Ack Ack Said The Instructor

Ack Ack said the instructor
bofors tommy gun lewis gun
(which has 156 different parts—
EACH THE GRANDEST BRIGHTEST BESTEST
EACH THE ONLY GOD–DAMN THING
ON THE MARKET
GUARANTEED WARRANTEED MONEY BACK IF NOT SATISFIED)
and this thing here's called the cruciform
(didn't any of you bastards
ever go to church?)
as you can see it's shaped like a cross

Yes said the instructor
blow his bloody brains out with
(our recognized brands the best that are made)
he's trying to blow your bloody brains out with
(OUR RECOGNIZED BRANDS THE BEST THAT ARE MADE).

Donald Bain

War Poet

We in our haste can only see the small components of the scene
We cannot tell what incidents will focus on the final screen.
A barrage of disruptive sound, a petal on a sleeping face,
Both must be noted, both must have their place;

It may be that our later selves or else our unborn sons
Will search for meaning in the dust of long deserted guns,
We only watch, and indicate and make our scribbled pencil
    notes.
We do not wish to moralize, only to ease our dusty throats.

Hugh Barty-King

Horses

*(After going into the old stables and finding the names of the horses that
once lived there still nailed above the stalls)*

'Ginger' 'Veracity' 'Visitor' 'Target',
    Where have they taken you? Far far away?
'Ginger', 'Veracity', 'Visitor', 'Target',
    Where have you taken your gallop to-day?
Was it the Signals who caused your eviction,
    Ruthlessly, powerfully? Was it the war
(Or death long ago) that has emptied your stables
    Once lived in and slept in and loved by you four?
Only the legends in flowery writing
    Painted in gold at the head of your stalls,
Set in a frame, out of place, ornamental,
    Only the marks of your hoofs on the walls,
Stay to remind us that we're the usurpers,
    Locum tenentes till Peace brings you back;
Help us to picture this place in its hey-day,
    Filled with your whiff, with your clickety-clack.
Fresh from the canter, unwieldy, impatient,
    Sweating and steaming, you're led through the door,
Shown to the guests after church on a Sunday,
    Gentle and tidy, the pride of The Moor.

Would there had never been cause for our coming!
    Look what a muddle we humans have made!
Would there had never been cause for us strangers
    – We too uprooted – to throng, to invade
This scene of your triumphs, your beautiful stable
    Occupied rowdily, quite out of hand,
First by the Quarter, then by 'B Cable'!
    Why? Surely if we can't, *you* won't understand.

Tom Beaumont

The Colonel's Eye

Lampshades thinly veiled
In silver dust:
Rifles richly scaled
With ornate rust:
Respirators, modest and ascetic,
Free from Pickering's obscene cosmetic:
Bottles on some airy shelf bestowed
Which, till the previous midnight, flowed
With good McEwans Ale: the mystic grain
Of frosty foliage on the window pane.
All these I love. So why
Should they offend the Colonel's eye?

Beds and blankets ranged
In staggered lines,
And on them, forming strange
Surrealist designs,
Books, bayonets, button-sticks and soap;
Improper coils of black-out shutter rope:
Immaculate class officers arrayed
In far-from-regimental shoes of suede:
All these . . . and more . . .
I, but not Authority, adore.

Thank God that I
Have not the Colonel's eye.

O.C.T.U. Malta Barracks Aldershot

David Bourne

St Valery – May 1940

Slip-shod waves scramble the shore
And lick the claw
Of rock. Dumb the beach
Once loudly strewn to bleach
Their bodies; knuckle-smooth
Sea-flanged.
Green-coifed cliffs are lately red;
(The spectral plaything of the sky is fed
With cold breaths)

Lights through the trees,
And the cliffs are white again
Praying on their knees
For peace again.

John Buxton

The Tarn

'We'd better split now. Keep behind the trees
Down to the tarn's edge. If there's a plane, come back
And meet me here: don't fire, they'll have MGs.
– We'll need to get as close as we can get.'
I heard the silky rustle of the skis
And stood stock-still, listening till it had gone.
I threaded one stick through the ring and strap
Of the other, and held them so in my left hand.
I cocked my tommy-gun – so loud, so loud
That little click! Zigzag from tree to tree,
Straining for any other sound beyond
The swishing of my skis, I ran to the tarn.
Between the black, still branches of a spruce
I looked across the ice: only the wind
Had made black random furrows in the snow.

Norway 1940

William Clarke

Military Cemetery[1]

Such discipline on parade
Would put to shame a Guards' Brigade;
So long, so rigid, to remain like this
And still no order to dismiss.

[1]Menin Cemetery, World War One

G.E. Cocker

Nickel Raid . . . 1940.

'Sprog crew. . . . .
What's the flamin' Air Force coming to. . .
To risk a precious kite on such a night. .
To drop a load of bum paper over France. .
While the Jerries dance and whoop it up. . .
And the French sit in the dark and shiver. .'

The Chiefy binds away. .
And the ground crew mutely listen. .
Plug in the starter. . .
Peer out of balaclavas. .
Cough, spit, and shuffle in the snow. .
'The Air Force isn't what it was. .
Before those political bods
Thought to even the score
With another war. . . .'

He kicks the starboard tyre. .
Walks around the tail
And kicks the port. .
'Pilot's O.K. . . . . pre war. . .
Survived the Heligoland show. . .
Another bloody disaster
To add to our victories. . . .'

We climb aboard. . .
A crew of sprogs. . .
Stiff in new issue flying togs. . .
Self-conscious, cold and wondering. . .
The ground crew stamp their feet. .
Impatient to get back to the warm fug
Of the crowded N.A.A.F.I. . . .
And what's left of New Year's eve. . .

The engines cough, snarl and roar. . .
The Wimpy shakes, quivers, and vibrates. .
And just when it seems
That it must tear itself apart. .
The noise subsides. .
The chocks are pulled. . .
And waving torches guide us to the fray. . .

Somewhere ahead the Germans drink French wine. .
Toast the Fuehrer in brandy. . .
Sing '*Gott strafe England*'. . .
Write letters home. . .
And man the guns. . .
We freeze at minus thirty. . .
Curse the cold, the Air Force,
And the war. . . .
Drone on, and on across endless clouds. . .
And see nothing. . . .

R.N. Currey

Firing with Heavy Guns

They laugh like fallen archangels, these four guns,
Utter their searing blasphemies of flame
And thunder that seeks to take in vain the name
And power of God; they flash hot vivid suns

From every side, and all four firing at once
In one clean salvo separately clout
Your head from side to side; they laugh and shout
And make the sandbags leap with their loud tones.

They are the fallen archangels, this the hour
In which they taste some memory of the power
With which they stormed the frontiers of heaven.
The four rounds burst together, seven miles high,
Quite close – good shooting, but they have not even
Begun to climb the immense heights of the sky.

Unseen Fire

This is a damned inhuman sort of war.
I have been fighting in a dressing-gown
Most of the night; I cannot see the guns,
The sweating gun-detachments or the planes;

I sweat down here before a symbol thrown
Upon a screen, sift facts, initiate
Swift calculations and swift orders; wait
For the precise split-second to order fire.

We chant our ritual words; beyond the phones
A ghost repeats the orders to the guns:
One Fire . . . Two Fire . . . ghosts answer: the guns roar
Abruptly; and an aircraft waging war
Inhumanly from nearly five miles height
Meets our bouquet of death – and turns sharp right.

This is a damned unnatural sort of war;
The pilot sits among the clouds, quite sure
About the values he is fighting for;
He cannot hear beyond his veil of sound,

He cannot see the people on the ground;
He only knows that on the sloping map
Of sea-fringed town and country people creep
Like ants – and who cares if ants laugh or weep?

To us he is no more than a machine
Shown on an instrument; what can he mean
In human terms? – a man, somebody's son,
Proud of his skill; compact of flesh and bone
Fragile as Icarus – and our desire
To see that damned machine come down on fire.

We've most of us seen aircraft crash in flame,
Seen how the cruel guardians of height,
Fire and the force of gravity, unite
To humanize the flying god and proclaim

His common clay; by hedge and field we came
Running through the darkness, tried to fight
The solid wall of heat. Only the white
Lilac of foam could get us near that frame –

That frame like a picked fish-bone; sprawled beneath –
Charred bodies, more like trunks of trees than men;
The ammunition began to go up then,
Another and more glittering type of spray;
We could not help them, six men burned to death –
I've had their burnt flesh in my lungs all day!

Gavin Ewart

Sonnet: The Hymn-Singers

We're officer cadets in 1940 –
and some of us won't get out of this war alive.
There's snow, and ice, on the gun park. With freezing hands
we bring the gun into action (so many seconds flat).
Later, in pubs, we sing the rugger songs,
establishing the warmth of wartime camaraderie,
like women's sewing bees, one sex together,
making a joke of love we're frightened of. . .

Years later will come the impotent polymaths
to say we shouldn't have sung them. Though very young men
think women and battle are equally tests, they'll say
it's homosexual. But we were a Congregation,
hymn-singing in that darkness – so would you!
Those sex-linked Spartans knew a thing or two!

Sonnet, 1940

The point where beauty and intelligence meet,
Where intersecting lines cross and divide –
Happy were I to lie between those feet
Or by that rare and warm and lovely side –
You are the centre of my moving world,
The cold ideal to which I daily move
Although iron flags of battle are unfurled –
You are not yet, though might still be, my love.
And I, before the happy tough battalions
Engulf me or the frozen seas of Norway,
Have still my dreams of cities and of dalliance,
But most of you as standing in a doorway,
Who might, though I so dissipate my life,
Be mistress or, fear of the young, a wife.

The Bofors AA Gun

Such marvellous ways to kill a man!
An 'instrument of precision', a beauty,
The well-oiled shining marvel of our day
Points an accusing finger at the sky.
– But suddenly, traversing, elevating madly,
It plunges into action, more than eager
For the steel blood of those romantic birds
That threaten all the towns and roads.
O, that man's ingenuity, in this so subtle,
In such harmonious synchronization of parts,
Should against man be turned and he complaisant,
The pheasant-shooter be himself the pheasant!

Alun Lewis

All Day It Has Rained

All day it has rained, and we on the edge of the moors
Have sprawled in our bell-tents, moody and dull as boors,
Groundsheets and blankets spread on the muddy ground
And from the first grey wakening we have found
No refuge from the skirmishing fine rain
And the wind that made the canvas heave and flap
And the taut wet guy-ropes ravel out and snap.
All day the rain has glided, wave and mist and dream,
Drenching the gorse and heather, a gossamer stream
Too light to stir the acorns that suddenly
Snatched from their cups by the wild south-westerly
Pattered against the tent and our upturned dreaming faces.
And we stretched out, unbuttoning our braces,
Smoking a Woodbine, darning dirty socks,
Reading the Sunday papers – I saw a fox
And mentioned it in the note I scribbled home; –
And we talked of girls and dropping bombs on Rome,

And thought of the quiet dead and the loud celebrities
Exhorting us to slaughter, and the herded refugees;
– Yet thought softly, morosely of them, and as indifferently
As of ourselves or those whom we
For years have loved, and will again
Tomorrow maybe love; but now it is the rain
Possesses us entirely, the twilight and the rain.

And I can remember nothing dearer or more to my heart
Than the children I watched in the woods on Saturday
Shaking down burning chestnuts for the schoolyard's merry
    play,
Or the shaggy patient dog who followed me
By Sheet and Steep and up the wooded scree
To the Shoulder o' Mutton where Edward Thomas brooded
    long
On death and beauty – till a bullet stopped his song.

Jack Lindsay

Squadding

The sergeant's roar, interpreted aright
by instinct of fear, dies bouncing on the asphalt.
The squad, grey-denimed in the distinct light
stand-easy, adjust a cap or finger a belt.

Shedding its shell, a crab must feel like this,
lost between two worlds, not so much scared as wary.
They consider the sergeant without prejudice
and accept the insulting candour of his stare.

Why is it then that with arms and legs loosened
out of a random rhythm they are forced to move
in a strange unison? Apart from the nuisance,
there is a buoyancy, even a kind of love.

Yet still, as the clue's emerging, they feel again
that pull of difference splitting each life into two.
More than the sergeant, each stands apart. The brain
is numbed with a semi-defiance. It isn't true.

It isn't true, each insists. It isn't happening.
This is not me. But it is. And you grin to find
the will re-welded, richer. You lose your cap,
feel foolish; and an urgency raps your mind –

tightened, look, in the buckle of belt and sling,
jestingly sealed in each momentous trifle,
stamped now, clamped in the bolt and the bayonet-ring,
fondled and final in the uplifted rifle.

K.W. Parkhurst

The Padre[1]

The Padre's got a cushy job, he roams about all day,
He doesn't work, he merely talks and wastes his time away.
He wears his collar back to front, and looks professional
But don't you let him take you in, he doesn't work at all.

It's War, boys, and we've got to fight, and that's our job for
    now;
The C.O. and the officers are here to tell us how,
The M.O's here to patch us up – we'll need him in this war –
But is there anybody who knows what a Padre's for?

The Army must be mechanised if we're to make a show
And every Fusilier admits we want an M.T.O.[2]
A Quartermaster there must be to superintend the store,
But only the Almighty knows just what the Padre's for.

And yet I've just been thinking, chaps, that surely he was sent
To do a job of some kind, for he's not an ornament;
I've heard it said by friends of mine who met a few in France
That Padres can come up to scratch if men give them a chance.

I get my problems and my thoughts, I get temptations, too,
And secret fears I'd like to share with someone, Bill, don't you?
We're not the only ones like that, there must be many more,
And so I've sometimes wondered if that's what Padre's for.

Mind you, I'm not afraid to die, and I don't ask for fuss,
But we've got girls or wives and kids who think the world of us
And if I get knocked out to-night and laid I don't know where,
Although I'm not a churchy chap I wouldn't mind a prayer.

Take that young fellow over there who's getting on so well –
If he gets shot his mother's heart is going to ache like hell;
If Padre wrote it couldn't bring him back, for nothing could,
And yet she'd be relieved to know that someone understood,

That someone understood, you know, someone who was
   nearby,
Who lived with him, and knew his name, perhaps who saw him
   die,
And every mother in the hour of bitterness and loss
Might like to know that someone tried to help the boy across.

I've asked you what a Padre's for: well now, I wonder, Bill
If he's been sent by Jesus Christ to help us up the hill?
He's not a saint and yet it's grand, tho' some might think it odd,
That we should have a fellow here to make us think of God.

[1]Written when Padre with the Royal Welch Fusiliers, 1940
[2]Mechanical Transport Officer

Henry Reed

Lessons of the War (To Alan Michell)

> *Vixi duellis nuper idoneus*
> *Et militavi non sine gloria*

I – Naming of Parts

Today we have naming of parts. Yesterday,
We had daily cleaning. And to-morrow morning,
We shall have what to do after firing. But to-day,
To-day we have naming of parts. Japonica
Glistens like coral in all of the neighbouring gardens
    And today we have naming of parts.

This is the lower sling swivel. And this
Is the upper sling swivel, whose use you will see
When you are given your slings. And this is the piling swivel,
Which in your case you have not got. The branches
Hold in the gardens their silent, eloquent gestures,
    Which in our case we have not got.

This is the safety-catch, which is always released
With an easy flick of the thumb. And please do not let me
See anyone using his finger. You can do it quite easy
If you have any strength in your thumb. The blossoms
Are fragile and motionless, never letting anyone see
    Any of them using their finger.

And this you can see is the bolt. The purpose of this
Is to open the breech, as you see. We can slide it
Rapidly backwards and forwards; we call this
Easing the spring. And rapidly backwards and forwards
The early bees are assaulting and fumbling the flowers:
    They call it easing the Spring

They call it easing the Spring; it is perfectly easy
If you have any strength in your thumb: like the bolt,
And the breech, and the cocking-piece, and the point of balance,
Which in our case we have not got; and the almond-blossom
Silent in all of the gardens and the bees going backwards and
    forwards,
For today we have naming of parts.

Vernon Scannell

War Song

A lesson that their children knew by heart
Where it lay stonily in that September.
Conscripted man, anonymous in hot
Brown or blue, intoned his rank and number.
The discs, strung from his neck, no amulet
Against the ache of loss, were worn in darkness
Under grave blankets in the narrow cot
After the bugle's skirmish with night's silence.
In trembling cities civil sleep was probed
By the wild sirens' blind and wounded howling;
White searchlights hosed the sky; black planets throbbed;
All night all buildings put on total mourning.
And when dawn yawned, the washed skies were afloat
With silver saveloys whose idle motion
And conference with puffed clouds appeared to mock
Bereaving night and morning's lamentation.
And then, down country lanes, the crop-haired sons
And nephews of the skeletons of Flanders
Made séance of their march, as, on their tongues,
The old ghosts sang again of Tipperary,
Packing kit-bags, getting back to Blighty,
But soon, bewildered, sank back to their graves
When other songs were bawled – a jaunty music
With false, bragging words: The Siegfried Line
Transformed with comic washing hanging from it,

Sergeants and Corporals were blessed, the barrel rolled;
But behind the grinning words and steady tramping
The Sergeant of the dark was taking names
And marking time to that lugubrious singing.
We're saying goodbye to them all: and, far away
From gunpit, barrack-square and trench, the mother
Sewed the dark garments for tomorrow's mourning.

Francis Scarfe

25-Pounder

O little dragon
Best seen from behind,
You have no paragon
In dragon-kind
For you can kill
Wherever you will
Without the bother
Of climbing a hill.

This much you have
In common with love.

Richard Spender

The Officer Cadet

My life darts
Like a worried cocking handle
From bored hotel lounges
Where angular and 'modern' officers' wives
Sit, and sip, and stitch nervously,
Talking confidential nothings

To their loudly precocious sons
In long grey flannel shorts
And to their so grown-up plain daughters
With big-buttocked tartan skirts.

My life jerks,
Like an unwanted casing
Pushed in the back by an ungrateful ejector,
To a pile of stale blankets and damp kit-bags,
Where everything smells of metal and of metal polish,
And where one's world,
Suddenly so remote from anything rational,
Revolves round boot polish and a brighter shine.

I cannot understand why
To fight for a few simple things
Necessitates polishing the toes of one's boots
'Until you can see your face in them.'
I have no wish to see my face;
And there are mirrors.
Neither do I see the cause nor wisdom
Of teaching supple bodies to behave like crank-shafts
And walk about like the most stupid
And self-opinioned wood pigeon in that little spinney
Where I once fell off the old white pony.
But that was in the days when
A bright wit and a clean neck
Were more important than polished buttons and shiny badges.

I have learnt wisdom here.
One can learn to love through opposites.
Sometimes I have unquenchable longings to lie
On the warm grass, perhaps by Binton Woods,
And watch the timid primrose smiling from her bed.

I love most the primrose
When I am surrounded by her opposites;
I can find nothing more unlike
A primrose
Than a Coldstream Guard Sergeant-Major.

Gervase Stewart

Parting

At main line junctions where such journeys have beginning
Blue tinted partings made we, with hooded trains above us
Hovering and like the fatal cobra hissing.

And we two of two hundred platform lovers
Trundled in wagons, making good our kissing
Until the moving train our parting covers

With the smoke, the garrulous lady, the soldier cursing,
The figure on the platform growing smaller,
And I not daring to withdraw my head lest the women nursing

The sightless child shall offer consolation,
But watch the china potted poles grow taller,
Hearing her sad lips' music in vibration

Of wide-strung wires against the background of the night,
And when at last dry-throated close the window,
To sit cornerwise beneath a smudge of light.

In an aroma of tobacco, sorrow
Collects, as mist about the outer moments of the moon,
And I am left to follow

The katabatic chatter of the train,
And wonder with a calculating eye
Would it be worth five pounds to pull the chain.

Douglas Street

'We're gonna set fire to the sea'[1]

I heard through the office window
The usual rider from Div –
A glib knowall with the sideboards
Of a typical cartoon spiv –
I heard him say in a casual way 'Sarr'nt Major!'
As he slurped a mug of our tea,
'I kid you not, Top Secret, we're gonna set fire to the sea'.

I was called to C.O.'s orders in a hush–hush sort of way;
'No notes, gentlemen, just listen! and what I've got to say
Is frightfully, frightfully secret,' he said, 'There are plans' –
and paused for effect, I suppose –
'With oil and gadgets and pipes and hose,
It all seems quite crazy to me,
Yes plans, to set fire, yes fire, to this our sector of sea.'

I called in at 'The Trip to Jerusalem' –
I'd noticed the brewers' dray;
The landlord was a friend of ours, a Home Guard Corporal he;
I drank my pints and chatted, and then he slipped to me,
Wrapped up, two bottles of whisky in a hush–hush sort of way.
'For God's sake keep these quiet,' he whispered – pause – 'Do we,
Like most of my customers say,
Have plans, daft plans, to burn up
Our stretch of the wet North Sea?'

Somewhere in Essex, 1940

[1]This anti-invasion plan was more advanced on the South Coast. The 'leak' was
partly due to the fact the local council workers had to be involved so that the
sewage outfall pipes could be used. The 'black' propaganda people used this when
it became almost public knowledge.

'Non-walking wounded will be left with civilians where possible.'

Wellington was reputed to have said, 'Gentlemen, the difference between a retreat and a rout, is that in a rout the wounded are left behind.'

Madame had told us she'd take them,
So on mattress, bed-spring, door,
We carried them clumsy, tender,
And laid them, on the Pension's cellar floor;
We lit the four tall candles
We'd nicked from the shell-shocked church;
We left them some water and toffees
   and some really horrible fags;
Each one of us felt he was half a man
As we guessed from their eyes that they knew it was lies
The yarn that I told, and the day grew old
   and the evening's shelling began.

Madame came down with her walking cane
Testing each cellar stair;
She had a cameo brooch, and a fine proud comb
In the back of her silvering hair;
She creaked me an old world curtsy
When I gave her my smartest salute;
She bent by the ginger-haired corporal –
The one with the hideous burn –
Looked up and said in her Flemish slang
I'd learned at my Grandma's knee,
'You bloody lot get moving, one day you will return!'
So we hurried out to the stink of rout
   and the sight of the blessèd sea!

Belgium, May 1940

Henry Treece

To Certain Ladies, On Going To The Wars

Goodbye ladies, O ladies sweet, goodbye,
No more the gentle flowers,
Another life I'll try.
No more the scented evenings,
The tussles in the hay,
It's time that I was leaving
To live another way.

O, there'll be blood, my ladies
(And not all mine, I hope),
And damp beds under hedges
And washing without soap.
Black lice will bite the body
That knew your friendly limbs;
In barrack-blocks I'll envy
Your silken-sheeted rooms.

But goodbye ladies, O ladies don't complain,
It's time I learnt to shoot straight
Or fly an aeroplane.
So many lads I knew once
Are rotting under sods:
I owe them this one journey –
So farewell, pretty birds.

John Waller

The Meaning Of War

How frequently the last time
Comes and we do not know
That this is indeed the last time
Before all shadows flow
Into a snow of memory
Where memory locks the gates
Of that ice-bound palace garden
Where a few wander like ghosts.

Childhood days by a river
To khaki dreams on a beach
Are usual recollections
That you or I may reach;
But those who deal in hazards
And take what dealing gives
Can never know the last time
In good or fatal moves.

The last time I see people
Is simple as goodbye,
Peter on Weymouth station
Or Kay going home to die.
Goodbye is always a warning
Till the next time we meet
That death is most wary, lurking
Behind unwary feet.

Leon Atkins

Dunkirk

*To One who survived long enough to die of
wounds in an English Hospital.*

BACKS to the Sea!
O bitter the word 'Retreat'
and bitterer yet—'Evacuate';
and nobody told the soldier why!
While Jerry's planes played merry hell
and laughed loud at our wounded pride:
Falling back with reluctant paces;
while Stukas spat death in our faces;
falling back – further back -
steadily back to the Sea . . . .
O God the crime!
(O blast the Sun!)
Pointing speechless guns
at contemptuous Huns
and five dud rounds
in our pouches . . . .

And nobody told us why!

My God,
How they cried,
how the wounded cried
as they staggered and sagged and died –
disarmed, in fierce anger and pride
on those lead-swept Dunes
in the Sun, on the way
to the Sea!

And nobody told them why!

God, how they cried
in their anger and pride,
in their impotence crucified!

Yea, loudly they cried as they'll cry anon
in the Day that will tell them why . . . .
when the scourge of Time
shall smite the crime,
the refuge of Lies
and the gilt-edged crime
that slew them
before their time!

O the crimson crime
that was yours and mine;
the crime that could dice
on the 'contract price'
of a Tank
and a Tommy Gun!
Spinning 'Put and Take'
for Judas's stake
and the profit
on Aeroplanes!

O despicable crime
that was yours and mine;
who could wine and dine
at home – so immune to the storm
in upholstered security;
while men fought with their fists
aye, with stones and sticks;
red mad in their anger and pride;
till they staggered and died
for the men that had lied,
on those lead-swept Dunes
in the Sun, on the way
to the Sea!

Tomorrow will tell them why!

B.G. Bonallack

Dunkirk (extract)

All through the night, and in the next day's light
The endless columns came. Here was Defeat.
The men marched doggedly, and kept their arms,
But sleep weighed on their backs so that they reeled,
Staggering as they passed. Their force was spent.
Only, like old Horatius, each man saw
Far off his home, and seeing, plodded on.
At last they ceased. The sun shone down, and we
Were left to watch along a dusty road.

That night we blew our guns. We placed a shell
Fuze downwards in each muzzle. Then we put
Another in the breech, secured a wire
Fast to the firing lever, crouched, and pulled.
It sounded like a cry of agony,
The crash and clang of splitting, tempered steel.
Thus did our guns, our treasured colours, pass;
And we were left bewildered, weaponless,
And rose and marched, our faces to the sea.

We formed in line beside the water's edge.
The little waves made oddly home-like sounds,
Breaking in half-seen surf upon the strand.
The night was full of noise; the whistling thud
The shells made in the sand, and pattering stones;
The cries cut short, the shouts of units' names;
The crack of distant shots, and bren gun fire;
The sudden clattering crash of masonry.
Steadily, all the time, the marching tramp
Of feet passed by along the shell-torn road,
Under the growling thunder of the guns.

The major said 'The boats cannot get in,
'There is no depth of water. Follow me.'
And so we followed, wading in our ranks
Into the blackness of the sea. And there,
Lit by the burning oil across the swell,
We stood and waited for the unseen boats.

Oars in the darkness, rowlocks, shadowy shapes
Of boats that searched. We heard a seaman's hail.
Then we swam out, and struggled with our gear,
Clutching the looming gunwales. Strong hands pulled,
And we were in and heaving with the rest,
Until at last they turned. The dark oars dipped,
The laden craft crept slowly out to sea,
To where in silence lay the English ships.

Alan Rook

Dunkirk Pier

Deeply across the waves of our darkness fear
like the silent octopus feeling, groping, clear
as a star's reflection, nervous and cold as a bird,
tells us that pain, tells us that death is near.

Why should a woman telling above her fire
incantations of evening, thoughts that are
older and paler than history, why should this lark
exploring extinction and oneness of self and air

remind us that, lonely and lost as flowers in deserted
weed-mastered gardens, each faint face averted
from the inescapable confusion, for each of us slowly
death on his last, most hideous journey has started?

What was our sin? – that heartless to the end
falls now the heavy sickle on foe, on friend,
and those that we love, value and regret
surrender quickest to death's empty hand.

Failure to suffer? We who in years past
have suffered, yes, in this or that, but in the last
irrevocable act of suffering, as a dog suffers deeply,
blindly, completely, are not versed.

What hope for the future? Can we who see the tide
ebbing along the shore, the greedy, lined
with shadows, dare with puny words support
a future which belongs to others? Dare we bind

now, at this last moment of sunshine above
the crests of oncoming events, like waves which move
remorselessly nearer, future generations
with sacrifice? *We* who taught hate, expect them to
        love?

The Middle East

Almendro

Night Preceding Battle

Spoamy,
Slashing at the shore,
Salt skimmering in the moonlight,
And always that roar
Like a family quarrel. Tonight
I look across the disarranged sea,
Undulating unaltered, only I,
Different and detached, divining Me
Formulated as a breathing question-mark
Crivelling in lust-pregnated casing,
Like bee seducing pollened virgin,
Questions 'Why?'

Why dust-born society advancing dust's decay,
Cradled in metal-moulded rhetoric, insane
Distortion of armed arbitration?
With this 'Why?' pounding, thumping in my brain
I demand God end His holiday
And influence the situation.

Yesterday I embraced my plough with masochistic pleasure,
Worrying if my economic seeds would be enough
To feed the hungry. Soil and work were the measure
Of my education.

Today I killed a man. God forgive me!
Tomorrow I shall sow another political corpse,
Or be dead myself. And strangely
I am satisfied to be applauded killer.
Holy Mary plead my dutied sin's legality.
Is there no end, reason, answer? Damn the sea!

Spoamy,
Slashing at the shore,
Salt skimmering in the moonlight,
And always that roar

Like a family quarrel. Tonight
They are rolling up the guns for tomorrow's battle.
I must not be late to hear Death rattle
In my enemy's throat.

The flame of Hell pythoning
Around my trigger finger insinuates coercion,
And feeling body's blooded-reeds contracting,
Dispose of humanity's humiliated feelings
And know that I am ready.

Christ, it's cold tonight!

Martin Bell

Reason for Refusal

Busy old lady, charitable tray
Of social emblems: poppies, people's blood –
I must refuse, make you flush pink
Perplexed by abrupt No-thank-you.
Yearly I keep up this small priggishness,
Would wince worse if I wore one.
Make me feel better, fetch a white feather, do.

Everyone has list of dead in war,
Regrets most of them, e.g.

Uncle Cyril; small boy in lace and velvet
With pushing sisters muscling all around him,
And lofty brothers, whiskers and stiff collars;
The youngest was the one who copped it.
My mother showed him to me,
Neat letters high up on the cenotaph
That wedding-caked it up above the park,
And shadowed birds on Isaac Watts' white shoulders.

And father's friends, like Sandy Vincent;
Brushed sandy hair, moustache, and staring eyes.
Kitchener claimed him, but the Southern Railway
Held back my father, made him guilty.
I hated the khaki photograph,
It left a patch on the wallpaper after I took it down.

Others I knew stick in the mind,
And Tony Lister often –
Eyes like holes in foolscap, suffered from piles,
Day after day went sick with constipation
Until they told him he could drive a truck –

Blown up with Second Troop in Greece:
We sang all night once when we were on guard.

And Ken Gee, our lance-corporal, Christian
        Scientist –
Everyone liked him, knew that he was good –
Had leg and arm blown off, then died.

Not all were good. Gross Corporal Rowlandson
Fell in the canal, the corrupt Sweet-water,
And rolled there like a log, drunk and drowned.
And I've always been glad of the death of Dick
        Benjamin,
A foxy urgent dainty ball-room dancer –
Found a new role in military necessity
As R.S.M. He waltzed out on parade
To make himself hated. Really hated, not an act.
He was a proper little porcelain sergeant-major –
The earliest bomb made smithereens;
Coincidence only, several have assured me.

In the school hall was pretty glass
Where prissy light shone through St George –
The highest holiest manhood, he!
And underneath were slain Old Boys
In tasteful lettering on whited slab –
And, each November, Ferdy the Headmaster

Reared himself squat and rolled his eyeballs upward,
Rolled the whole roll-call off an oily tongue,
Remorselessly from A to Z.

Of all the squirmers, Roger Frampton's lips
Most elegantly curled, showed most disgust.
He was a pattern of accomplishments,
And joined the Party first, and left it first,
At OCTU won a prize belt, most improbable,
Was desert-killed in '40, much too soon.

His name should burn right through that monument.

No poppy, thank you.

Max Bowden

Myriad Destiny in Neat Black Shoes . . .

With minimum bow-wave
The convoy glides persistently
Determined sheep guarded by brawny shepherd
Swallowing opposed distance

Sweating ghosts from reeking troop-decks
Man bleak unsmiling guns
Like devils' fingers jeering at God
And all balanced on a restless eiderdown
That gives no rest

Eyes like women's fingers
Attempted to smooth ruffled surfaces
Lay a constant stare by day and night
Focusing the impossible
Optic nerves ache and minds dull
At constant illusion of small waves

This monstrous iron womb
Teeming with obscure life
Holds tortuous course
Steered by epaulettes flanking a teak face
Grey pulp throbbing in bony cup
Under bald head and peak cap
Myriad destiny in neat black shoes.

Jocelyn Brooke

Landscape Near Tobruk

This land was made for War. As glass
Resists the bite of vitriol, so this hard
And calcined earth rejects
The battle's hot, corrosive impact. Here
Is no nubile, girlish land, no green
And virginal countryside for War
To violate. This land is hard,
Inviolable, the battle's aftermath
Presents no ravaged and emotive scene,
No landscape à la Goya. Here are no trees
Uprooted, gutted farms; the unsalvaged scrap –
The scattered petrol-cans, the upturned
And abandoned truck, the fallen Heinkel; all
The rusted and angular detritus
Of war, seem scarcely to impinge
Upon the hard, resistant surface of
This lunar land: ephemeral
As trippers' leavings, paper-bags and orange-peel
Upon Ben Nevis. Sun and sand
Inhibit here the mind's habitual
And easy gestures; hand and eye
Perform their functions with a robot-cunning –
The sly and casual movements of
The shadowed thief. The soldiers camped
In the rock-strewn wadi merge

Like lizard or jerboa in the brown
And neutral ambient: stripped at gunsite,
Or splashing like glad beasts at sundown in
The brackish pool, their smooth
And lion-coloured bodies seem
The indigenous fauna of an unexplored,
Unspoiled country: harmless, easy to trap,
And tender-fleshed – a hunter's prize.

J.E. Brookes

Tobruk 1941

His Company was in the second wave.
ADVANCE! Unfortunately something gave
him 'Gyppo Tummy', water melons p'raps,
and as a consequence occurred a lapse
of social etiquette if not the sin
of breaching military discipline.
Public Exposure! Desert Waste Defaced
By Private Soldier! Infantry Disgraced?

Then pulled his trousers up, pulled down his hat,
and checked his safety-catch. And after that
he caught the others up. To leave no doubt
in anybody else's mind about
the nature of the incident because
they might think he was shit-scared (which he was),
he started whistling *British Grenadiers*
as if he'd been a fighting man for years.

Norman Cameron

Green, Green Is El Aghir

Sprawled on the crates and sacks in the rear of the truck,
I was gummy-mouthed from the sun and the dust of the track,
And the two Arab soldiers I had taken on as hitch-hikers,
At a torrid petrol-dump, had been there on their hunkers
Since early morning. I said, in a kind of French
'*On m'a dit, qu'il y a une belle source d'eau fraîche,
Plus loin, à El Aghir.*' It was eighty more kilometres
Until round a corner we heard a splashing of waters,
And there, in a green, dark street, was a fountain with two facets
Discharging both ways, from full-throated faucets
Into basins, thence into troughs and thence into brooks.
Our negro corporal driver slammed his brakes,
And we yelped and leapt from the truck and went at the double
To fill our bidons and bottles and drink and dabble.
Then, swollen with water, we went to an inn for wine.
The Arabs came, too, though their faith might have stood
    between;
'After all,' they said, 'it's a *boisson*,' without contrition.

Green, green is El Aghir. It has a railway-station,
And the wealth of its soil has borne many another fruit,
A mairie, a school and an elegant *Salle de Fêtes*.
Such blessings, as I remarked, in effect, to the waiter,
Are added unto them that have plenty of water.

Roy Campbell

Snapshot of Nairobi

With orange-peel the streets are strown
And pips, beyond computing
On every shoulder save my own,
That's fractured with saluting.

May 1943.

Heartbreak Camp

To Major S.C. Mason of the Nigerian Regiment

Red as the guardroom lamp
The moon inspects the trees:
High over Heartbreak Camp,
Orion stands at ease:

With buttons lit, for Sentry,
He challenges who's there
Acceding all the entry
Whose passport is Despair.

All joys are privates there
Who seldom go on leave
And only sorrows wear
Three chevrons on their sleeve:

But boredom wears three pips,
A fiend of monstrous size,
With curses on his lips
And circles round his eyes.

All round, for league on league
And labouring up the hills,
The clouds are on fatigue,
Collecting damps and chills.

Sir Dysentery Malaria,
A famous brigadier,
Commands the whole sub-area,
And stalking in his rear,

A more ferocious colonel
Lord Tremens (of the Drunks)
To whose commands infernal
We tremble in our bunks.

Here, till the pale aurora
Dismiss the stars from drill,
I dream of my Señora
Behind the guardroom grille.

In the outcry of crickets
And the silence of guitars,
I watch the lonely pickets
And the slow patrol of stars.

Our vineyard and the terrace
By the Tagus, they recall,
With the Rose of the Sierras,
Whom I love the best of all!

My heart was once her campfire
And burned for her alone,
Fed with the thyme and samphire
That azure days had grown.

My thoughts for their safari
Have scarcely taken wings·
Through spaces wide and starry
To hear her stroke the strings:

But ere one word be spoken
A fiend my elbow jogs,
The reverie is broken
By the tomtom of the wogs:

And, all illusions killing,
Upon the stillness jars
A far hyaena drilling
His company of stars.

Louis Challoner

Alternative

The question rises almost daily
In the gunpit, grimly, gaily –
Is it the shelling you prefer
Or the bombing? – All the air
Crouching in silence, tensely waiting –
The distant thud – the daily hating –
The whining scream – the crashing roar,
Forever nearer, – ever more
Intimately:

Then are the strong weak and the brave
Lie flattened low in their sandy grave,
Counting the leaden seconds dropping
Heavy as heart-beats, slowly – stopping –
Knowing each moment, dearer, clearer, –
Death creeps methodically nearer –

Or shall we stand, hands to our eyes
And watch the foeman in the skies,
Knowing the peril but unheeding
For the sheer beauty of the speeding
Planes that dive and, turning, mount again –
Light of their silver load – count again
The known numbers, note foreseen effect,
The chaos, sand and limestone wrecked
Into a halo round the sun
A cloud about our friendly gun?

I'd rather look death in the face
Born by a bomber's speed and grace –
Swinging down its rainbow arc
Like a falcon to its mark –
Than grovel like a nerveless slave
With nothing but his skin to save,
Crouching beneath the ugly Hell
Made by the calculated shell.

Michael Croft

Leaving the Med.

We came this way before
In different ships
Which knew no casual watch.
The hills rose crimson from the brooding coast
As at the guns we watched the light's last span
Shrink with the fatal sun
To night, and eyes the night concealed
Peering from black waters.

Historical islands
Familiar as midday bombers
Pass, known by their battle names,
Islands with the dead we once had watched
When dawn was shell–plunged
Dragged by gaunt islanders down jagged graves
Or buried in torn groves.

Now leaves are green and ruins are arranged
To soothe the tourist on the languid cruise;
Bored elegance can gaze,
Admire the luscious view, the beach,
And ask, when guides are hired in hills,
Which bones are which.

We have raced periscopes
Slanting for murder
From neat waves, seen water lap blood's blue serge
From gun decks when ships screamed,
And when night's bombs had ceased,
The sick convoy, limbs floating in loose scarves,
And bobbing aimless caps.

Soon even the love we learnt will be lost,
Blotted from memory like the ports of Egypt,
Buried in obscure images of distant poetry.

This was our way.
We know faith's private history
Alone defines a way.

1945.

John Cromer

Asleep in War

I called you once, but you were sleeping,
Gold in your hair the moonlight gleamed.
I stood quite still, but my heart was leaping
Though I knew not what were the dreams you dreamed.

I called you again, you still were sleeping,
Pale was your face, no smile was there.
Your eyes were tired with too much weeping,
The splendid lustre had left your hair.

I called once more, you were not sleeping,
A trickle of blood lay by your head.
The sky was clear, no searchlights sweeping;
Raiders had passed – but you were dead.

D.M. Davin

Cairo Cleopatra

No mighty Caesars helpless gasp
In these lubricious thighs.
Plain soldiers in their practised grasp
Grunt inexpensive sighs.

Simple and short her shift,
Cheap is her price.
All that she has in gift
Is pubic lice.

You who have sobbed above
This mortal core,
Cast off your agonied love
On this jetsam shore

Recall to your coward heart,
Remind your despair,
This used Egyptian tart
May also ask where,

Where is there peace at last,
Peace from all lust?
The quiet of the womb long past,
What of the dust?

Or worse, no questions sear
This public flesh.
Enjoying each desperate dear,
She is content in the mesh.

Cairo, July 1942.

Grave near Sirte

No poppies bleed above his blood.
His diary closed before last spring.
Upon his cross there greens no second bud.
He feels no more the sandstorm's sting.

The sweating dew upon his helmet's steel
Dries through each day to rust.
Caressing sand he cannot feel
Has blanketed his lust.

Eyes look no longer to the sea
His hope had often crossed.
Rocks shade his bones, and no dark tree,
No thaw for this death's frost.

Not British and not German now he's dead,
He breeds no grasses from his rot.
The coast road and the Arab pass his bed
And waste no musing on his lot.

December 1942.

Erik de Mauny

News from Home

Here under the neutral, distempered wall
Of the shuttered hut in a transit camp
Or waiting in tent at pebbly dusk
Impatient as a traveller at an empty station
I have lived, hardly aware of you at all.
Stray thoughts of home make leaguer and decamp
Between the exile's smile and gesture.
For here I have learned another intonation:
The shadow of the year passes like a bird's,
Dark, treacherous and smooth across the banquet,

Life's bright plateaux and shining mountains.
(I'm sorry I sent you just a picture postcard:
The legions foundered in the snow.)
These are my trophies: beads and dead leaves,
An island mask and the programme of a show,
Pension receipts from the foreigners' foreshore –

Can I tell the girl who gave, the waves' thunder
As the moon sank? These you cannot know.
These, like the dreams of ruin or delight,
Happened to the jar and thrill of the fife,

Are pent for the bullet's or the fever's spending.
This last of ecstasy, life and no life
I will bring to bury in peace among you.
You will say: 'There is another day gone by.'
And I will smile and shrug: say yes
To a dear stranger's happiness.

C.P.S. Denholm-Young

Dead German Youth

He lay there, mutilated and forlorn,
Save that his face was woundless, and his hair
Drooped forward and caressed his boyish brow.
He looked so tired, as if his life had been
Too full of pain and anguish to endure,
And like a weary child who tires of play
He lay there, waiting for decay.
I feel no anger towards you, German boy,
Whom war has driven down the path of pain.
Would God we could have met in peace
And laughed and talked with tankards full of beer,
For I would rather hear your youthful mirth
At stories which I often loved to tell
Than stand here looking down at you
So terrible, so quiet and so still.

Keith Douglas

How to Kill

Under the parabola of a ball,
a child turning into a man,
I looked into the air too long.
The ball fell in my hand, it sang
in the closed fist: *Open, open
Behold a gift designed to kill*.

Now in my dial of glass appears
the soldier who is going to die.
He smiles, and moves about in ways
his mother knows, habits of his.
The wires touch his face; I cry
NOW. Death, like a familiar, hears

and look, has made a man of dust
of a man of flesh. This sorcery
I do. Being damned, I am amused
to see the centre of love diffused
and the waves of love travel into vacancy.
How easy it is to make a ghost.

The weightless mosquito touches
her tiny shadow on the stone,
and with how like, how infinite
a likeness, man and shadow meet.
They fuse. A shadow is a man
when the mosquito death approaches.

Tunisia-Cairo, 1943.

Elegy for an 88 Gunner

(Published elsewhere under the title 'Vergissmeinicht')

Three weeks gone and the combatants gone,
returning over the nightmare ground
we found the place again and found
the soldier sprawling in the sun.

The frowning barrel of his gun
overshadows him. As we came on
that day, he hit my tank with one
like the entry of a demon.

And smiling in the gunpit spoil
is a picture of his girl
who has written: *Steffi, Vergissmeinicht*.
in a copybook Gothic script.

We see him almost with content,
abased and seeming to have paid,
mocked by his durable equipment
that's hard and good when he's decayed.

But she would weep to see today
how on his skin the swart flies move,
the dust upon the paper eye
and the burst stomach like a cave.

For here the lover and the killer are mingled
who had one body and one heart;
and Death, who had the soldier singled
has done the lover mortal hurt.

Homs, Tripolitania, 1943.

Cairo Jag

Shall I get drunk or cut myself a piece of cake,
a pale Syrian with a few words of English
or the Turk who says she is a princess; she dances
by apparent levitation? Or Marcelle, Parisienne
always preoccupied with her dull dead lover:
she has all the photographs and his letters
tied in a bundle and stamped *Décédé*.
All this takes place in a stink of jasmin.

But there are the streets dedicated to sleep,
stenches and sour smells; the sour cries
do not disturb their application to slumber
all day, scattered on the pavement like rags,
afflicted with fatalism and hashish. The women
offering their children brown paper breasts
dry and twisted, elongated like Holbein's bone signature.
All this dust and ordure, the stained white town
are something in accord with mundane conventions.
Marcelle drops her Gallicism and tragic air,
suddenly shrieks about the fare in Arabic
with the cabman; and links herself
with the somnambulist and the legless beggars.
It is all one, all as you have heard.

But by a day's travelling you reach a new world,
the vegetation is of iron.
Dead tanks and gun barrels split like celery
the metal brambles without flowers or berries;
and there are all sorts of manure, you can imagine
the dead themselves, their boots, clothes and possessions
clinging to the ground. A man with no head
has a packet of chocolate and a souvenir of Tripoli.

On a Return from Egypt

To stand here in the wings of Europe
disheartened, I have come away
from the sick land where in the sun lay
the gentle sloe-eyed murderers
of themselves, exquisites under a curse;
here to exercise my depleted fury.

For the heart is a coal, growing colder
when jewelled cerulean seas change
into grey rocks, grey water-fringe,
sea and sky altering like a cloth
till colour and sheen are gone both:
cold is an opiate of the soldier.

And all my endeavours are unlucky explorers
come back, abandoning the expedition;
the specimens, the lilies of ambition
still spring in their climate, still unpicked:
but time, time is all I lacked
to find them, as the great collectors before me.

The next month, then, is a window
and with a crash I'll split the glass.
Behind it stands one I must kiss,
person of love or death
a person or a wraith,
I fear what I shall find.

Egypt-England, 1943–44.

Lawrence Durrell

Alexandria

To the lucky now who have lovers or friends,
Who move to their sweet undiscovered ends,
Or whom the great conspiracy deceives,
I wish these whirling autumn leaves:
Promontories splashed by the salty sea,
Groaned on in darkness by the tram
To horizons of love or good luck or more love –
As for me I now move
Through many negatives to what I am.

Here at the last cold Pharos between Greece
And all I love, the lights confide
A deeper darkness to the rubbing tide;
Doors shut, and we the living are locked inside
Between the shadows and the thoughts of peace:
And so in furnished rooms revise
The index of our lovers and our friends
From gestures possibly forgotten, but the ends
Of longings like unconnected nerves,
And in this quiet rehearsal of their acts
We dream of them and cherish them as Facts.

Now when the sea grows restless as a conscript,
Excited by fresh wind, climbs the sea-wall,
I walk by it and think about you all:
B. with his respect for the Object, and D.
Searching in sex like a great pantry for jars
Marked 'Plum and apple'; and the small, fell
Figure of Dorian ringing like a muffin-bell –
All indeed whom war or time threw up
On this littoral and tides could not move
Were objects for my study and my love.

And then turning where the last pale
Lighthouse, like a Samson blinded, stands
And turns its huge charred orbit on the sands
I think of you – indeed mostly of you,
In whom a writer would only name and lose
The dented boy's lip and the close
Archer's shoulders; but here to rediscover
By tides and faults of weather, by the rain
Which washes everything, the critic and the lover.

At the doors of Africa so many towns founded
Upon a parting could become Alexandria, like
The wife of Lot – a metaphor for tears;
And the queer student in his poky hot
Tenth floor room above the harbour hears
The sirens shaking the tree of his heart,
And shuts his books, while the most
Inexpressible longings like wounds unstitched
Stir in him some girl's unquiet ghost.

So we, learning to suffer and not condemn
Can only wish you this great pure wind
Condemned by Greece, and turning like a helm
Inland where it smokes the fires of men,
Spins weathercocks on farms or catches
The lovers at their quarrel in the sheets;
Or like a walker in the darkness might,
Knocks and disturbs the artist at his papers
Up there alone, upon the alps of night.

Donald Everett

Envoi

The show was over, we did not know
how long it had been over.
There was a slow drift from shelters,

some thought we were dead, all knew
that we were mad. The oaths were strong
the sullen stub was lit, but sleep
soon re-assumed
its overweaning power.

We awoke as the dogs licked our faces –
dawn was a woman in violet
wearing a red sash –
we worshipped her.

Ian Fletcher

Naked Africa

Naked Africa I lie on you
– the fruit-like body of woman

think of your women, philtres of midday,
dark cinders of their gaze

pressing an earthiness
of eastern flesh upon us

hiding fear between
pincers of their salamandrine sex

this is the source,
emptiness, a nothing
through which we enter on ourselves
gravid the desert

two eyes on a thin khaki stalk
still surprised
like foetuses the dead are coiled.

1944.

Soldiers at the Base

Among lupine faces on the rabid posters
'V.D. is dangerous to the Family' and
'Buy National Savings Now', in their blunt postures,
Ranked, numbered, moved, removed, the squaddies stand.

Those who past polemical terrain
Bumbled by tank and lorry to the front
But hazard if their day may bloom again
In quiet-keyed living, the menial stunt.

Others in flycapped kitchens, office and hutment, band,
Dressing the sick sweet altars of the Latrine;
Outflanked by boredom, sliverings of sand;
Sensed, the high rigours of the lost campaign.

So I, raw poet, notionally quite least
Of such uncompassed travellers, come
By war, all langour, on this middling east
And jeopard in survival's trivium.

A carrier, standing for its convoy;
I talk to a serious trooper. All these ends.
O Predellas, Aumbries, Archlutes, arcs of joy;
Over there, up the Blue, is freedom, death and friends.

Base, all base, in our off-coloured dreams,
Clawed not those waxed infantas, dimly kind;
But divas in froth velvet, whose bare screams
Skewed us like shot. *We have fallen too far behind*.

Geneifa, January 1944.

G.S. Fraser

Egypt

Who knows the lights at last, who knows the cities
And the unloving hands upon the thighs
Would yet return to seek his home-town pretties
For the shy finger-tips and sidelong eyes.

Who knows the world, the flesh, the compromises
Would go back to the theory in the book:
Who knows the place the poster advertises
Back to the poster for another look.

But nets the fellah spreads beside the river
Where the green waters criss-cross in the sun
End certain migratory hopes for ever;
In that white light, all shadows are undone.

The desert slays. But safe from Allah's justice
Where the broad river of His Mercy lies,
Where ground for labour, or where scope for lust is,
The crooked and tall and cunning cities rise.

The green Nile irrigates a barren region,
All the coarse palms are ankle-deep in sand;
No love roots deep, though easy loves are legion:
The heart's as hot and hungry as the hand.

In airless evenings, at the café table,
The soldier sips his thick sweet coffee up:
The dry grounds, like the moral to my fable,
Are bitter at the bottom of the cup.

An Elegy for Keith Bullen[1]

(Headmaster of Gezira Preparatory School, Cairo, and a friend to English poetry and poets.)

A great room and a bowl full of roses,
Red roses, a man as round as a ripe rose,
Lying in a bowl of sun. And who supposes
Such a sad weight could support such a gay pose,

Flying his sad weight like a round baby's
Petulant balloon! He has blue pebbles for eyes,
Petulant, bewildered, innocent eyes like a baby's;
Like a great baby or a clipped rose he lies

In a white bowl of light in my memory;
And expands his tenuous sweetness like a balloon;
I shall die of feeling his dear absurdity
So near me now, if I cannot cry soon.

Keith was particularly Sunday morning,
Red roses, old brandy, was unharrying Time,
Was that white light, our youth; or was the fawning
Zephyr that bobs the gay balloon of rhyme,

He bobbed incredibly in our modern air;
With his loose jacket, his white panama hat,
As he leaned on his walking stick on the stone stair
He seemed a balloon, moored down to the ground by that.

As he leaned at the bar and ordered us pink gin
Or arranged a flutter on the three-fifteen
He seemed a child, incapable of sin:
We never knew him prudent, cold, or mean.

Or tied to the way the world works at all
(Not even tied enough for poetry);
All that he was we only may recall,
An innocent that guilt would wish to be,

[1]Founder of The Salamander Society, Cairo

A kind, a careless, and a generous,
An unselfseeking in his love of art,
A jolly in his great explosive fuss;
O plethora of roses, O great heart!

Alan Freedman

August

Flood-swift and brown with earth-break,
Rock-spun, bridge-cleft and clamouring,
In one great turbulence – thus the Nile.

Down to the arms of the aching delta
Swirls the green-wrack silently.
Yet, river entire, there is no quiet
For water is reft and the whole length
Surfaced with sail and flutter of birds.
But rarely now the weighted oars
And plash of fishnets dropping.
All things wait, feeling the turn
Of season and the coming up of cloud.
Enough and enough of heat and aridity!
Seep, pour, drench down the coolness,
Stride in the bluster of evening breeze
For this is the sign, the months develop
And soon the quick and the cold and the clean.

Underneath the mosque
The cistern cellar is splash
With flooding and still mounting,
While on the palms the tight date clusters
Redden and ripen.
Root sprung with roaring sediment
All things conceive.
Night after night the banks are mad
With multiple voices

And the maize fields yelling with frogs.
Pulse after pulse, like blood beat
Of desire, moves the strong life,
Beats upwards. This is the river
Whose autumn is a strange new spring.

Brian Gallie

To a German Airman

Who flew slowly through the British Fleet

Perhaps you knew not what you did,
That what you did was good;
Perhaps the head I saw was dead,
Or blind with its own blood.

Perhaps the wings you thought you ruled,
With sky and sea beneath,
Beat once with love for God above –
And flew you to your death.

Perhaps: but I prefer to think
That something in you, friend,
No inch would give to land and live,
But conscious chose the end.

That something in you, like a bird,
Knowing no cage's bars,
Courage supreme – an instant dream
Of mind beneath the stars:

Misguided, arrogant, or proud,
But – beyond telling – great,
Made you defy our fire and fly
Straight on, to meet your fate.

Steel-capped, we cowered as you went,
Defiant and alone;
A noble thing, we watched you wing
Your way to the unknown.

You passed us, still a mile from death,
Rocked by the wind of shell;
We held our breath, until to death
Magnificent you fell.

Whatever comet lit your track –
Contempt, belief, or hate –
You let us see an enemy
Deliberately great.

John Gawsworth

The Fallen

When they fall, men grasp at feathers,
Cheat the knowledge of their doom
With hot hopes, and see all weathers
Fine, not overhung with gloom.

They have failed, and there's no falling
Further. Uncrowned heads are light.
Ambition no more is calling.
Restlessness has passed with fright.

None but fools offer their pity
To the fallen who at last,
Driven from their tyrant city,
Into freedom have been cast.

E.F. Gosling

Mechanization

Only seven months have passed but what a change they've
    made.
Remember how it used to be when troops got on parade?
'See those bits are fitted right!
See those girths are tight!
Mind you shake the blankets out before you put 'em on!'
How the nose-bands caught the light, how the steel-work
    shone!

All that's very different now. We dress like garage hands;
Gone now the clink of bit and spur; no trumpets now, no bands.
'Petrol, oil and water right?
All the wheel-nuts tight?
Did you check the levels up before you got aboard?'
No more, alas, the head-tossed foam, the fretful foot that
    pawed:
Oh glory that was Tetrarch's might, oh drabness that is Ford!

Deòrsa Caimbeul Hay (George Campbell Hay)

Mochtàr Is Dùghall

Sgeula-Dhàn Fada Neochrìochnaichte

Mhochtàir is Dhùghaill, choinnich sibh
    an comann buan gun chòmhradh.

B'iad fraighean an taigh-chèilidh dhuibh
    an cactus ceuste, leònte.

B'i 'n aoigheachd an dèidh furain dhuibh
    làn beòil den duslach ròsta.

B'i fàilte an ùir chomainn sin
    guth obann, cruaidh ' mhòrtair.

Am fear a sgrìobh an dùnadh
    le bloighdean, bùirich 's ceò dhuibh.

Am fear a sgaoil an urchair,
    cha bu shuilbhear e no deònach.

A bhrù gu 'chur gu tuireadh
    le droch-uisge plodach lòintean.

A shùilean dearg is sreamach
    le cion cadail 's an *schnapps* a dh'òl e.

Is e a' speuradh is a' mallachadh
    an stùir, an teas 's a' chòirneil.

A bheil fhios ciod e'n dubh chumhachd
    a chuir cruinn sibh air an sgòrr seo?

A stiùir thar bheann 's thar chuan sibh,
    gur cruadhachadh le dòrainn?

Nur triùir – sibh fhèin rinn bràithreachas
    's an làmh a naisg bhur n-eòlas.

(George Campbell Hay)

Mokhtar and Dougall

Mokhtâr and Dougall, you have met in an everlasting fellowship
    without conversation.
The walls of your gossiping house were the tortured, wounded cactus.
The hospitality that followed welcome for you was the fill of your
    mouth of hot dust.
The greeting of your new companionship was the sudden, hard voice of
    the mortar.
The man who wrote the closing words of your song with splinters,
    roaring and smoke. . .
The man who fired the shot, he was no cheerful, eager warrior.
His belly driving him to weep with the bad, tepid water of the flats.
His eyes red and watering with want of sleep and the schnapps he had
    drunk.
He blaspheming, and cursing the dust, the heat and the Colonel.

Who knows what dark power brought you together on this pinnacle.
That guided you over mountains and oceans, hardening you with
    misery.
The three of you – you two who formed your brotherhood, and the hand
    that bound you together in acquaintance.
Sneaking, crawling on all fours, snaking like beasts of prey.
The Gefreiter who gave you your death, and pulled out, leaving you
    together. . .
He was captured with the scream in his throat, a madman on Cape Bon.
Der Krieg ist Scheiss – der Führer Scheiss! – that was his Sieg Heil
    in the end.
But you stayed on the battlefield amongst the djumar of this swarthy
    mountain.
Here are the 'lousy Arab' and the 'dirty Roumi' together.
Was that the speech you used when you used to meet on the highways?

A' sèapail is a' màgaran,
    a' snàgail mar bhèisdean feòlachd.

An *Gefreit* a thug am bàs dhuibh,
    's a thàrr as gur fàgail còmhla,

Dh'fhalh e crom is gearanach
    fo 'eagal 's luchd a' mhòrtair.

Ghlacadh, 's an sgreuch 'na mhuineal,
    'na fhear cuthaich air Ceap Bòn e.

'*Der Krieg ist Scheiss! Der Führer Scheiss!*'
    b'e sin an *Sieg Heil* fa dheòidh aig'.

Ach dh'fhuirich sibh san làrach
    measg *diumàir* an *debeil* chròin seo.

An seo tha'n 'trusdar Arabach'
    's an '*Rùimi* rapach' còmhla.

Am b'e sin a' chainnt a bh'agaibh
    nuair a thachradh sibh sna ròidean?

No 'n do nochd sibh daonnachd chaidreabhach
    san aiteal am bu bheò sibh?

Daoine nach gabhadh fionnaireachd
    le *burnus* no dath còta?

Nach coma! Air an leathad seo
    rinn sibh mu dheireadh còrdadh,

Is chan eil foirfeach no *marbat*
    a thearbas sibh le 'eòlas;

Tàileab, iomàm no ministear
    chuireas ioghnadh, crith no bròn oirbh.

Fear-rèite treun is tìoranach
    deagh shìbhealtachd na h-Eòrpa!

Or were you humane and affable in the glimpse of time you were alive?
Men who would not turn coldly hostile on account of a burnouse or the
    colour of a coat.

What does it matter? On this hillside you agree at last.
There is no elder or marabout *who can estrange you with his*
    knowledge.
Taleb, imam *or minister to fill you with wonder, or trembling or*
    sorrow.
A powerful, tyrannous reconciler is the goodly civilisation of Europe.

Hamish Henderson

Seven Good Germans

*The track running between Mekili and Tmimi was at one time a kind of
no-man's-land. British patrolling was energetic and there were
numerous brushes with German and Italian elements. El Eleba lies
about half-way along this track.*

Of the swaddies
who came to the desert with Rommel
There were few who had heard (or would hear) of El Eleba.
They recce'd,
or acted as medical orderlies
or patched up their tanks in the camouflaged workshops
and never gave a thought to a place like El Eleba.

To get there, you drive into the blue, take a bearing
and head for damn-all. Then you're there. And where are you?

– Still, of some few who did cross our path at El Eleba
there are seven who bide under their standing crosses.

The first a Lieutenant.
When the medicos passed him
for service overseas, he had jotted in a note-book

*to the day and the hour   keep me steadfast   there is only
the decision and the will
the rest has no importance*

The second a Corporal.
He had been in the Legion
and had got one more chance to redeem his lost honour.
What he said was
*Listen here, I'm fed up with your griping –
If you want extra rations, go get 'em from Tommy!
You're green, that's your trouble. Dodge the column, pass the buck*

and scrounge all you can – that's our law in the Legion.
You know Tommy's got 'em . . . He's got mineral waters,
and beer, and fresh fruit in that white crinkly paper
and God knows what all! Well, what's holding you back?
Are you windy or what?
                    Christ, you 'old Afrikaners'!
If you're wanting the eats, go and get 'em from Tommy!

The third had been a farm-hand in the March of Silesia
and had come to the desert as fresh fodder for machine-guns.
His dates are inscribed on the files, and on the cross-piece.

The fourth was a lance-jack.
                    He had trusted in Adolf
while working as a chemist in the suburb of Spandau.
His loves were his 'cello, and the woman who had borne him
two daughters and a son. He had faith in the Endsieg.
THAT THE NEW REICH MAY LIVE prayed the flyleaf of his
    Bible.

The fifth a mechanic.
                    All the honour and glory,
The siege of Tobruk and the conquest of Cairo
meant as much to that Boche as the Synod of Whitby.
Being wise to all this, he had one single headache,
which was, how to get back to his sweetheart (called Ilse).
– He had said
                    Can't the Tommy wake up and get weaving?
If he tried, he could put our whole Corps in the bag.
May God damn this Libya and both of its palm-trees!

The sixth was a Pole
                    – or to you, a Volksdeutscher –
who had put off his nation to serve in the Wehrmacht.
He siegheiled, and talked of 'the dirty Polacken',
and said what he'd do if let loose among Russkis,
His mates thought that, though 'just a polnischer Schweinhund'
he was not a bad bloke.
                    On the morning concerned
he was driving a truck with mail, petrol and rations.

The MP on duty shouted five words of warning.
He nodded
     laughed
           revved
               and drove straight for El Eleba
not having quite got the chap's Styrian lingo.

The seventh a young swaddy.
           Riding cramped in a lorry
to death along the road which winds eastwards to Halfaya
he had written three verses in appeal against his sentence
which soften for an hour the anger of Lenin.

    Seven poor bastards
    dead in African deadland
(tawny tousled hair under the issue blanket)
     wie einst Lili
    dead in African deadland
             einst Lili Marleen

So Long

*(Recrossing the Sollum Frontier from Libya into Egypt, 22nd May,
1943, in a lorry carrying captured enemy equipment.)*

To the war in Africa that's over – goodnight.
  To thousands of assorted vehicles, in every stage of
    decomposition,
  littering the desert from here to Tunis – goodnight.
To thousands of guns and armoured fighting vehicles
  brewed up, blackened and charred
from Alamein to here, from here to Tunis – goodnight.
To thousands of crosses of every shape and pattern,
  alone or in little huddles, under which the unlucky bastards
    lie –
    goodnight

Horse-shoe curve of the bay,
        clean razor-edge of the escarpment,
    tonight it's the sunset only that's blooding you.

Halfaya and Sollum: I think that at long last
    we can promise you a little quiet.

So long. I hope I won't be seeing you.

To the sodding desert – you know what you can do with
        yourself.

To the African deadland – God help you – and goodnight.

Quintin Hogg

Night Patrol

Muttered the sea, the hill
And silent wadis lay
Black in the moon, when we to kill
Went on our silent way.

Whispers of listless wind
Hissed in the drifting sand
And ancient names gaunt bushes signed
In a forgotten hand.

Menacing ill the wrack
Of last year's battle frowned
Grim in the dark, most like the mark
Of Cain upon the ground.

Silent, we came, we killed.
One blow, and quiet he lay.
One cry, and all was stilled:
Then silent we crept away.

John Jarmain

At a War Grave

No grave is rich, the dust that herein lies
Beneath this white cross mixing with the sand
Was vital once, with skill of eye and hand
And speed of brain. These will not re-arise
These riches, nor will they be replaced;
They are lost and nothing now, and here is left
Only a worthless corpse of sense bereft,
Symbol of death, and sacrifice and waste.

El Alamein, 30th October, 1942.

El Alamein

There are flowers now, they say, at Alamein;
Yes, flowers in the minefields now.
So those that come to view that vacant scene,
Where death remains and agony has been
Will find the lilies grow –
Flowers, and nothing that we know.

So they rang the bells for us and Alamein,
Bells which we could not hear.
And to those that heard the bells what could it mean,
The name of loss and pride, El Alamein?
– Not the murk and harm of war.
But their hope, their own warm prayer.

It will become a staid historic name,
That crazy sea of sand!
Like Troy or Agincourt its single fame
Will be the garland for our brow, our claim,
On us a fleck of glory to the end;
And there our dead will keep their holy ground.

But this is not the place that we recall,
The crowded desert crossed with foaming tracks,
The one blotched building, lacking half a wall,
The grey-faced men, sand-powdered over all;
The tanks, the guns, the trucks,
The black, dark-smoking wrecks.

So be it; none but us has known that land;
El Alamein will still be only ours
And those ten days of chaos in the sand.
Others will come who cannot understand,
Will halt beside the rusty minefield wires
and find there, flowers.

E.D. Jordan

Maqil: I wanna go home

The greying Captain brooded
over his long drink. Then suddenly
he tossed the liquid into
the whining fan. Although
bespattered by the spray,
no one stirred, no one was shaken.
Silently he rose and gloomed
out of the hut. His boon companion,
a raffish white-tailed duck,
flopped from the bar
and staggered after.

Western Desert: Aftermath

Goggle-eyed, with faces stiff
concreted by driven sand and sweat,
we strode across the searing waste.
    As we approached, the driver grinned
a silent welcome,
lolling upon the bare springs
of his burnt-out truck.
    And as we stood,
out from the empty sockets
of his gaze
a lizard dropped.

Sidney Keyes

War Poet

I am the man who looked for peace and found
My own eyes barbed.
I am the man who groped for words and found
An arrow in my hand.
I am the builder whose firm walls surround
A slipping land.
When I grow sick or mad
Mock me not nor chain me;
When I reach for the wind
Cast me not down
Though my face is a burnt book
And a wasted town.

March 1942

The Expected Guest

The table is spread, the lamp glitters and sighs;
Light on my eyes, light on the high curved iris
And springing from glaze to steel, from cup to knife
Makes sacramental my poor midnight table,
My broken scraps the pieces of a god.

O when they bore you down, the grinning soldiers,
Was it their white teeth you could not forget?
And when you met the beast in the myrtle wood,
When the spear broke and the blood broke out on your side
What Syrian Veronica above you
Stooped with her flaxen cloth as yet unsigned?
And either way, how could you call your darling
To drink the cup of blood your father filled?
We are dying tonight, you in the aged darkness
And I in the white room my pride has rented.
And either way, we have to die alone.

The laid table stands hard and white as tomorrow
The lamp sings. The west wind jostles the door.
Though broken the bread, the brain, the brave body
There cannot now be any hope of changing
The leavings to living bone, the bone to bread;
For bladed centuries are drawn between us.
The room is ready, but the guest is dead.

Advice for a Journey

The drums mutter for war, and soon we must begin
To seek the country where they say that joy
Springs flowerlike among the rocks, to win
The fabulous golden mountain of our peace.

O my friends, we are too young
To be explorers, have no skill nor compass,
Nor even that iron certitude which swung
Our fathers at their self-fulfilling North

So take no rations, remember not your homes –
Only the blind and stubborn hope to track
This wilderness. The thoughtful leave their bones
In windy foodless meadows of despair.

Never look back, nor too far forward search
For the white Everest of your desire;
The screes roll underfoot, and you will never reach
Those brittle peaks which only clouds may walk.

Others have come before you, and immortal
Live like reflections. Their still faces
Will give you courage to ignore the subtle
Sneer of the gentian and the ice-worn pebble.

The fifes cry death and the sharp winds call;
Set your face to the rock; go on, go out
Into the bad lands of battle, the cloud-wall
Of the future, my friends, and leave your fear.

Go forth, my friends, the raven is no sibyl
Break the clouds' anger with your unchanged faces.
You'll find, maybe, the dream under the hill –
But never Canaan, nor any golden mountain.

Uys Krige

The Taking of the Koppie

No, it was only a touch of dysentery, he said. He was doing fine
   now thank you . . . What the hell were the chaps grousing
   about anyhow?

He was sitting on the edge of his hospital cot clad only in a slip
    with both his feet on the floor,
his strong young body straight and graceful as a tree, golden as
    any pomegranate but only firmer,
its smooth surface uncracked, gashed with no fissure by the
    burning blazing sun of war;
and with his muscles rippling lightly
like a vlei's shallows by the reeds touched by the first breath of
    the wind of dawn,
as he swung his one leg over onto the other.

He was telling us about the death of the colonel and the major
whom all the men, especially the younger ones, worshipped.
'The colonel copped it from a stray bullet. It must have been a
    sniper . . .
just a neat little hole in the middle of his forehead, no bigger than
    a tickey, and he dropped dead in his tracks.
The major was leading us over some rough open ground
    between the gully and the far koppie
when a burst of machine gun bullets smacked from the kloof,
    tearing him open;
he was a long way ahead of us all and as he fell he shouted:
'Stop! Stay where you are! Don't come near me! Look out for
    those machine guns! There's one in the antheap and one on the
    ledge . . .
    Bring up the mortars! The rest take cover!'
Then he rolled over on his back, blood streaming all over his
    body, and with a dabble of blood on his lips he died – Christ,
    what a man he was!'

The boy reached for a match box, then lighting a cigarette, he
    continued:
'We came on them about ten minutes later, three Ities curled up
    on some straw in a sort of dugout
– as snug as a bug on a rug – and they were sleeping . . .
The two on the outside were young, I noticed. They were all
    unshaven. The bloke in the middle had a dirty grey stubble of
    beard – and that's all I noticed . . .'

As the boy stopped talking he moved, his hair falling in thick
    yellow curls over his forehead, his eyes.

And as I caught the soft gleam of blue behind the strands of gold
I was suddenly reminded of quiet pools of water after rain
among the golden gorse that mantle in early summer
the browning hills of Provence.

'Then I put my bayonet through each of them in turn, just in the
    right place, and they did not even grunt or murmur . . .'

There was no sadism in his voice, no savagery, no brutal pride
    or perverse eagerness to impress,
no joy, no exultation.
He spoke as if he were telling of a rugby match
in which he wasn't much interested
and in which he took no sides.

And as I looked at his eyes again
I was struck with wonderment
at their bigness, their blueness, their clarity
and how young they were, how innocent.

Addis Ababa, May 1941.

L.K. Lawler

Poem

I have remained in the café
Long since the sour red wine
Sank to black dregs in my glass
And think if the chair next to mine
Will again be tenanted, who will come in
Before the café's beetle dark begins.

You, coming first with crinkled eyes
Into the yellow shout of light
And the stale smell, suddenly

From the unreceptive night's
Old fingers which our own new war unties
To blind in blackout streets the cars' weak eyes;

Sitting at my table, pretending
That no one watches you,
Hesitant, beginning politely to speak
How empty the time, having nothing to do;
Why were you quick-eyed frightened,
So that at each newcomer your throat muscles tightened?

Later the woman with a sloppy mouth,
Humped in the chair next to mine,
Not very hopeful amateur tart
Whose cheap hot smell spoilt the taste of wine;
Why were your meaty hands not still,
Not for a moment still?

I do not want your body
Or your soul, or your creed,
You have no glance, nor grace
Nor love that I need;
Though from the eyes the soul is fever ill
And the hands are never still.

Being nothing to me these are brethren,
Sloppy mouth, moth hands and loose eyes
These are the friends I have and will hold
In our hate and sentimental lies;
We are the ancient easy game, we are yet cheap
For power and slaughter; these are the friends I will keep.

Because I hate and want no reason,
No more of words or scientific logic,
No more the regretful, relentless
Equation of the economic;
These are my friends, whose eyes were put out
By those they do not know to hate.

Somhairle Macgill-eain (Sorley Maclean)

Curaidhean

Chan fhaca mi Lannes aig Ratasbon
no MacGill-Fhinnein aig Allt Eire
no Gill-Iosa aig Cuil-Lodair,
ach chunnaic mi Sasunnach 'san Eiphit.

Fear beag truagh le gruaidhean pluiceach
is glùinean a' bleith a chéile,
aodann guireanach gun tlachd ann –
còmhdach an spioraid bu tréine.

Cha robh buaidh air ''san tigh-òsda
'n àm nan dòrn a bhith 'gan dùnadh',
ach leóghann e ri uchd a' chatha,
anns na frasan guineach mùgach.

Thàinig uair-san leis na sligean,
leis na spealgan-iaruinn beàrnach,
anns an toit is anns an lasair,
ann an crith is maoim na h-àraich.

Thàinig fios dha 'san fhrois pheileir
e bhith gu spreigearra 'na dhiùlnach:
is b'e sin e fhad 's a mhair e,
ach cha b' fhada fhuair e dh' ùine.

Chum e ghunnachan ris na tancan,
a' bocail le sgriach shracaidh stàirnich
gus an d' fhuair e fhéin mu 'n stamaig
an deannal ud a chuir ri làr e,
bial sìos an gainmhich 's an greabhal,
gun diog o ghuth caol grànnda.

(Sorley Maclean)

Heroes

I did not see Lannes at Ratisbon
nor MacLennan at Auldearn
nor Gillies MacBain at Culloden,
but I saw an Englishman in Egypt.

A poor little chap with chubby cheeks
and knees grinding each other,
pimply unattractive face –
garment of the bravest spirit.

He was not a hit 'in the pub
in the time of the fists being closed,'
but a lion against the breast of battle,
in the morose wounding showers.

His hour came with the shells,
with the notched iron splinters,
in the smoke and flame,
in the shaking and terror of the battlefield.

Word came to him in the bullet shower
that he should be a hero briskly,
and he was that while he lasted
but it wasn't much time he got.

He kept his guns to the tanks,
bucking with tearing crashing screech,
until he himself got, about the stomach,
that biff that put him to the ground,
mouth down in sand and gravel,
without a chirp from his ugly high-pitched voice.

Cha do chuireadh crois no meadal
ri uchd no ainm no g' a chàirdean:
cha robh a bheag dhe fhòirne maireann,
's nan robh cha bhiodh am facal làidir
's có dhiubh, ma sheasas ursann-chatha
leagar móran air a shàilleabh
gun dùil ri cliù, nach iarr am meadal
no cop 'sam bith á bial na h-àraich.

Chunnaic mi gaisgeach mór á Sasuinn,
fearachan bochd nach laigheadh sùil air;
cha b' Alasdair à Gleanna Garadh –
is thug e gal beag air mo shùilean.

No cross or medal was put to his
chest or to his name or to his family;
there were not many of his troop alive,
and if there were their word would not be strong.
And at any rate, if a battle post stands
many are knocked down because of him,
not expecting fame, not wanting a medal
or any froth from the mouth of the field of slaughter.

I saw a great warrior of England,
a poor manikin on whom no eye would rest;
no Alasdair of Glen Garry;
and he took a little weeping to my eyes.

Latha Foghair

'S mi air an t-slios ud
latha foghair,
na sligean a'sianail mu m' chluasan
agus sianar marbh ri mo ghualainn,
rag-mharbh – is reòta mur b'e 'n teas –
mar gum b' ann a' fuireach ri fios.

Nuair thàinig an sgriach
a mach as a' ghréin,
á buille 's bualadh do-fhaicsinn,
leum an lasair agus streap an ceathach
agus bhàrc e gacha rathad:
dalladh nan sùl, sgoltadh claistinn.

'S 'na dhéidh, an sianar marbh,
fad an latha;
am miosg nan sligean 'san t-strannraich
anns a' mhadainn,
agus a rithist aig meadhon-latha
agus 'san fheasgar.

Ris a' ghréin 's i cho coma,
cho geal cràiteach;
air a' ghainmhich 's i cho tìorail
socair bàidheil;
agus fo reultan Africa,
's iad leugach àlainn.

Ghabh aon Taghadh iadsan
's cha d' ghabh e mise,
gun fhoighneachd dhinn
có b' fheàrr no bu mhiosa:
ar liom, cho diabhlaidh coma
ris na sligean.

Sianar marbh ri mo ghualainn
latha foghair.

An Autumn Day

On that slope
on an autumn day,
the shells soughing about my ears
and six dead men at my shoulder,
dead and stiff – and frozen were it not for the heat
as if they were waiting for a message.

When the screech came
out of the sun,
out of an invisible throbbing;
the flame leaped and the smoke climbed
and surged every way:
blinding of eyes, splitting of hearing.

And after it, the six men dead
the whole day:
among the shells snoring
in the morning,
and again at midday
and in the evening.

In the sun, which was so indifferent,
so white and painful;
on the sand which was so comfortable
easy and kindly;
and under the stars of Africa,
jewelled and beautiful.

One Election took them
and did not take me,
without asking us
which was better or worse:
it seemed as devilishly indifferent
as the shells.

Six men dead at my shoulder
on an Autumn day.

Calvin Makabo

Desert Conflict

Written by Sgt Calvin Makabo 1946 Coy. A.A.P.C. (Basuto), on the occasion of King George VI's visit to the Western Desert in 1943 after the defeat of Rommel. Sgt Makabo was drowned west of Tripoli later in 1943. Translation by Sgt Alexander Qoboshane.

Cast your eyes and look over to the ocean and see ships.
It is far, you cannot see with your naked eyes.
Had it not been so, you could see the track of a big sea snake.
It is dusty, it is where the sea dogs play.
Raise the waves and hide yourselves, for you see the country has
    changed.
England and Berlin are in confliction.
It is where we saw bulls in a rage,
Each one being proud of its equipment.

A woman left the baby and ran away,
The women up north are crying,
They cry facing towards the east,
And say 'There our husbands have disappeared'.
Keep silent and listen to the war affairs.
Year before last in September,
There were great flashes towards the west.
It is there the enemy were troublesome.
The Resident Commissioner heard from home,
He heard about great deeds done by Africans,
He heard they were victorious.
Rommel neglected his duties.
The son of Makabo has taken part in those deeds.
The Chiefs at home heard – Chiefs Theko, Litingoana, Seele
    Tane and Mahabe

You always deceive us and say that
His Majesty King George VI is not seen.
A telegraphic message was sent from England to Tripoli.
It was received in the morning,

And delivered to the companies on Saturday, 21st June.
All Companies according to their race and colour
Coming to cheer the King.
There were those with three stars on their shoulder,
And those who had a crown in their hands.

The General Lyon[1] went down by the main road being silent.
There was wireless round his motor car,
And cannons guarding him on all sides;
Then the soldiers cheered the King as he passed and shouted
   HURRAH!

[1] 'General Lyon' was the code name for the King.

H.B. Mallalieu

State Of Readiness

    The moon rises late:
After sudden warning we wait,
The guns manned, searching among the stars.
At last, perhaps, our hour has come. Cars
Shoot past with urgent messages. We stand
Eager and glad, rifles steady and cool in hand.
For months nothing has happened. Now the sky
Turns hostile. Around us searchlights pry
Into thin clouds. Tonight the enemy, unseen,
Is real. We know these tedious past days have been
Prelude to battle: and if the time is near,
No dearer thoughts shall resurrect our fear.
For this we have waited. If the air should fill
With mushroom parachutes we will
Forsake all memory, all promises to break
On future days, for battle's compelling sake.
We have been ready. Though the warning prove
As false as any, we have abjured our love,
All dreams or hopes, to keep alert and sure.
The drone of planes continues and clouds endure

The searchlight's naked steel. Flares fall,
Hang in the sky. Flashes of guns appal
The quiet air. But as the minutes pass
Talk dies out, rats scurry through the grass.
We grow tired, long for cigarettes. Our minds return
To windows where familiar lights still burn.
Our thoughts resume their island voyages:
Raiders give place to homelier images.
            The moon is full and shines
On tree and hill. In the farm a dog whines;
The routine of life continues while we wait;
Less eager and less certain. Our moons rise late.

J.G. Meddemmen

L.R.D.G

He threw his cigarette in silence, then he said:

You can't predict in war;
It's a matter of luck, nothing less, nothing more.
Now here's an instance. Darnley copped it in the head
His third day up the blue although he'd seen the lot
In Dunkerque, Greece and Crete –
The sort that went in tidy and came out neat;
He copped it when the going wasn't even hot.
And there was little Pansy Flowers,
Machine-gunned through the guts; he bled
(And not a murmur from him) for hours
Before he jagged it in.

                    And you remember Bowers?
Bowers got fragmentation in the lungs and thigh;
We couldn't do a thing: the moon was high
And a hell of a bright
On that particular night.
Poor sod, he won't kip in a civvy bed.

It's queer . . . I've even laughed
When blokes have chucked it in and gone daft.
I remember one that scarpered bollock-nude
One midnight, out across the dunes, calling for Mum;
You'd have thought him blewed.
He wasn't seen again – not this side of Kingdom Come.

One job that I really funked
Was when Fat Riley bunked
From a Jerry leaguer on a getaway.
We found him blind, with both hands gone.
When we got him back inside the lines
He'd only say,
Over and over, 'the mines, the mines, the mines'.
It's the lucky ones get dead:
He's still alive. I wonder if his wife understands
How you can't even shoot yourself without your hands.

March 1942.

N.T. Morris

It's Always Mealtime

Oh, they're queueing up for breakfast, they have rattled on the
    gong;
Hear the mess tins jingle-jangle. Let us go and join the throng.
There is porridge made from biscuits. There's soya for the fry.
There is tea that tastes of onions; there is bread that's rather dry;
And the cooks are looking browned off as they pass the grub
    along.
Oh, that look they get from cookhouses and drinking tea too
    strong.

Oh, it must be time for tiffin. What d'you think it is today?
Well, there's fish and meat and pickle mixed in some peculiar
    way.

There is yellow cheese as usual, and marg., and that's the lot –
Oh, help yourself to biscuits, 'cos the weather's ——— hot.
And the cooks are looking browned off as a dollop each one
   deals,
The look they get from arguing and never eating meals.

You can tell it's time for dinner by the fidgets in the queue.
And it's world-without-end bully meat mocked up as pie or
   stew,
And if you're mighty lucky, there'll be flour in the 'duff,'
But the chances are it's rice again, and rice is . . . rough.
So the cooks are looking browned off, slightly woebegone and
   worn,
The look that comes from cards all night, and lighting fires at
   dawn.

William E. Morris

The Captured

Barrage silk cast shadows where we sat
on kit bags gas mask and tin hat embedded in a crusted sand.
We sat swatting Egypt's flies with a peaked hat.
Our R.T.O.[1] was having someone on the mat,
still we sat, watching rusted prows of
sunken ships – grim reminder this was war,
a harbour bombed a little while before –
now Tewfik slumbered, as we reclined
uncomfortably on an alien shore.

Marching four abreast in column array
Hitler's beaten army halted for transport in the Bay,
tired features creased by particles of desert dust
shabby uniforms infested by its all embracing crust,
dust – entrenched itself in ridges on head gear sadly worn,
irritated sweated forelocks closely shorn.
Down-at-heel boots made no imprint in sand
fringing polluted land – ugly born.

[1] Railway Transport Officer

Bleak eyes had this sullen band
arrogant in their shifting sideways stare,
eyes that had witnessed swift victory in other lands –
then reluctant surrender chill despair
a valedictory to high hopes
to triumph that was never really there.
Where shifting dunes shimmer under Libya's molten sky
vultures cast shadows flying high
over rock cairned graves where comrades lie.
'Neath windswept desert's rim barb wire had hemmed them in;
between reaching fingers of twisted wire
threadbare prisoners huddled as cattle in a byre
their hearts racked with questioning doubt,
minds seared from barb's reality.
Beings filled with but one desire
to throw twigs on a home hearth fire.
Sentry go on sentry beat made mockery of a dream complete –
they scrambled for the 'cigs' we threw –
then cursed us 'cause there were so few.

Egypt, 1941.

G.C. Norman

Halt for Lunch

A light wind whips the flame to furnace heat.
'It's on the boil, throw out the milk and tea,'
Says Atkins, 'what we going to have to eat?'
Somebody stirs the petrol-sodden sand;
The dixie-lid spurts steam.
                                        'There's M and V'
I say, 'as good as anything. And canned
Pineapple.'
                    They agree. The cans are stood
In water on the fire-tin. Mercifully
The dust storm has died down.

                                             'There is some wood
Somewhere inside the truck' says Cpl Dean.
The air is very still. A smell of bully,
And chips and onions fried in margarine
Comes from a truck a hundred yards from ours.
The sky would match a Suffolk sky at home,
Pale blue and cloudless. Small sweet-scented flowers
Make sweet pretence of Spring. The burnt-out husk
Of a wild idea conceived in distant Rome
Stands near at hand, where desert scrub and musk
Have given place to strange, hewn wooden plants,
Whose harvest has been plucked, and whose rough branches
Are done with Spring forever.
                                        Two spidery ants
With triply bulbous bodies come and go
In aimless haste.
                        Some men are digging trenches
Unhurriedly. McCartney tries to sew
A button on his trousers at the back,
And turns round like a corkscrew.
                                        'Take 'em off'
Says Atkins.
                        'What, in front of you?' says Mac,
And tries to blush. He does not find that easy,
Being older than us all in years and love,
Three times in jail, and twelve years in the Army.
I lean against the wheel and close my eyes,
The water in the tin is bubbling softly.
Two amorous and persistent desert flies
Whine in my ears. Small sounds can sometimes quell
The roaring of great silences.
                                        Then faintly
A new sound strikes the air, a surge and swell
Like angry breakers on grim distant shores –
A sullen hateful sound, evil, portentous,
That grows in wrath and volume, till it roars
Its hatred and defiance overhead.
From half a score fierce throats.
                                        'Look out, they're Stukas!'
'Where's my tin hat?'

Ghent has already fled.
We jump into a trench. The mighty throbbing
Is changing key. Two of us have a Bren
And one a rifle. Ghent is almost sobbing,
From breathlessness and panic. It is the first.
The planes turn round into the sun, and then:
A sudden pause.
These moments are the worst.
Five dreadful seconds, five eternities,
Five bars of trembling silence.
Nothing stirs.
Breathless and tense we listen. Here it is:
A throb, a hum, a deep full-throated roar,
The whistling of rushing air, and now our ears
Are helpless in the turmoil and furore
Of impact and explosion. As they land,
Bursting and crashing to a wild crescendo,
The bombs send up great founts of smoke and sand.
Wandering shrapnel whistles through the air,
Uttering a long-drawn sigh, as if in sorrow
At finding no soft mark or target there.
The planes are past us now. The last bombs fall,
The roaring dies away; and it is over.
We clamber up and dust ourselves. 'That's all,'
Says Atkins, 'that's our lot. Cups up for tea.'
And when the smoke has lifted we discover
One truck ablaze; one torch for Liberty.

F.T. Prince

Soldiers Bathing

The sea at evening moves across the sand.
Under a reddening sky I watch the freedom of a band
Of soldiers who belong to me. Stripped bare
For bathing in the sea, they shout and run in the warm air;
Their flesh, worn by the trade of war, revives
And my mind towards the meaning of it strives.

All's pathos now. The body that was gross,
Rank, ravenous, disgusting in the act or in repose,
All fever, filth and sweat, its bestial strength
And bestial decay, by pain and labour grows at length
Fragile and luminous. 'Poor bare forked animal,'
Conscious of his desires and needs and flesh that rise and fall,
Stands in the soft air, tasting after toil
The sweetness of his nakedness: letting the sea-waves coil
Their frothy tongues about his feet, forgets
His hatred of the war, its terrible pressure that begets
A machinery of death and slavery,
Each being a slave and making slaves of others: finds that he
Remembers his old freedom in a game
Mocking himself, and comically mimics fear and shame.

He plays with death and animality;
And reading in the shadows of his pallid flesh, I see
The idea of Michelangelo's cartoon
Of soldiers bathing, breaking off before they were half done
At some sortie of the enemy, an episode
Of the Pisan wars with Florence. I remember how he showed
Their muscular limbs that clamber from the water,
And heads that turn across the shoulder, eager for the slaughter,
Forgetful of their bodies that are bare,
And hot to buckle on and use the weapons lying there.
– And I think too of the theme another found
When, shadowing men's bodies on a sinister red ground,
Another Florentine, Pollaiuolo,
Painted a naked battle: warriors, straddled, hacked the foe,
Dug their bare toes into the ground and slew
The brother-naked man who lay between their feet and drew
His lips back from his teeth in a grimace.

They were Italians who knew war's sorrow and disgrace
And showed the thing suspended, stripped: a theme
Born out of the experience of war's horrible extreme
Beneath a sky where even the air flows
With lacrimae Christi. For that rage, that bitterness, those blows,
That hatred of the slain, what could they be
But indirectly or directly a commentary

On the Crucifixion? And the picture burns
With indignation and pity and despair by turns,
Because it is the obverse of the scene
Where Christ hangs murdered, stripped, upon the Cross. I
     mean,
That is the explanation of its rage.

And we too have our bitterness and pity that engage
Blood, spirit, in this war. But night begins,
Night of the mind: who nowadays is conscious of our sins?
Though every human deed concerns our blood,
And even we must know, what nobody had understood,
That some great love is over all we do,
And that is what has driven us to this fury, for so few
Can suffer all the terror of that love:
The terror of that love has set us spinning in this groove
Greased with our blood.

                    These dry themselves and dress,
Combing their hair, forget the fear and shame of nakedness.
Because to love is frightening we prefer
The freedom of our crimes. Yet, as I drink the dusky air,
I feel a strange delight that fills me full,
Strange gratitude, as if evil itself were beautiful,
And kiss the wound in thought, while in the west
I watch a streak of red that might have issued from Christ's
     breast.

Enoch Powell

The Net

The net like a white vault, hung overhead
Dewy and glistening in the full moon's light,
Which cast a shadow-pattern of the thread
Over our face and arms, laid still and white
Like polished ivories on the dark bed.

The truck's low side concealed from us the sight
Of tents and bivouacs and track-torn sand
That lay without; only a distant sound
Of gunfire sometimes or, more close at hand,
A bomb, with dull concussion of the ground,
Pressed in upon our world, where, all else banned,
Our lonely souls eddied like echoing sound
Under the white cathedral of the net,
And like a skylark in captivity
Hung fluttering in the meshes of our fate,
With death at hand and, round, eternity.

John Rimington

Danse Grotesque

The Devil played the drums when Peter died
An overture of bombs and crashing sound
   A whirling slip of splinter caught his side
   And deftly set his body spinning round

Alas! He missed his final curtain calls
A khaki Harlequin in 'Danse Grotesque'
   With just a single vulture in the stalls
   To witness so superb an arabesque.

The Flap

It pains me deeply to relate
The sad and truly frightful fate
Of James Augustus Livermore,
A driver in the Service Corps.

One day they sent him down the road
Instructing him that he must load
A Honey tank at Alex. Docks
And take it to GAZALA BOX.

Now James Augustus it appears
Had been a soldier several years,
But up to now had failed to see
A sign of any enemy.
He set out, then, with courage high,
Resolved to DO THE JOB or DIE!

He drove by day, he drove by night –
And not a German came in sight.
The nights were cold, the days were hot –
And no one fired a single shot;
'Pooh-pooh' said Driver Livermore
    'If this is called a *total war*
'The thing will last for fifty years. . .'

Now, at that moment, it appears,
The German Field Artillery,
(Who'd shaved, and washed, and had their tea)
Decided that they might as well
Stand To, and fire another shell;
Alas! For James Augustus came
Precisely on their point of aim!

He heard the bang, he heard the whine
And, fearing he was in the line
Of fire, and that he might be trapped,
He did the only thing – HE FLAPPED!

As fast as a homer he shot past ACROMA,
Past MONUMENT CROSSING as quick as a flash.
The road that he took brought him straight through TOBRUK
Where he nearly removed a policeman's moustache!

He was very soon put on the road to GAMBUT
And tore up the road past the Y.M.C.A.
And as he drew near to the town of BARDIA
He nearly wrenched one of the bridges away!

Then he put down his foot, so the men in CAPUZZO
Were hardly aware that he'd come, when he'd gone!
Going down HALFAYA, he burst a rear tyre
But the others stayed up – so he went flapping on!

A few saw him zoom round the bay of SOLLUM,
And he entered the straight with a deafening roar,
And at SIDI BARRANI, not giving a darn, he
Went straight by a Redcap at seventy-four!

He very nigh flew into MERSA MATRUH
The dust fairly blinded the onlookers' eyes
And passing through FUKA, an enemy Stuka
Was left far behind, to the pilot's surprise!

At DABA his load tumbled off on the road.
But, not stopping, he let the thing lie;
And the only thing seen as he passed ALAMEIN
Was a dust-cloud, two hundred feet high!

As he passed EL IMAYID his engine backfired.
HAMMAM went by in a shake.
As he came to the DELTA, the people took shelter
From stones that flew up in his wake!

Then he came to the town; he began to slow down.
And he put on his footbrake at last.
Drawing into the side. 'Good old ALEX!' he cried
Convinced that the danger was past. . .

But my tale is not o'er: as he opened the door
He slipped, and fell out on his head.
The R.A.M.C. brought him hot, sweetened tea,
But too late! James Augustus was DEAD!

R.M. Roberts

Troop Train

Dark has fallen on the crowded troop train
Lumbering slowly through the Egyptian night,
Cold as the smooth steel of the coaches.
We in our thin drill shorts huddle close
The thin ribbed wooden seats,
Wrapped each in his single blanket,
Staring unseeing with large pupilled eyes
Mirrored in the pool of black glass windows,
Drugged and heavy with the dust of Africa
And the sweet desire of sleep.
The broken rhythm of the jolting carriage wheels
Brings to the soldier a fitful slumber
And the lights that flare with the passing
Of each unknown clamorous station
Paint grotesque pictures of living light
Flickering on the shrouded waxen faces
And as the train in its relentless funeral pace
Slowly rumbles through the dim lit bays,
Arab shirted close cropped urchin hawkers
Shriek their wares with all the discord of the east,
Trailing the red glow of receding tail lamp
With fading high pitched half tone echoes
That shiver the sleepers and walk the skin
With the spiders' icy feet.
Deep into the night and waste lands
The sleeping coaches roll,
With the firelit clanging monster
Probing one-eyed its grinding way
Until the biting cold dew of the desert
Glistens on the swaying steel,
Etching the twin threads of railroad
Converging under a pale moon far to the west,
And the east breaks in a fan of brittle light
Flooding the lonely plain.
We the shrouded sleepers in a golden train

Wake, beard rough and dust rust eyed,
Stamp the cold from stiffened limbs
And boisterous blood beats in shouting life
Chasing the phantoms of the spell ridden night,
While the train presses on to the west and the camps
To the unknown but rumoured future.

John Ropes

Voluntary Ladies of the Town

The scene: Any soldiers' club in Cairo just before opening time. Three Cairene matrons are seen putting the final touches to the tea tables. They sing:

VERSE:
Though many years ago, we said goodbye to beauty,
We've a most important duty to fulfil.
Every Saturday at three,
We serve the soldiers tea
And put their half piastres in the till.
And when the shadows lengthen, and the light begins to pale,
We do a splendid trade in bottled ale.

CHORUS:
We're voluntary ladies serving voluntary beer
To voluntary soldiers compulsorily here.
We try to do our bit
To keep them fighting fit
Though we don't encourage any horseplay here.

We're voluntary workers selling voluntary eggs
To keep the men's attention from those voluntary legs.
A lightly toasted bun
Is just as jolly fun
As draining Passion's goblet to the dregs.

Some of the men are jokers, you can very quickly spot 'em.
They ask for fancy pastries when they know we haven't got
     'em
And last Tuesday Mrs Smithers had a sergeant pinch her
     bottom
Because she's such a voluntary lady.

So if ever you want some ping-pong, some billiards or a bath
Without military policeman and a nasty aftermath
We'll try to keep your footsteps on the straight and narrow
     path,
We're the voluntary ladies of the town.

SECOND CHORUS:
    We're voluntary ladies serving voluntary food
    To servicemen to whom we hope to do a little good.
        We dispense Egyptian bangahs
        To the heroes from the hangars
    To distract their minds from Nature in the nude.

    We're voluntary talkers to the soldiers as they eat,
    The boys all like to talk to any girl that they can meet,
        Though a man the other day
        Took it quite the other way
    And said a word I really can't repeat.

    It's interesting to hear them and the stories that they bring,
    I listened to a corporal for half an hour last spring
    After which I much regret, he did a most peculiar thing,
    He tried it on a voluntary lady.

    But we never fuss or worry and we're none of us
        complaining,
    After this evacuation, we're the only ones remaining,
    And the fellows must go somewhere to complete their early
        training
    With the voluntary ladies of the town.

THIRD CHORUS:
    We're voluntary ladies in voluntary clubs
    Keeping rather browned-off soldiers from the cabarets and
        pubs,
      When you've nothing else to do,
      Just come and have a brew
    With Merrie England's tea-dispensing tubs.

    We're voluntary ladies going voluntary gay
    Being rather free and easy in a voluntary way,
      Though we gaily love to flirt,
      We draw the line at dirt,
    And we leave at nine o'clock to hit the hay.

    All the same, its pretty risky if you see behind the scenes,
    They draw the rudest pictures on the backs of magazines,
    And the words . . . well, we can really only guess at what it
        means,
    Because we're such voluntary ladies.

    So whether you're from the desert or the greenness of the veldt,
    Australian, New Zealander, a Scotsman or a Celt,
    Play the game like British soldiers, and don't hit below the belt
    Of these voluntary ladies of the town.

Alf Samson

Back to the Beginning

Inspired after our cook had been jilted.

    Again the same old story
      Of the girl that's left behind,
    When her fellow has to go off to a war,
      She writes for him she's yearning,
    Living just for his returning,
      But the waiting, it really is a bore.

So just to stop her fretting
   She goes off to a dance,
When the cat's away, the mice will surely play,
   Meets a chap who is most charming,
Makes her heart beat most alarming,
   After that she sees him nearly every day.
Her letters then get scarcer
   To her man across the sea,
He blames the post and swears like bloody hell,
   Then a card he gets to say,
'Darling, let's call it a day',
   He's been jilted and he knows it very well.

Is he sad and broken-hearted?
   Well at first he feels depressed,
But time soon heals the aching pain,
   On his leave he meets a girl,
She sets his heart off in a whirl,
   After that he sees her time and time again.
Now this girl too, had a lover,
   Who sailed across the sea,
To help the mother country fight a war,
   She was the apple of his eye,
But to him she writes goodbye,
   And he knows she doesn't love him any more.
He says his life is ruined,
   For him it is the end,
Until one day he meets a pretty dame,
   No longer he feels blue,
He is sure this one is true,
   After all, *all women really aren't the same*,

And the pretty dame she sighs,
   As she writes a letter-card,
To a boy, who thought that he and she would wed,
   She explains her life's her own,
And as he had to roam,
   There was nothing more between them to be said.
. . . BACK TO THE BEGINNING . . .

Charles Smith

Field Hospital

Agnostic: so the ticket on the bed
along with army number name and rank
as guide for priest or parson in a ward
of pole and canvas wounded men and sand,
the clergy heedful of that pothook scrawl
of nurse who checked the spelling as she wrote
and then forgot on pocketing the pen,
blood having levelled or exalted all.

She'd neither time nor space to write below:
'This casualty retains implicit faith
in timeless pulse of life, a shadow-tide
evading creed and microscope, beyond
analysis in plasm sap and egg,
a gut conviction deep below belief –
and therefore credible. He harbours doubt
of God in nightgown and prophetic voice
invariably male, and fancy dress
performances of strictly human rite –
but now, confused by pain, depends upon
a mothering nurse who cannot spell.'

Casualties

Shellcrack . . . and for some oblivion,
for some an ambulance but for these two
the transit camp toward too-busy death.
Needle . . . good God why aren't the bastards dead,
poor bloody bastards squalling as they go
in search of dignity. They'll never know
the fight they made to keep on sucking breath.

Minqar Qaim, 1942.

Bernard Spencer

Base Town

Winter's white guard continual on the hills;
The wind savaging from the stony valleys
And the unseen front. And always the soldiers going,
Soldiers and lorries beating the streets of cobble,
Like blood to where a wound is flowing.

War took friends, lights and names away. Clapped down
Shutters on windows' welcome. Brought those letters
Which wished to say so much they dared not say.
The proud and feminine ships in the harbour roads
Turned to a North-East grey.

Curious the intimacy we felt with Them;
We moved our meals to fit Their raids; we read
Their very hand across each bomb-slashed wall.
Their charred plane fallen in the cratered square
Held twisted in it all

Their work, Their hate, Their failure. Prisoners
Bearded and filthy, had bones, eyes and hair
Like other men in need. But dead like snow,
Cold like those racing winds or sirens' grief,
Was the hate which struck no blow:

The fear of speaking was a kind of tic
Pulling at the eyes. If stranger drank with stranger
It seemed thief drank with thief. Was it only every
Night, the fall of the early and lampless dark?
I remember it so often. And the lie,
The twist of reason,
The clever rumour planted in the nerves,
The dossier infecting like a coccus;
All these became for us the town, the season.

These, and the knowledge that to die,
Some stony miles north of our wintering
Was a more ordinary thing.

Theodore Stephanides

Western Desert – Two Years After

The ancient melancholy of the moon's
Pocked face peers earthwards with unhoping eyes;
The moon – a tragic mask hung in the skies,
Pale mirror of a myriad buried noons,
Dead light from a dead world. The world below
In that dead radiance lies a lifeless sea,
Its long low swells of immobility
Congealed to silver silence. In that glow
All is pure whiteness rolling to the round
Eternity of the horizon's rim
Ringed by the galaxy's eternal haze.

All is pure whiteness, save alone where strays
One blackness on the sands: the shadow slim
Of alone cross on a forgotten mound.

Tobruk, 1944.

Duologue

(Between two graves side by side on the battlefield)

'Did *you* slay me, or did *I* strike you dead?
In that mad welter who could ever tell!'
– 'It matters not, O Brother, how we fell,
For now we share in concord the same bed!'

Frank Thompson

Day's Journey

Starting at early light from the old fort
Across the dry flaked mud, you remember,
We left the well on our right and the crosses,
Drove west all day through the camel-scrub,
Tossing in convoy like a mobile orchard,
An olive-yard on wheels, irregular,
Spaced over miles: were bombed: were bombed again,
Until the air was dust: drove on due west
Past the sheikh's tomb of stones, past the dry spring,
Until at dust from the escarpment
Rumbled and boomed the guns' resentment,
Impersonal, the protest of a Titan
Impartially disgusted, while the sun
Signed off in angry flames.
                    We halted,
Quietly, in the close leaguer, half ashamed.

Terence Tiller

Lecturing To Troops

They sit like shrubs among the cans and desert
                    thistles
        in the tree's broken shade and the sea-glare:
strange violent men, with dirty unfamiliar muscles,
sweating down the brown breast, wanting girls and
                    beer.
The branches shake down sand along a crawling air,
                and drinks are miles towards the sun
                and Molly and Polly and Pam are gone.

Waiting for my announcement, I feel neat and shy,
    foreign before their curious helplessness,
innocence bought by action, like the sea's amnesty:
all my clean cleverness is tiny, is a loss;
and it is useless to be friendly and precise
              – thin as a hornet in a dome
              against the cries of death and home.

How can they be so tolerant – they who have lost
    the kiss of tolerance – and patient to endure
calm unnecessity? They have walked horror's coast,
loosened the flesh in flame, slept with naked war:
while I come taut and scatheless with a virgin air,
              diffident as a looking-glass,
              with the fat lexicon of peace.

The strangeness holds them: a new planet's uniform,
    grasped like the frilly pin-ups in their tent
– something without the urgency of hate and harm,
something forgotten.
              But that is not what I meant:
I should have been the miles that made them
              innocent,
           and something natural as the sun
           from the beginning to everyone
           though Harry and Larry and Len are gone.

Coastal Battery, Tripolitania

Flying to Tripoli

Pages of sand; the slow black tape of road;
hills with salt and wreckage in their laps;
the canvas Mediterranean a guide
to windy Tripoli and the listing ships.
It is a kind of death, this vanishing:
the country or the flier? Blue flight; then
after oblivious landmarks, fall with dipped wing
like angels and with power, among men.

Down by the harbour over drooping wires,
on amazed marble bathers in the bowl,
the gloating of the sun is drops or flowers:
the oleanders and the fountains fall.
And what is real enough to touch? – we who
have died so fast along the death and fire,
following where we cannot possibly go,
dazed by the violence of that mine of air?

Oh flowery white and military town,
gapped like a boxer's mouth and pink with trees;
twirled by the ugly finger of the gun,
a restless bowl: or with dogs' humble eyes
upon the quiet coarseness of a rein
strong enough to be gentle. Where the lulled
ships nestle deeper; masonry scuttles down
from gash or scaffold; houses have been killed.

Flags that shrug and huddle in the wind,
summer of war, colour of tree and sky,
break us your angry bread; and for this land
that swarms with supplication not to die
– hunger of withering spaces where the crops
are dragged like salvage sunwards; of men and
        hills
with death with salt with wreckage in their laps;
and of this town of hesitating walls:

the injury and shyness of a guilt,
four eyes askance, held steady like a house
by dug-out, buttress, rifle, barbed–wire–belt,
where all turns downward, sweet and ruinous:
beauty that paints and wavers; fall of men;
dropping of strangers from enormous heights;
soft imprisoned terror in the sun.
Death and living have torn down their gates.

And agony ended here: dream into dream
by water–clock and flower–clock; rest with
the grey quay curving like a lover's arm
and as unsure. Pattern of peace and wrath.
For the guns tell the time: the earth falls
roaring and flowering from us; we are huge:
the tiny quilt of camps and farms and hills;
the road of urgent news; the turning page.

1943

N.J. Trapnell

Lament of a Desert Rat

I've learnt to wash in petrol tins, and shave myself in tea
Whilst balancing the fragments of a mirror on my knee
I've learnt to dodge the eighty–eights, and flying lumps of lead
And to keep a foot of sand between a Stuka and my head
I've learnt to keep my ration bag crammed full of buckshee food
And to take my Army ration, and to pinch what else I could
I've learnt to cook my bully–beef with candle–ends and string
In an empty petrol can, or any other thing
I've learnt to use my jack–knife for anything I please
A bread–knife, or a chopper, or a prong for toasting cheese
I've learnt to gather souvenirs, that home I hoped to send
And hump them round for months and months, and dump them
   in the end
But one day when this blooming war is just a memory
I'll laugh at all these troubles, when I'm drifting o'er the sea
But until that longed–for day arrives, I'll have to be content
With bully–beef and rice and prunes, and sleeping in a tent.

James Walker

From
Portrait And Background

Tobruk way were the graves. Not many,
As numbers go, as casualties in war,
Though in the isolating moon they seemed
Milestones over the world, and in the sunlight
Their identities oppressed, as all things did
In that meticulous vivisecting light.
Most were anonymous, the scattered ones,
With stones heaped over them to keep their bones
Longer, a little, from jackals and the raven.
'*Ein unbekannter englischer Soldat*'
Held a wild place where there were flowers and larks.
But that was gracious. Most were '*Unbekannt*',
'*Incognito*', 'Unknown'. These haunted most.
For these were us. This was the end we came to,
Whether our bones went underground or not.
Love's individuality became
Ein unbekannter englischer Soldat.
So we despised our bodies, whose too-tired flesh
No longer brought us in its old delights.
And sometimes in the dark, running for shelter,
We stumbled over them, and cursed these dead
Equally with the living, lying still.

R.N. Walker

Living and Dead

These crimson bandages speak and move feebly,
But quickly establish their identity and enquire for others from
  their home town.
Becoming tender acquaintances instantly:
They wring the heart.
But the dead –
Makeshift mortuaries full, uncounted,
Uncountable –
The mind claps down its shutter, excludes the realization
That they ever lived, and ascribes the scene
To frenzied work left unfinished
In a waxworks factory.

John Waller

Convoy

Like lazy ducks upon a placid pond
Only deep blue, and the sun drenching
Against shadows a hard dry light, the ships rule
Whose purpose is so firm and feminine,
Now power but heart lazy, the cool limbs
Safe on a certain journey, an end sure.

Now for a moment distance intensifies
Each personal tragedy, lends wings to wish,
New favour to frail. Certain moments
Make pictures for always, continual summer
On a separate island, over each heart
An enchanted figure, someone to adore.

John Warry

To a W.A.A.F.

Even that wretched uniform she wears
Cannot prevent her being beautiful.
I met her in the train, where as a rule
I travel second class with third class fares.
And now my heart is in need of repairs,
For she, part Greek and three parts Austrian,
Apparelled as a sort of ersatz man,
Seemed worthy of her warrior forbears.
And though the language of Themistocles
And that of brave Don John who sailed his galleon
Against the Turkish menace at Lepanto,
Are both unknown to her, she speaks Italian,
English and French. Nay, but her voice would please,
Though she could speak no tongue save Esperanto.

Darrell Wilkinson

Drifting at Sea

Look! my beloved, the sea-waves are rocking,
softly the eddies hurry past the boat;
here are no moments, we are not caught
in the dance of hours, and are excused
the sounding of the chimes.

For there to be time there must be sense
and consequence; the perception that rotates
in the changing of the symbol;
the opening and closing of the flower,
the scent of honeysuckle drifting in the wind,
the swoop of predatory birds
and the interminable agonizing instant

drained of precision, when the ferret
comes slinking towards the rabbit.

Such is the time of landsmen; but here
is only the continuous indifference of the sea
and the inconsequential rocking
while the cold, tireless moon
reiterates her journey in the sky.

Alexander J. Will

Hope Deferred

The camel train is coming throttle down
Or think of a red light just anywhere
Better to stop. A lady lithe and brown
Thanks with a smile, flashing and debonair.

In groups of six the one-humped camels pass
Roped tail to nose, Somali boys in charge.
Last comes Himself, the owner of the lass
Camels and merchandise, but why enlarge?

The caravan is gone, a musty scent
Of camel and a dusty cloud remain,
Their baggage for Hargeisa. That indent
Sent in a year ago, was it in vain?

Hargeisa 1942

Anonymous

Ode to a Gezira Lovely

They call me Venal Vera,
I'm a lovely from Gezira[1],
The Fuehrer pays me well for what I do,
The order of the battle,
I obtain from last night's rattle,
On the golf course with the Brigadier from 'Q'.

I often have to tarry,
In the back seat of a gharry,
It's part of my profession as a spy,
Whilst his mind's on fornication,
I'm extracting information,
From the senior G.S.O. or G.S.I.

When I yield to the caress,
Of the D.D.W.S.
I get from him the lowdown of the works,
And when sleeping in the raw,
With a Major from G.4.
I learn of Britain's bargain with the Turks.

On the point of his emission,
In the 26th position,
While he quivers in exotic ecstasy,
I hear of the location,
Of a very secret station,
From an over-sexed S.C. from 02E.

So the Brigadiers and Majors,
And the whiskey soaked old stagers
Enjoy themselves away from Britain's shores,
Why should they bring Victory nearer,
When the ladies from Gezira,
Provide them with this lovely f—— War?

[1]Island in the Nile, location of sports club.

Anonymous

Leave, Compassionate, Children, Production, for the use of

*At the end of the war Sir James Grigg, Minister of War, authorized
leave for fathering children*

In distant lands the stalwart bands of would-be fathers wait,
Certificates to join their mates upon affairs of State,
For para 3 (appendix B) will authorize a chap,
to reproduce, for scheduled use, the species homo sap.

When good Sir James takes down their names in files, to
    procreate,
This caveat the unborn brat must circumnavigate:
'All who have wives (past thirty-five) and children unbegot
And certified that they have tried, are able, and have not

'May stake a claim. But if their aim is not, or has succeeded,
we can't allow that here and now their services are needed.'
All who apply must certify that they can understand
What lies behind the subtle mind of the Middle East Command.

The Middle East has now released a gallant group of men,
Of future Dads, like Galahads, who have the strength of ten,
And every dame must be the same, for it is infra dig,
That they should dare a child to bear uncertified by Grigg.

1945.

Anonymous

Cairo Love Song

Now Johnson joined the Army not so very long ago
They sent him out to Egypt right away.
He didn't like it first because he couldn't quench his thirst,
At least he didn't get that rate of pay.
Now one fine day in June, he thought he'd like to spoon
So to a little Gippo bint he cried:
Sayeeda bint, I love your charming manner
To walk with you would be my pride and joy.
Your dainty little yashmak, your finger nails of henna
Make me say to other bints muskeen: mafeesh filoos.
Two eyes of fire, that make me stanna swire
I'd give the world to have you call me dear
So I think I'll call you Lena
'Cos I think it rhymes with talla heena
You're my little Gippo bint, you're quois ketir.

Glossary

Sayeeda *Hallo*
Bint *Woman*
Muskeen *(I'm) poor*
Mafeesh filoos *I've no money*
Stanna swire *Wait a little (gharry driver's order to his horse – or swaddy's order to the gharry driver).*
Talla heena *Come here*
Quios ketir *A bit of all right (lit. 'plenty good').*

The Home Front

Stephanie Batstone

Poem

The stolen, crowded moments fly,
Too fragile is this breathing space;
Too soon his eager frame must lie
Forlornly in some foreign place;
My heart cries out that he will die,
And I have never seen his face.

For these few weeks he wanders free,
Yet dimly comprehends the choice
Which he has made, forsaking me;
No memories my hours rejoice;
A world of silent grief I see,
For I have never heard his voice.

Bitter it is that he must die,
Before our love was young and glad;
Yet though I know that, in him, I
Must lose the things I never had,
Harder it is to feel that he
Will never know those things in me.

D. Van den Bogaerde

Steel Cathedrals

It seems to me, I spend my life in stations.
Going, coming, standing, waiting.
Paddington, Darlington, Shrewsbury, York.
I know them all most bitterly.
Dawn stations, with a steel light, and waxen figures.
Dust, stone, and clanking sounds, hiss of weary steam.
Night stations, shaded light, fading pools of colour.
Shadows and the shuffling of a million feet.

Khaki, blue, and bulky kitbags, rifles gleaming dull.
Metal sound of army boots, and smoker's coughs.
Titter of harlots in their silver foxes.
Cases, casks, and coffins, clanging of the trolleys.
Tea urns tarnished, and the greasy white of cups.
Dry buns, Woodbines, Picture Post and Penguins;
and the blaze of magazines.
Grinding sound of trains, and rattle of the platform gates.
Running feet and sudden shouts, clink of glasses from the buffet.
Smell of drains, tar, fish and chips and sweaty scent, honk of
    taxis;
and the gleam of cigarettes.
Iron pillars, cupolas of glass, girders messed by pigeons;
the lazy singing of a drunk.
Sailors going to Chatham, soldiers going to Crewe.
Aching bulk of kit and packs, tin hats swinging.
The station clock with staggering hands and callous face,
says twenty-five-to-nine.
A cigarette, a cup of tea, a bun,
and my train goes at ten.

1943

Winifred Boileau

Sounds

The Heinkels drone their dismal nightly dirge,
The guns spit forth their salvoes, sharp and harsh,
And whistling bombs and dull explosions merge
With thunderous land mines, out across the Marsh.

The clanging tocsin of the fire brigade
Rings in your ears. Through weary hours you lie
And listen, trying not to be afraid,
Yet fearing most to be afraid to die.

The sirens shrill their high-pitched note at break
Of day. A grey half-light appears,
And drowsiness steals through your weary brain.
You sleep. Then suddenly you are awake
To comfortable music in your ears,
The friendly shunting of a railway train.

A.A. Battery, Hackney Wick, London, 1940

R.P. Brett

Point of View

[*Heard in a butcher's shop, Bolton, Lancs.*]

'It's slaughter – nothing more nor less –
The bombing in this war. . .
A dreadful thing . . . you'd never guess
The shocking sights we saw
In London, when the Blitz was on . . .
A leg hung from a tree;
A body with the top half gone
And nowt below the knee;
A hand with wedding ring and all;
Two feet in socks and boots;
A baby's head stuck to a shawl;
An arm torn by the roots;
While here and there was flesh in lumps
They shovelled into sacks.
It proper left us in the dumps . . .
Sent shivers down our backs.'

'It's slaughter, sir. I've seen a bit
Of what those swine can do.'
His chopper fell and fiercely split
A sheep's head clean in two.

'It's downright murder to attack
Defenceless folk who can't fight back!'
. . . . And swinging dumbly on a hook,
A dead pig gave him such a look.

Norman Cameron

Punishment Enough

They say that women, in a bombing-raid,
Retire to sleep in brand-new underwear
Lest they be tumbled out of doors, displayed
In shabby garments to the public stare.

You've often seen a house, sliced like cheese,
Displaying its poor secrets – peeling walls
And warping cupboards. Of such tragedies
It is the petty scale that most appals.

When you confess your sins before a parson,
You find it no great effort to disclose
Your crimes of murder, bigamy and arson,
But can you tell him that you pick your nose?

If after death you pay for your misdeeds,
Surely the direst and most just requital
Would be to listen while an angel reads
Before a crowd your endless, mean recital:

Golf scorecards faked, thefts from your mother's purse. . .
But why should Doomsday bother with such stuff?
This is the Hell that you already nurse
Within you. You've had punishment enough.

Elsie Cawser

Salvage Song (or: The Housewife's Dream)

My saucepans have all been surrendered,
The teapot is gone from the hob,
The colander's leaving the cabbage
For a very much different job.
So now, when I hear on the wireless
Of Hurricanes showing their mettle,
I see, in a vision before me,
A Dornier chased by my kettle.

Robert L. Chaloner

Home Front: 1942

Marching in step, the Battery subalterns
Moving along the footpath of the main road,
Chat about minor military concerns;
Bracing their shoulders as to take a load,
Swinging their canes, eyeing each girl that passes,
Feeling distinctly distant from the masses.

Grudgingly sidecapped gunners give salutes,
Murmur obscenities beneath their breath,
Gossiping news and public house disputes:
Tired of the drag of service, tired to death.
Their only thought to catch a bus as far
As the local town hall dance or cinema.

These carry now the future in the heads
Fouled with the daily drug of great events;
Discuss it in their buttockbiting beds
Or argue in the damp despair of tents
While hired wireless sets dictate aloud
The paths which must be followed by the crowd.

Unheeding now through summer days they give
Their drilled attention to the killer's art
Rehearsing in their minds the life they'll live
When some day soon their second life will start,
And ripping, every time they thrust, the drab,
Embittered present with a bayonet jab.

Sitting in the Mess, the Battery subalterns
Spreading their legs around a firelit hearth,
Distant from Army Orders and returns
Carry their talking down a well trod path.
'When this is finished we'll . . .', is all the theme
Of their age-old and never realised dream.

William Clarke

Return To Base

The place had not changed to the extent
That here and there you couldn't recognise
Signs of its occupation during the war,
The backstreet billets and the pubs you spent
Off-duty hours in after an exercise,
The Sergeant's Mess over the Co-op store
And the old mansion in its yew-tree shade
That served as headquarters of the brigade.

It all looked pretty much the same and yet
Was not the same because the people there
Seemed unapproachable or chose to ignore
What brought you back that made you stand and stare,
The young too young to remember or forget;
The old too old to care much anymore.

G. Haslett Connor

Remembrance Sonnet, 1941

We knew them as our comrades. We shall raise
    Heads that are proud with sorrow when men tell
    Of brave young souls that stood and fought and fell
And left to us their heritage of days.
We shall remember, on the paths we blaze,
    The land, the hopes they loved and guarded well.
    We shall be still, touched deeply by the spell
Of gratitude they leave with us always.

The future is not ours to take or squander;
    These comrades of our boyhood, it is theirs.
        Where freedom lives, where poverty is slain,
There shall their spirit dwell, their footsteps wander
    Over our hills; and in our thoroughfares
        Their selfless accents shall be heard again.

Joy Corfield

First Night in Barracks

Don't cry, young woman,
In your badly made bed;
Pull the grey blanket
Over your head.

Your mother cries, too,
On your first night from home,
Fearing your safety
Now you're on your own.

Take comfort, young woman.
If only you knew
Most of the others
Are crying, too.

Guildford, 1944.

I Didn't Believe It . . .

Two weeks in uniform
Strangers now friends.
Rosa teaching us to polish shoes;
Senga, the expert, pressing skirts.
Every morning
Jacky rushes to help me make my bed:
Three biscuits, neatly stacked.
On top, sheets and pillows wrapped
In one big grey blanket.

Two weeks confined to barracks
Then let free.
Best-dressed, checked in the guardroom,
Then off to town.
Self-conscious, shy,
We glanced in darkened windows
At our familiar faces in unfamiliar clothes,
Straightening our hats and shoulders,
Laughing when caught.
We shared chocolate, fish and chips,
And returned sober and properly dressed
In good time.

But three girls stayed out.
They'd been seen in a pub
With some Americans.
'They're fast,' someone whispered.
I couldn't believe it.
Seemed nice and friendly.

They were brought back by M.P.s
At lunchtime next day.
Dirty, untidy, defiant;
One wearing a U.S. army jacket.
They collected their things and left.
Never saw them again.

Someone shocked me saying,
'They boasted they'd each had thirty men.'
I didn't think it possible
So I didn't believe it, then.

Guildford, 1944.

Morse Lesson

A cold, cold room with cold, cold girls
In buttoned greatcoats, scarves and mitts;
Frozen fingers try to write
The letters for the dah–dah–dits.

'Faster, faster,' says the sergeant;
Slower, slower work our brains.
Feet are numb, our blood is frozen,
Every movement causing pains.

Yet – four of us swam in the sea
Just last week, on Christmas Day,
Through frosty foam and fringe of ice,
Warmer than we are today.

Isle of Man, 1945.

Timothy Corsellis

'I' Always 'I'

I passively acquiesce in the avalanche of death
Under my breath I lose the sincere feeling
That while hands are dealing in sin the soul is free.
No harm to me, justifying the material deed
With the new born seed of a higher emotion,
A sudden devotion to a greater thing than imperial expansion.

'I' always 'I' in this turmoil of souls;
God above holds millions of lives in his arms
Yet the word harm means only one thing to this mind.
Help me to find an idea successive to soliptic I!
Let them all die; one day a bullet inscribed with my name
Shall find the same written upon my heart with shame.

Why in the middle of complete conflagration,
Involving a nation, must the solipsist idea
Rise? To conquer fear? To hide from a wrangling soul
The extinction of the whole? Give me part of God's
    unselfishness,
From the centre of unrest make me realize
That no man dies; not the souls that once spoke from behind
    gristle eyes.

Norah Cruickshank

Posting

Once more, the train; the wet,
Grey, hauled-on, flying fields,
The sadness, the cold. This year
For the second time I set
Behind me the far from dear
Place with a strange regret.

A tale as hard to begin
And finish as *War and Peace*,
A system of people, ends.
For a breathing-space, within,
You walk and speak, my friends,
Before the loud others win.

I see a leaf that grips
A twig lodged in a stream,
Tugged at, as good as gone,
When I think of these years' friendships:
The straggling tide sweeps on;
The face from fond-thought slips.

The time is salt with farewells.
But, calling the better years,
But, tuned to the rushing train,
My stumbling verse tells:
In this body of death and pain
Were green, rebellious cells:

Were cells of kindness, whose sum
Worked softly to lift the whole,
To leaven this doughy lump
Our sighing world, this numb
Sin-tip, devil's dump,
And make the good kingdom come.

Hate thickens. But who will take
Back the same feckless heart,
Having seen in many places
The dull, cold, sealed crowd make
Way for names, for faces,
And liking and laughter break?

Good luck! A safe return
To city or glen or vale
At no distant day.
Heaven bless your return.
May tides be gentle, may
The tide of the world turn.

Paul Dehn

At The Dark Hour

Our love was conceived in silence and must live silently.
This only our sorrow, and this until the end.
Listen, did we not lie all of one evening
Your heart under my hand.

And no word spoken, no, not even the sighing
Of pain made comfortable, not the heart's beat
Nor sound of urgency, but a fire dying
And the cold sheet?

The sailor goes home singing, the sleepy soldier
May pin to the lit wall his lover's face.
Boys whistle under windows, and are answered;
But we must hold our peace.

Day, too, broke silently. Before the blackbird,
Before the trouble of traffic and the mist unrolled,
I shall remember at the dark hour turning to you
For comfort in the cold.

Madge Donald

Sonnet: To Albert in a Pub on New Year's Eve

'I would not have her second-hand,' he said,
As gaze to gaze we drained a glass of beer.
I paused, and could not get it from my head –
What bitterness to drink to the New Year.
The thought came slow that this was sacrilege:
Love, like a worn-out garment handed down,
Love, which is bounded by no bond or pledge,
Patterned to this man's form – that woman's gown.

Ah no, if you have kissed beneath the stars
And felt the spirit striving through the clay
Remember that eternity was yours
Though love but lasted for a single day:
What matter if she loved a thousand more
Yet gave you love alone in that one hour.

Cheadle, January 1942.

Keith Foottit

Two Pairs Of Shoes

Draw back the curtains,
Dim the electric light.
Now the stage is set for
Our impromptu first night.

We've had no rehearsals,
We don't need the cues,
And out in the corridor
Are two pairs of shoes.

If I could find the time, dear,
By looking in your eyes,
I'd never find the time for
God and apple pies.

If love was set to music,
And played at Albert Hall,
Man would love his neighbour,
There'd be no war at all.

Whisper, dear, you love me:
That's all you need to say.
Tomorrow I must leave my heart
For you to take away.

There's no time to lose, dear,
There's no time to lose.
Already they are polishing
Our two pairs of shoes.

Wilfred Gibson

The Shelter (extract)

In the air-raid shelter of the Underground
Stretched on the narrow wire racks ranged around
The walls, like corpses in a catacomb
With brows and cheeks cadaverous in the light,
By enemy raiders driven from hearth and home
War-weary workers slumber in the thick
Close atmosphere throughout the Summer night.
But, wakeful in the glitter of glazed white brick,
Dan sees a figure stumble down the stair,
A girl with wide eyes dazzled by the glare
Who pauses near the bottom; then with a moan
Sways helplessly, and, dropping like a stone,
Crumples up at the stairfoot. Hastily
The lad leaps down; then carefully makes his way
Among the sleepers huddled on the ground
To where she lies unconscious with still grey
Eyes staring. Stooping down, Dan hears a sound
Of heavy breathing; and, assured that she
Still lives, he seeks assistance speedily;
And skilfully the nurses bring her round;
When she sits up, bewildered, stroking back
The strands of chestnut hair from her white face.
Then, at a question where room can be found
To make a bed for her in that packed place,
The lad insists that she must have his rack.
So now he helps them as they carry her
And lay her on his berth; where presently,
After a puzzled glance at the unknown lad

Whose kind eyes look on her so anxiously,
Wrapt in Dan's overcoat she falls asleep,
Wornout by terror and shock, and does not stir;
In a fatigue-drugged slumber, dreamless and deep,
Recovering her vitality; while he
Against the rack leans resting, eager and glad
To think that he should have her in his care –
That he, among the sleepers who toss and groan
And mutter in their dreams, should watch alone
In sole charge of this slumbering unknown
Young creature come to him out of the night.

The Morass

His tank had stuck,
Bogged deep in the morass –
A stationary target – just his luck!
And, when the guns should get the range, like glass
They'd shatter it, or, leastways, knock it out,
Battered like an old kettle kicked about
From boy to boy across the grass
Of his old village-green . . . And he, well he
Was too done-in to worry; and, seemingly,
For evermore would be
Just part of the morass.

He Took Life Easy . . .

He took life easy in the days of peace
And never of its worst made much ado:
So, when chance caught him in the thick of fight,
He took death easy, too.

Employment

In wartime no one need be unemployed –
At least while aught is left to be destroyed.

George T. Gillespie

Promotion

In Room Four-Five Staff Captain X
received a file 're fireproof flex'.
He took a piece of paper and
began, as usual, 'Yours to hand. . .'
and ended up in mild reproof,
'This office deals with flex, rainproof.
In course of time your file will be
forwarded to FFP.
Meanwhile, for information and
attention, passed to Flexes, Land.'
Thus, ah thus, it all commenced.
Each office, in a form condensed,
added remarks and chits and quotes,
and half a hundred knowing notes,
until the file, now leather-bound,
chock full of 'seen' and 'no trace found'
and 'passed to you' and 'acked with thanks',
and 'flex, suggested use in tanks',
'not known' and 'see my urgent tel.'
and 'vide flex, electric bell',
is five years old and come to rest
with him who understands it best.
In Room Four-Five now Colonel X
has opened up a 'Part Two, Flex'.

London, July 1945

John H. Goss

Lance Corporal

Though there ain't a snouted sergeant in this god-forsaken Force
But whose ma knew less of wedding rings than sexual
    intercourse,
The bloke that gets my dander, – who I'm shortly going ter
    swipe, –
Is the belly crawling lance-jack with the solitary stripe.

Though the R.S.M. has s.o.l.[1], though Quarters' got no nous,
And there ain't a flaming Corporal whose guts would fill a
    louse,
The day my trigger-finger slips when cleaning of my hipe,
The cow that cops the bullet will only wear one stripe.

Though way down from the Colonel to the thievin'
    babbling-brook
There's not a flaming one of them that's worth a second look,
When I go out a-sniping the first thing I shall snipe
Is the tail-end of a bandicoot, with just one blinking stripe.

The jumping-jack one-striper, who puts his mates away!
And does it 'cos he loves to, for he gets no extra pay!
When the M.O. finds a bullet where green apples used ter gripe,
The cot-case wot's a-groaning there will wear a single stripe.

The ridin', crimein' lance-jack, he'll never cross the Bight,
If he should lean upon the rail one dark and dirty night:
And if the sharks don't get him or the whales don't make him
    tripe,
A squid will suck the harder – or a marlin wear one stripe!

[1]s.o.l. – 'sod all intelligence'

Grace Griffiths

Doodlebugs

A bomb, last night, fell close by Radlett.
The pulsing engine stopped right overhead.
Four minutes to the crash. Slowly we counted;
One girl cried 'Oh God! Dear God!'
The tension grew to bursting point; the blast
Shattered the windows. We breathed again.
Always the bombs come over in early evening
Just before we go on shift. We talk of rush-hour traffic
But underneath the fear remains. Death can come
From so many angles. Tomorrow, next week, next month
It may not pass us by.

(Shenley, Herts., 1944)

Charles Hamblett

Bombs on my Town

for T.

The farmers I spoke of that night
In London, drive into High Street
A roundabout way,
Their stunted, aggressive features
More death-vacant than ever,
Since yesterday.

Quiet, an empty dray
Only to mark for this scooped-hollow
Yeomanry, its past proud chatter,
Its market clatter
Of carriage and horse,
Now a sad echo,
An exhumed decay.

The tradesmen I've known for years
Bow with civic ponderosity
Over smashed pavements, to collect
Their stock, swept, with their integrity,
Beneath the quick stroke
Of an uncaring raider,
Whose fifth-rate dentistry tore
Our houses from the long, gaping maw
Of High Street.

Michael Hamburger

Sentry Duty

His box is like a coffin, but erect,
the night is dull as death; he must not sleep,
but leans against the boards. The night winds creep
around his face, while the far stars reflect
the awful emptiness of heart and brain,
and trembling wires wail a requiem.
(If they were Sirens he would follow them
to the sweet morgue, their magical domain.)

But no one passes; a stray cat cries out,
the moon emerges from a cloud's dark rim,
and vanishes; he walks, and turns about.

Next day no sad unrest bewilders him
who'd seen the planets fall into a trance,
the earth shed lustre and significance.

W.J. Harvey

Maps

Maps are terrible, dangerous things;
for one man's death beneath the gathering waves
and one girl's agony of heart
are but two meeting lines, abstract,
a point in space upon a barren chart,
a common symbol for a thousand graves.

O shall we always be deceived
by geographic fictions – never see
the lie behind the cross, the arrowhead,
and think, not of advance or frontier,
but rather of the Russian soldier dead
and hopeless, helpless German refugee?

Portsmouth

I remember this town
by the decaying piles of wood on the deserted quays,
by the slack-lipped pallid women,
and the humourless latrinary obscenities.

Love is mechanical here,
worshipped in sticky cinematic cuddles,
by brutish gestures in shop doorways, and under arches
where the old whore flaunts; the cripple huddles.

People are all walking in circles,
their villas a wilderness of anonymity;
northwards the bright lights, the flickering dance halls,
southwards, the grey corrugations of the sea.

To the east lie the merchants and their bankers,
and cringing upon the fringes of respectability
a multitude shrinking from the omniscient historical embrace;
yet, as Auden observed, some of these people are somehow
   happy.

Desmond Hawkins

Night Raid

The sleepers humped down on the benches,
The daft boy was playing rummy with anyone he could get,
And the dancing girl said, 'What I say is,
If there's a bomb made for YOU,
You're going to get it.'
Someone muttered, 'The bees are coming again.'
Someone whispered beside me in the darkness,
'They're coming up from the east.'
Way off the guns muttered distantly.

This was in the small hours, at the ebb.
And the dancing girl clicked her teeth like castanets
And said, 'I don't mind life, believe me.
I like it. If there's any more to come,
I can take it and be glad of it.'
She was shivering and laughing and throwing her head back.
On the pavement men looked up thoughtfully,
Making plausible conjectures. The night sky
Throbbed under the cool bandage of the searchlights.

F.A. Horn

Reveille – 1943

The day calls coldly, and the billet stirs
To habit-grafted routine; yawning men
Tousle their hair, stretching like sleepy curs
Roused by the boot of duty from their den
Of frowsy, warm and timeless luxury,
Sit up, light cigarettes, cough, and scratch,
Salvage their coin, and count their penury;
Or, rolling over, seek again to catch
The dim last moments of their morning dreams –
Of women fairer, kinder than they've known
In waking life; sun-splintered moorland streams,
And good brown ale in pewter, and the sown
And wrinkled ploughlands, cheeky music-halls,
Lampfall on cobbles and the peace that's found
With slippered ease among evening sound;
The candid noise of children laughing . . . to his own
Each dreamer would go back . . . go back. No good.
Boots clump on wood. A coarse roar batters on the hood
Of blankets, in mock rage; the squirrel cage
Of duty spins; day calls; and Now begins.

Train Piece– 1943

Riding the corner of the corridor,
The big pink officer sways and brays
To the pretty school-teacher on holiday.
Shortage of seats leading to communion of souls,
They rock, smile, and chatter to each other,
Mutually condemning Blackpool
And agreeing that Shakespeare is nice.
He loves Bristol and the Warsaw Concerto
And she thinks Walbrook something rather less than male.
Very carefully well-bred, they talk sociology,

And discuss in detail the weather in Gloucestershire,
While all the time, under the cloak of dialogue
Oh, so remote from any thought of bed,
They sniff and nibble at the edge of sex,
And the talk doesn't matter a damn.

She leaves the train at Sheffield,
Seduced, flushed, and faint with masculine platitudes,
And he finds refuge from frustrations in the 'Telegraph'
Sitting in one of many long, long empty seats.

Patricia Ledward

From
Air-Raid Casualties: Ashridge Hospital

On Sundays friends arrive with kindly words
To peer at those whom war has crushed;
They bring the roar of health into these hushed
And solemn wards –
The summer wind blows through the doors and cools
The sweating forehead; it revives
Memories of other lives
Spent lying in the fields, or by sea-pools;
And ears that can discern
Only the whistling of a bomb it soothes
With tales of water splashing into smooth
Deep rivers fringed with ferns.
Nurses with level eyes, and chaste
In long starched dresses, move
Amongst the maimed, giving love
To strengthen bodies gone to waste.
The convalescents have been wheeled outside,
The sunshine strikes their cheeks and idle fingers,
Bringing to each a sensuous languor
And sentimental sorrow for the dead.

One by one the wards empty, happiness goes,
The hospital routine, the usual work
Return for another week;
The patients turn upon themselves, a hundred foes
Imagined swell their suffering;
Fretfully hands pick at sheets
And voices meet
Discussing symptoms and the chance of living.
Only the soldier lies remote and resolutely sane,
Remembering how, a boy, he dreamt of folk
With footballs. Maturity dispelled the dream – he woke
To know that he would never walk again.

Geoffrey Matthews

Nocturne

Smoke from the municipal dump blows sleepily over
Newmarket; racehorses on the heath are ridden down
To breathy paddocks, and the last lights are all covered.
Evening in Air Force blue leans at the end of the town.

Lovers in slacks and battledress on their physical errands
Loiter past, unfocus, sombre are no longer seen.
Thigh-deep already in shadow the cinemas stand
Posing, where the dun staff-cars founder like plasticine.

Far out along the sea-coloured coasts of Norfolk,
From ruts and estuaries, the searchlights raise their arms
Palms uppermost, pressing up against the cloud-pack,
Withholding the heavy sky from camp and farm.

Two factory-chimneys a long way away fume and labour,
Tops black against duck's-egg, trunks in cinnamon.
A concert of travelling stars. Bomber after bomber
Steps overland to rehearse the destiny of man.

Embarkation Song

Behind are the guns drilled by their daughters,
Hills ahead like fumes in a retort,
Salt water beside me, an endless bay of water
Is there a way out?

A girl I know would hide me: she's no angel,
With a tribe's blood on her nails and lips.
We'd love and drown the war and then be single
At the war's end, perhaps.

Or ask the chemist, delving in the daylight
Of shelves crowded with bitter looks.
Here's peace for sixpence: I can have myrrh and aconite
If I write in the book.

I'm joking, dear, and I shan't ask what you're doing
While I'm abroad, or how you wait.
But quick, tell me once more why I am going,
Before it is too late.

Neil McCallum

Stand-To

The sea at dawn is grey, sombre as metal,
With dull unburnished strength.
The light expands till the horizon,
Once more defined, encircles our day.
In the tufted grass and the sea-pinks
Our rifles lie, clean, with bolts oiled,
Our pouches hard with rounds.
A metal world of rifle, sea and sky.

The cramped limb moves; the eyes stare outwards.
Only behind is life where the fields stretch
And new smoke lifts from silent houses.
We forget the pre-vigil days
The time of fretting and proposition
Of clamorous words and fear be-devilled plans.
Perhaps we were wrong then,
And all the holy words
Were cried in a madman's dream:
Peace and freedom
Dwelled in the clarity of delirium;
The scales of justice balanced neatly
Not now, but in the future of a mirage.

We have returned to faith
For the argument did not reach its conclusion.
The words were buried by bullets, and the guns
            drowned our songs.
Here, leaning on the side of the weapon-pit,
A trickle of sand on our boots
There is only the tense eye and the tired mind
That does not plead or suffer but has learned patience.

James Monahan

Kentish Lines in War

A saddle cornfield burnished Van Gogh-bright,
a tumble of clashing rooks, rooks regathering
their rapscallion squadrons; their independent flight
to the harbour oak, to flap a dismissive wing
and caw themselves surfeited of the battle-game.
Through thinnest blue the silver, rigid birds
unwaveringly trace their pencilled aim
at France; their unrelenting voice is heard
like a tiny shaking of the firmament.

And evening, and the sunlight's luxury
spent to the afterglow; just now night sent
her horsemen, chilly-javelined, brushing by,
probing the valley. Above the valley swells
a longer wind through that remoter sky –
wind bursting the tufty clouds to particles,
dawn fragile beyond visibility.
An incurious hawk floats, shivers, floats again,
and rides the evening on a loosened rein.

April 1942.

Kenneth Smith

A Rose By Any Other Name
(dedicated to all the 'W.R.E.N.S.'[1])

Dainty, peace-time, silken step-ins
Were not proof against men's weapons,
   But the Regulation Knicker,
   Stronger, durable, and thicker,
Shapeless, ugly, long, and black,
Keeps the forward suitor back!

High-heeled shoe, and flesh-tight stocking,
Twinkling legs so madly shocking
   Leering eyes of lustful male –
   All is hidden 'neath a veil –
Under cylinders of cotton
Tantalising is *verboten*.

And a maiden's shapely breast
'Neath its woollen, issue, vest
Jiggles gently (lovely words)
   But in vain. – So think Their Lords. –
Yet despite these old curmudgeons
Not two in fifty Wrens are virgins!!!

[1] Women's Royal Navy Service

A.H. Watkins

The Tragic Mystery of Corporal Plum

Wherever a group of men is seen –
Gallant Home Guardsmen, sturdy and keen –
At the village pub, or in the canteen,
You will hear them discuss, with visage glum,
What they conjecture might have become
Of their gallant old comrade Corporal Plum.
This really remarkable, tragical mystery
Has, until now, been muffled in history.
Now the Security Officer gives his consent,
I can give you the dope on the whole sad event.

Plum, an old soldier, manly and tall,
Was one of the first to answer the call
(Made some of the slackers look a bit small).
Soon all the neighbours turned out to see
Plum marching homeward as proud as could be,
With his manly arm labelled 'L.D.V.'
He attended parades, and he worked very hard.
Mr. Churchill altered the name to 'Home Guard.'
Then, in overalls, denim, we meet our old chum.
Henceforth to be known as Corporal Plum.

'This sewing on bits is the plague of my life'

Then things began to move with an urge;
From the Quarter Bloke's store we saw Plum emerge
Bravely arrayed in Battle-dress, serge.
Then a Cap, F.S., was the next to appear
Perfectly poised upon his right ear.
Boots, ankle, pairs one, and Anklets, leather
(Useful things these in the dirty weather),
And a nice leather belt to hold him together.
Dressing, field, one, Ointment A.G.,
A packet of Eyeshields containing three.
Then he found they hadn't done with him yet;
There was Rifle and Bayonet, and Frog, bayonet.
Then, on parade, a few minutes later,
The R.S.M. said, 'Where's your Respirator?'

After every parade he called at the store
And they loaded him up with something more:
Kept sticking bits on from his head to his feet,
Till, at last, they made him a soldier complete.
'Twas his own idea that he'd look a bit bolder
With one of those lanyard things over his shoulder.

Then, Mrs. Plum's task was entered upon:
Titles, shoulder, Home Guard, she had to sew on.
Flashes and Numerals, Stripes, and so on.
She complained, though she had been a most dutiful wife,
'This sewing on bits is the plague of my life.
I don't understand, but it seems to me
They're making you look like a Christmas Tree.
Isn't there anything else you can cadge?'
'Yes, there's Conduct Stripes and Proficiency Badge.'

They gave him a Greatcoat, then called him back;
They'd forgotten to give him a Haversack.
Still they kept on with the jolly old game;
Bottle, water, one and Carrier for same;
Tin, mess, one; Gloves, worsted, one pair,
And then they decided while he was there
To fill up the few remaining spaces
With Webbing Equipment, Sleeve, Pouches and Braces.

He tried to make his escape, but alas!
They dished him out a Cape Anti-Gas.
'Sixty-nine items,' said the Quarter, 'I make it.'
Plum manfully murmured, 'O.K. – we can take it.'
Bravely, he shouldered the mountainous pack.
It was too much. Alas and Alack!
You remember the tale of the camel's back?
He could not support one little bit more;
That Cape Anti-Gas was the very last straw.

He staggered away down the roadway dark,
And just as he reached the gates of the park –
Some twenty minutes, I suppose had elapsed –
There came the end. Our hero collapsed!
He was lulled to his rest by the evening breeze
As the chestnut leaves fluttered from fading trees.

The following morning the milkman found
As he started out on his early round,
A sort of a new and peculiar mound.

'Sixty nine items,' said the Quarter, 'I make it . . .'

The Mediterranean, North Africa
Italy and the Balkans

Drummond Allison

'Come Let Us Pity Death'

Come let us pity not the dead but Death,
For He can only come when we are leaving,
He cannot stay for tea or share our sherry.
He makes the old man vomit on the hearthrug
But never knew his heart before it failed him.
He shoves the shopgirl under the curt lorry
But could not watch her body undivided.
Swerving the cannon-shell to smash the airman
He had no time to hear my brother laughing.
He sees us when, a boring day bent double,
We take the breaking point for new beginning,
Prepared for dreamless sleep or dreams or waking
For breakfast but now sleep past denying.
He has no life, no exercise but cutting;
While we can, hope a houri, fear a phantom,
Look forward to No Thoughts. For Him no dying
Nor any jolt to colour His drab action,
Only the plop of heads into the basket,
Only the bags of breath, the dried-up bleeding.
We, who can build and change our clothes and moulder,
Come let us pity Death but not the dead.

Verity

*In memory of Captain Hedley Verity, injured in Sicily. Taken
P.O.W., buried at Caserta. Pre-war, Yorkshire and England
slow left arm bowler.*

The ruth and truth you taught have come full circle
On that fell island all whose history lies,
Far now from Bramhall Lane and far from Scarborough
You recollect how foolish are the wise.

On this great ground more marvellous than Lord's
– Time takes more spin than nineteen thirty four –
You face at last that vast that Bradman-shaming
Batsman whose cuts obey no natural law.

Run up again, as gravely smile as ever,
Veer without fear your left unlucky arm
In His so dark direction, but no length
However lovely can disturb the harm
That is His style, defer the winning drive
Or shake the crowd from their uproarious calm.

Robin Benn

Dalmatian Islanders

These were peaceful people, and the hills, their world,
hedged in by changing seas, to rocky breasts
took prints of intimacy with gentle feet.
These rocks, white-piled a million gleaming cairns,
or walled around with meagre fields they hid,
saw silent fortitude reach dogged mastery,
and grimly watched, amazed, a people grow.
These waters, savaging the stranger craft,
conspiring with the rocks to spoil their keels,
took fathers to their death, and saw the sons
tight-lipped at dawn confront their rage anew.
Through centuries the thirsty sun beat down on them,
parching their vineyards; from their hard-hewn wells
spirited off the precious hoarded drops
of water. Yet they'll say they loved the sun.
For these were peaceful people. In their hearts
no bitterness that Nature was so harsh,
no whined complaint to Heaven in need they raised.
Man had not harmed them; therefore friends of Man,
and all men friends, their life was hard but glad.
And Man has struck them, vilely, from behind,
thinking to bend them, beaten, to his will.

These are quiet people, but their eyes are hard,
and sounds we know can number none to tear
and chill the heart as when their women mourn.

J. Bevan

Ubique

(Motto of the Royal Artillery)

The long barrel of the past is pointing towards me;
I peer down its spiral rifling, reflecting those times
so many mortgages, lectures, removals,
so many bombards, ranging rounds ago.
I can see those long five-fives with the vertical horns,
and the stencilled hundred-pounders we posted each day
from our cluttered dens in tents or farmhouse kitchens
to destinations we thought we knew,
a few thousand yards, years away in our future:
Forcoli, Campi Bizenzio, Astra Signa
swim through the donkey's ears;
that time with the guns straddling the Serchio
deeply snowed where David made a suspension footbridge,
and all those fireplans at two or three hundred hours
on Monte Rumici, Monte Caprara, Sole,
ringed in crayon on the talc, names of fear;
HEN (it is marked in red) when the Guards
ran into fixed-line fire on a night attack
and the casual company commander who had a look-see
beforehand from the O.P., dumped his valise there
and never came back to unroll it; that
premature on the hilltop
position at snug Bombiana, the gun-barrel peeled
back like a steel banana skin, circular saws
of jagged bits, plummeting down whining thousands of
    minutes later;
that first barrage in the Gothic Line

when everything suddenly blazed round the pivot gun,
haystack, boxes of cordite, and Gunner Lea
(who is it walking up with a mug of tea?
I wish I remembered the Number One's name who is pulling
his clothes off and kicking away the charges
and burning hay while the rest of the crew
lie about dazed in the scorched grass. The strong men
are all nameless in history);
and the night-move over to Castelfiorentino
where we lost a gun-tower on a mine;
I remember the goggled D.R.[1] on his motorbike
(squarehead concealed by crash-helmet)
who directed me into a minefield with the guns
and vanished without so
much as a *Leben Sie wohl*;
Those winters of deep ruts and wheels
spinning the trucks lop-sided, world of wires and phones,
a crazed polyphony of dozens of frequencies
marking the F.D.Ls[2]; the always arriving
always changing Meteor; slewing the grid, and shells coming up
from the wagon lines (strange
nineteenth-century name from horse-drawn days),
havens of sleek non-combatants three miles back,
with constant brews and pick of all the perks.
Where are all those thousands of indestructible metal
charge boxes, some in junk shops on Merseyside still?
Some under the curtained bunks on Appenine
farms; one in the garage at my last address;
and the summers, the scissor sharpeners busy all night in the
    quincunx
olive ranks; musk smell of the dusk,
and sudden flash-bang of the high-velocity
guns, dragged on the edge of dark over the ridges to fire
quick rounds with open sights from the forward slopes,
then limbered up and away before we could say Take Post;
the morning mist thinning at the feet
of Santa Maria, and black crosses on the grey

[1]Despatch Rider
[2]Forward Defence Lines

shapes I looked steeply down on, turning on tracks and
rumbling away to the cemetery (I hear
the drone of their lumbering exit);
shouting to the mike, hearing the battery, neat
miniature toys hidden in the next valley,
orders going out to the guns, the tiny
reduced voices of the Number Ones, then
Ready: No time for range tables, time of flight?
thirty seconds.
Fire! (and Fire! and, fainter, Fire!);
then waiting,
the shells already posted, for them to fly
over my head like whistling kettles, magnificent
loving response;
then below, four hundred yards away, land in a clump of
(puffs first) crumps;
and one tank, hated, like a rat in a wainscot,
stop and turn round and round and round
concussed
by a hit, then judder like a compass needle
and follow the others away with seeming unhaste.

Ah, those ithyphallic barrels, always exactly parallel,
pointing where someone's right and glory led us
through two long winters, over the Appenines,
across the Arno and beyond Verona
to the great plains and the lakes
(peregrino labore fessi), Garda and Como
where we fired our final rounds for ever and ever.
Can a few tree trunks, sawn and sloped to the sky
in a field on the eve of Good Friday, decades later
still fire such long-range salvos?
The soul saves what it needs
from the waste, halts time at its will.
Those gun positions, those facets, those parallel pieces
are ranging on me still.

J.E. Brookes

Thermopylae 1941

A private soldier doubtless suffers less
from his privations than from ignorance
of what is going on; in terms of chess,
he is a pawn. But the significance
of our deployment on the forward slopes
of this position was not lost on us.
No purpose served consulting horoscopes
at Delphi; students of Herodotus
would know withdrawal to Thermopylae
and putting up barbed wire could only mean
fighting a rearguard action Q.E.D,
as Euclid would have put it. We had been
deposited into the warlike lap
of ancient deities. I said to Blue,
my Aussie mate, 'There was this famous chap
Leonidas, he was the Spartan who
defended it with just 300 men
against an army.' Bluey took a draw
upon his cigarette. 'Well stuff 'im then!'
a pungent comment on the art of war.
Foreboding we looked back across the plain
which we had crossed, towards Lamia, towards
the north just as the Spartans must have lain
with spear and sword and watched the Persian hordes
amassing for the battle long ago.
It was deserted, a proscenium
where once Leonidas heard trumpets blow,
a theatre whose auditorium,
the home of gods, was mountains, and whose stage
was lapped by Homer's wine-dark seas as blue
as lapis lazuli, where in a rage
Poseidon wrecked Odysseus and his crew
and siren voices tempted. In the wings
of history we waited for a roll
of other drums and strident trumpetings

to usher in the gods of war. The soul
of Sparta stirred, could but the brave
Leonidas renew his mortal span
instead of merely turning in his grave,
and all his hoplites, perished to a man,
but resurrect themselves. . . . I said 'They wore
long hair, the Spartans, a visible proof
that they were free, not helots, and before
the battle they would gravely sit aloof
and garland it with flowers.' Bluey spat.
Continuing to watch the empty road
across the plain he took of his tin-hat
(a proof that he was bald) and said 'A load
of bloody poufdahs!' Thus he laid the ghost
of brave Leonidas. Herodotus
informs us Xerxes, leader of the host,
when told was equally incredulous,
though whether from a soldier's point of view
of army discipline or on the grounds
of social prejudice like my mate Blue,
was not elaborated. With the sounds
of planes we kept our heads down. After dark
we dug slit-trenches neath the April moon
in silence broken only by the bark
of some Greek shepherd's dog while our platoon
commander and the sergeant walked about
discussing fields of fire. We lit a smoke,
which made the section corporal shout 'Put out
that bloody light!' It was the Colonel broke
the news, like some deus ex machina
descending from above. THEY SHALL NOT PASS. . .
THE LAST LINE OF DEFENCE etcetera,
all sentiments of which Leonidas
would have approved, and as he disappeared
into the moonlight, with a martial air,
a crown and two pips, everybody cheered
instead of putting flowers in their hair,
but muted just in case the Germans were
in earshot and from feeling (for myself
at any rate) that we should much prefer

that history did not repeat itself.
And later with our cigarettes concealed
behind cupped hands we peered into the night
across the darkened plain and it revealed
first one and then another point of light,
and then a hundred of them, moving down
the distant backcloth, shining off and on
like tiny jewels sparkling on a crown
of moonlit mountains, a phenomenon
caused by the winding path of their descent
round hair-pin bends cascading from the heights
beyond Lamia, our first presentiment
of evil genius – they were the lights
of Hitler's war machines! So fate had cast
us in the role of heroes in the same
arena where the heroes of the past
had closed their ranks and perished in the name
of freedom. Was there one of those among
the Spartans who, at the eleventh hour
upon the eve of battle, while he hung
his hair with many a patient-wreathed flower,
prayed that some unpredictable event
like Xerxes dropping dead, some miracle,
might even yet occur and thus prevent
the battle being joined the oracle
at Delphi notwithstanding? 'Time to pick
the flowers, Blue, that bloom upon the steep
hillside' I said 'make daisy-chains and stick
the buggers in our hair!' He was asleep.
So all night long I watched and when the skies
had lightened with the dawn (doubtless the last
that I should ever see with mortal eyes
before we joined those heroes of the past
in the Elysian fields) and bold day broke
across the misted plain on mythic banks
of white and yellow asphodel he woke
and heard combustion engines. German tanks?

I said a private soldier suffers less
from his privations than from ignorance
of what is going on, but we could guess

that some extraordinary circumstance
had made the sergeant, full pack, rifle slung,
rise up before us blotting out the sun.
Phoebus Apollo? Götterdämmerung
more likely! GREEKS CAPITULATED . . . HUN
MIGHT CUT US OFF . . NO PANIC . . GET
EMBUSSED . . .
YES 3-TON TRUCKS HAVE JUST ARRIVED. . . I thanked
the Lord for it and meanwhile Bluey cussed
and our lance-corporal said he'd been outflanked
at Passchendaele and got away with it.
As Bluey put it 'if some bloody mug
brasshat had only warned us, used a bit
of common sense we never need have dug
that something something slit-trench!' (Stuff 'im then?)
But as we drove away I must confess
it felt like a desertion. Those few men
with flowers in their hair were heroes! Yes!

April 25, 1941

W.H. Burt

Stane Jock[1]

For the glory of the Highland Division
on the night of 23 October 1942

Atween the mune an' the yird[2]
   There is quick steel:
Atween the steel and the yird
There is quick stane!

The man-trap field is fu' o' men
   Walking saftly.
The man-eating mandrakes scream
   As they bite.

[1]Name of the stone memorial on the Western Front of World War One
[2]Earth

The stane Jock o' Beaumont Hamel
   Is fa'en doon.
There's nae mair pipes in France –
   Nae mair sweet croon.

But this nicht stane Jock,
   Walks in the sand!
This nicht I hear the pipes,
   I hear the band!

There's nane deid but his dead e'en
   Glower at the west.
There's nane living but stepping hard
   Towards the west.

For the stane fa'n in France
   Here rises a living stane –
For the mindin' o' men killed
   Here rises a killing stane!

Yon pinke'ed craw, the mune,
   Sees a field o' strange plants –
Fire and sand fused glassily
   Into flowers on a wall.

An' the wa' is o' stane,
   An' the wa' walks
Covered wi' red flowers –
   A stane striding to destiny!

Gallus laddies a'l
   Stanes o' destiny!
Stane Jock in the mantrap field
   Walking saftly.

James McAdam Clark

The Capture of Rome

We passed Rome by,
Grey silhouette against a greyer sky;
So with a sigh we passed Rome by.

Paramount, commanding Rome
we saw the dome, Saint Peter's dome
And passed it by.

But soon returned one day
To Rome; and to the Romans say
You are not worthy of our way.

Too sleek, too nonchalant you are,
Too selfish to deserve of war
Never a scar.

Can it be well for Roman pride
If we who rescued her decide
The Roman's soul has died?

That Peter's dome commands in Rome
An empty home, which with a sigh
The armies of mankind passed by?

June 1944

Les Cleveland

Cassino (Extract)

At the face of the smoking crag
a horde of screeching machines
labour at this season's assignment:
spurts of furious dust rise and fall,
curtaining flesh ripped and thwacked
by fanged rods of shrapnel:
Engines howl full throttle
and claw at wreckage of sandbags,
smashed beams, spilled stone and lumbering
paraphernalia of heavy infantry
programmed for the intensive industry
of siege warfare in winter.
Steel tracks rage over pulverised streets
as enemy armour-piercing, self-propelled artillery
lashes pointblank at our newborn organism scuttling,
limbs entangled, heads devoutly flattened to earth,
huddling together under the barrage.
Each man clasps his blood brother
on that ancient rock of community
till every autonomous fibre is willed
into one prostrate, protesting entity
as the ponderous imperatives of shellfire

Signal that the position has been outflanked.
We, the living, hitch at weapons and scrabble
under cover of counter-battery fire
over mud-greased heaps of masonry
crusting the wrecked street and congealed
in frozen, formless landscapes against jammed
doorways and bomb-avalanched walls to the next
instalment of death shown the Via Casalina.
The dying wane with the expected stoic calm
Toward their silent territory;
They are already cast out.

Stay with the mob, you can't go wrong.

Now that soldier in the rubble
flinches, and instantly I feel
the thump of shrapnel pillaging
my temporary brother's flesh:
he cries out for help, and grips me
in a child-like hold;
I break his arms from their embrace,
and unbuckle his web gear,
open coat and tunic
and look where his blood
soaks into the dusty stones.
Kaput, the stretcher bearers say,
Don't waste time on him: but I have to trace
the random processes of his death

I draw my knife and hack away the sodden cloth.
The carcase does not stir.

Flora of battlefields, discarded junk of casualties
strews the ground like trampled weeds:
I spread a dead paratrooper's camouflaged jacket
to cover both his stiff body
and the homelier shape sprawled underfoot . . .
The Spandau fire from close range!
A sharp, bone-snapping shock
splinters the smoked-clogged air:
we run,
while I formulate the usual lies,
the righteous words to ease guilt
and sanctify the ritual death
of the man whose abandoned body
has been an expendable shield,
a viable husk in the ruthless cycle
of the omnipotent organism.
We run,
And awkwardly, gun at the ready,
I try to wipe from my shivery hands
The salutary, scab-like clots
Of the necessary victim's blood.

H. Compton

On a Soldier Playing the Piano

The Naafi much admires
The lucky, gifted man
Who, lacking thought or plan,
Incites these weary wires,
Like rivals hoarse for votes,
To argue over pitch.
With long-habitual twitch
His left hand dully quotes
A ready-made, staccato,
And smudgy ostinato.
Unhampered by notation,
He learned to play by ear.
This leaves his right hand free
To ramble languidly –
To roam his private sphere
By free association,
And with subconscious bonds
To bind up odds and ends:
Remembered gramophones
That mingle with his dreams,
And visions in a trance
Of girls he saw in trams,
Dim evenings drowned in bars,
Embraces on the stairs,
An impulse at the dance,
The body's vain expense –
All these he now lays bare,
His wealth is here displayed.
O who will say he's hollow,
Whose drift we all can follow,
Or find in him a lack
Who, innocent of Bach,
Thus scatters on the air
The notes in which he's paid?

Robert Conquest

A Minor Front

The bridge attributed to Belisarius
Is blown, and we cross the stream on foot
Towards the little town.
          Absolute power
Has receded like a tide from the Thracian hills
And the people reappears, a streaming rock
Surrounded by dead monsters.
          Across the Struma
The German outposts can be seen, and their patrols
Still cross the river almost unopposed
For the retreat was caused by pressure elsewhere
And here no force of partisans can yet
Resist them. Half a dozen towns
Still lie in a no-man's land which small patrols
Alone can enter.
          The clouds appear
Fully created in the Aegean sky
And ahead of us the stony and half-empty
Struma glistens.
          Among the buildings
(Not too badly wrecked) people are moving.
An old man, carrying a wooden bucket
Full of goat's milk, staggers to his neighbour's.
– The quick withdrawal of that violent empire
Has left a vacuum of rule. Government is dead;
And after the executions by patrols the tired survivors
Learn, for a few days, to work together, to live.
The best are in the mountains with the partisans
Or rotting in Salonika jail. The worst come out
To loot or denounce. And among the others only,
Mediocre and stupid, in small and selfish cities,
Half-suffocated by starvation and disease,
The free life of the holiday camp arises.
Very dimly through a host of more immediate noises

They faintly hear the music of the stateless future
Like a distant waterfall.
       But there is too much.
Too much confusion! Too much metal!
They have gazed too long into a mirror of Europe
And seen the Minotaur reflections gnash their teeth,
And they cannot keep their eyes on the green star
Nor listen to the bells.
       The sky glitters, burning coldly.
The moment is losing its illumination;
The world of politics and rifles reappears;
In Seres, Drama, Sidhirokastron, life will revert
To the visionless present.
       We lower our field-glasses,
And walk back to the far end of the village,
And pull out our rations and begin to eat,
As by the failing light we try to interpret
The gilt inscription on the public monument
In front of which, their hands still tied behind them,
The bodies of two gendarmes lie in the street.

Erik de Mauny

Morning After Battle

As if for a first time I have seen
The breathless outburst of this winter morning
And never before knew sun so tender in bare trees.
Nor, under the naked branches, green so green
As the silent fields. And the silence is
The calm of the late reprieve. We cannot bear
This silence speaking: so, as if ashamed
To show our joy, are wordless as we turn
Away from that country of fear no one has named.
There are birds singing in the crystal air.
We forget the fear that like a spider's web
Brushed at our faces through the lonely night;
Forget the pall of guns forever spreading
On cities, lights and perfumes, and release
The small history clenched in the fist of fear.

Mutter: 'They copped old Tom (or Dick, or Joe)
Sleeping – just there, look – under the wild hedgerow.
Wouldn't it make you. . .' Yes, when Death nudges,
'Old Flatnose', they are always ready to go,
With a brief sigh, like children woken from dream:
With simple words like these for epitaph
Masking the bright deep fury without a name.

Before these nameless faces what can be said
For a courage that braves the eternally private hell?
Yet it seemed like the promise wrought, the miracle sign
When a girl smiled, drawing water at the well.

Italy, Winter 1944

Donald Everett

Kyrenia

Saw far below
glitter of white churches
among grey of Castle
grey of Mosque
and two piers enclosing
the blue deep harbour
with Pharos, the little guardian
sturdily standing.

We descended into the little city
bathed in cool of sea
beneath the Pharos
rested upon surface to see above
green of gardens
red of Bougainvillea
eyes reaching to inland crags
dominating the sky
to castles floating among the ranges.

Completeness of beauty
we had never known
an absolute of perfection
for us this once.

Gavin Ewart

War Dead

With grey arm twisted over a green face
The dust of passing trucks swirls over him,
Lying by the roadside in his proper place,
For he has crossed the ultimate far rim
That hides from us the valley of the dead.
He lies like used equipment thrown aside,
Of which our swift advance can take no heed,
Roses, triumphal cars – but this one died.

Once war memorials, pitiful attempt
In some vague way regretfully to atone
For those lost futures that the dead had dreamt,
Covered the land with their lamenting stone –
But in our hearts we bear a heavier load:
The bodies of the dead beside the road.

near La Spezia, April 1945

Sonnet

Armies, like homes once hated, feed and clothe
And occupy with certain dull routine,
Are Fathers, strict, and cannot ever soothe,
Nor see what lovers with clear eyes have seen.
Good at its job, the soldierly, keen eye
Combs fields for gun sites and the sky for planes;
Landscapes suggest campaigns – but you and I
Are too fine detail on those endless plains
Where generals are romping. 'Personnel'
Would be our label; we are on their files.
And where you are no flag will ever tell
Although my love for you should cover miles.
Known to the wise, for you I write it out –
There are two worlds, within us and without.

Roy Fuller

The White Conscript and the Black Conscript

I do not understand
Your language, nor you mine.
If we communicate
It is hardly the word that matters or the sign,
But what I can divine.

Are they in London white
Or black? How do you know,
Not speaking my tongue, the names
Of our tribes? It could be as easily a blow
As a match you give me now.

Under this moon which the curdled
Clouds permit often to shine
I can see more than your round cap,
Your tallness, great eyes and your aquiline
Nose, and the skin, light, fine.

The British must be wicked:
They fight. I have been brought
From our wide pastures, from
The grave old rules of conduct I was taught:
Like a beast I have been caught.

If only I could tell you
That in my country there
Are millions as poor as you
And almost as unfree: if I could share
Our burdens of despair!

For I who seem so rich,
So free, so happy, am
Like you the most despised.
And I would not have had you come
As I most loath have come.

Among our tribe, like yours,
There are some bad, some good –
That is all I am able to say:
Because you would not believe me if I could
Tell you it is for you, the oppressed, the good
Only desire to die.

West Africa

Robert Garioch

Kriegy[1] *Ballad*

Note: This is somewhat nearer to being a definitive edition than previous definitive editions have been. In fact, it is the definitive edition to end definitive editions in the meantime, under the circumstances.

CHORUS:
Toorally Oorally addy etc.
Here's hoping we're not here to stay.

Yes, this is the place we were took, sir,
And landed right into the bag,
Right outside the town of Tobruk, sir,
So now for some bloody stalag.

There was plenty of water in Derna,
But the camp was not very well kept,
For either you slept in the piss–hole,
Or pissed in the place where you slept.

And when we went on to Benghazi,
We had plenty of room, what a treat!
But I wish that the guard was a Nazi,
He might find us something to eat.

[1]German slang for P.O.W.

We sailed on the good ship Revalo,
She carried us over the sea,
You climbed up a forty-foot ladder
Whenever you wanted a pee.

And then we went on to Brindisi
With free melons in fields on the way,
Parades there were quite free and easy,
Except that they went on all day.

In transit-camp at Benevento
We stayed a long time, truth to tell,
It was there that we all got the shivers
And were all bloody lousy as well.

The sun it grew hotter and hotter,
The shit-trench was streaked red and brown,
The stew it was like maiden's water,
With gnatspiss to wash it all down.

With hunger we're nearly demented,
You can see it at once by our looks,
The only ones really contented
Are the greasy fat bastards of cooks.

And then we went on to Capua,
On hard ground we mostly did snooze,
The bedboards got fewer and fewer
As we smashed them up to make brews.

It was there that we got Red Cross parcels
With bully and packets of tea
Would you swop it for . . .
For want of some brew-wood? Not me!

And how it was late in the Autumn
And our clothes they were only a farce,
For torn K.D.[1] shorts with no bottom
Send a helluva draught up your arse.

[1]Khaki Drill

In Musso's fine box-cars we're riding,
All fitted with wheels that are square,
They park us all night in a siding,
But somehow we bloody get there.

At Musso's show-camp at Vetralla
They gave us beds, blankets and sheets,
They'd even got chains in the shit-house,
But still they had no bloody seats.

We were promised a treat for our Christmas
Of thick pasta-shoota, all hot,
But somehow the cooks got a transfer
And shot out of sight with the lot.

So somewhere they wish us good wishes
That we're not all feeling too queer,
And while they are guzzling our pasta
They wish us a happy New Year.

Letter From Italy

From large red bugs, a refugee,
I make my bed beneath the sky,
safe from the crawling enemy
though not secure from nimbler flea.
Late summer darkness comes, and now
I see again the homely Plough
and wonder: do you also see
the seven stars as well as I?
And it is good to find a tie
of seven stars from you to me.
Lying on deck, on friendly seas,
I used to watch, with no delight,
new unsuggestive stars that light
the tedious Antipodes.

Now in a hostile land I lie,
but share with you these ancient high
familiar named divinities.
Perimeters have bounded me,
sad rims of desert and of sea,
the famous one around Tobruk,
and now barbed wire, which way I look,
except above – the Pleiades.

Reg. T. Gilchrist

Sand Fly Fever

Beelzebub the God of all the flies
Has given me a hellish pain behind the eyes;
And God am I depressed?
I cannot read
I cannot feed
But I can lie and stare
With half-closed eyes upon the grey and green
Of colour wash upon these army billets
And paint from many sounds the outside scene.
Instead of pictures that the eye recalls – patterns that are form
And colour – comes the music that is Malta.
The patter of bare footsteps in the street;
The 'Donald Duck'-like sounds the goat man makes;
The shuffling movement of his herd; the bells
On goats and gharries; noise of scratchy brakes
On wooden wheels, and buckets clanking from the wells;
A snatch of song – Italian – something new
And then those sad discordant notes that grew
Old with Africa.
And over all
The murmuring of a mint of voices
Rising to a roar – each vocal chord
In conflict with its neighbour. And the screams
Of babies soundly smacked.

That is the theme of Malta music.
Raucous is the voice
Of this great but indisciplined race
Who breed like rabbits
And are much put upon by history.

Malta 1942

When all the din is done, and banshee wail
Of siren haunts the heavy air no more
Will I stand bail
For my imprisoned thoughts and let them loose
As liars – to wander back and reconstruct
The deeds of former days?
And will I bore
With tales how sunsets on far Jebels plucked
My spirit with their beauty – so that shell
And bombs and massing of dusk raiders seemed
Like something vague and distant I had dreamed
While beauty made a Heaven of that Hell?

I choose to think that if I talk at all
About those days I languished on the isle
I'll use no rant no grand heroic style
But humbly state the facts.
Island of Walls:
Oh, how I hated that first sight of you –
The brown and dusty fields devoid of grass
Cicadas, and the lizards, and the roads
Of powder, white as miller's dust, which blew
In choking clouds as sweating columns pass –
And tracks between the walls that wandered down
From squalid village into squalid town –
And all the smells, the bells, the yells that shock
The senses on that pock-marked rock.

Those first impressions – always to remain
Though seasons change and winter and the rain
Had stirred the latent powers of the dust
And filled the fields with crops that surely must
Break down the walls that hold the teeming growth.

Strange land of Peace and War – from office work
To labour gang – from club to cinemas
Gay comradeship to black depression.
I give my oath
That we were mad, the whole damned lot of us
Shut in upon ourselves with too much waiting.

Perhaps in that kaleidoscopic life,
Whose rhythm was the siren's up and down
And H.E. bombs, the commas, and the stops
And paragraphs that started with each raid,
New types of heroes lived – as different from the old
As quicksilver from gold.

In that great talking which must follow after
If someone says 'that was their finest hour'
I fear
One who served on Malta, with quiet laughter
Will add 'that was our longest year.'

Tony Goldsmith

The I.G. at War

I'm Captain Blenkinsop. I.G.[1],
Sent by mistake across the sea,
To land upon this dismal shore
And find myself involved in war.

[1]Inspector of Gunnery

Sad is the tale I have to tell –
For a man like me this war is hell.
For how can anyone expect,
My fall of shot to prove correct,
When everything I tell the guns,
Is interfered with by the Huns?
When bombs are dropping down in rows
How can I make my traverse close.
Or take a bearing on the Pole
While cowering in a muddy hole?
It's plain that the opposing forces,
Have not been on the proper courses.
But, worst of all, the other day,
When I was checking someone's lay,
The Germans rushed the gun position
Without the Commandant's permission.
I had to meet them, man to man,
Armed only with a Tetley fan.
O send me back to Salisbury Plain
And never let me rove again!
Larkhill's the only place for me,
Where I could live at ease and free
And frame, with sharpened pencil stroke
A barrage of predicted smoke.
Worked out for sixteen different breezes,
With extra graphs, in case it freezes,
For non-rigidity corrected,
And on a Merton Grid projected!
O take me to the R.A. Mess,
To dwell in red brick happiness,
Enfold my body, leather chair,
And let me fight the War from there!

Alec Grant

Randolph's Gethsemane

When Winston Churchill sent his son, Major Randolph Churchill, on a mission to Tito, the writer, one of the ground crew of his aircraft, watched him standing in the moonlight outside the Operations Room, in a strong wind, while he made the 'go – not go' decision.

A Churchill stands beneath the trees
Silent, while Adriatic breeze
Sends scudding clouds across the moon,
Decision now, and 'take-off' soon.

'My Father sends me, his Only Son,
Save Comrade Tito from the Hun.
The Red Flag to be my Calvary?
This moment, my Gethsemane?'

624 Squadron (Halifaxes)
S.D. (Special Duty) C.M.F.

Michael Hamburger

For the Dead

I

What is it that cries in the silence? not
where the dead are only, the crippled
towns, Cassino's stubble of stone where a child
waits for the train, the engine potent as hope,
bread in the trucks, the salute of handkerchiefs,
to the survivors stranded on dead soil;
not only in the trampled fields where wrecks
of tanks lie rusted, nor in the docks of Naples
clogged with bulk of ships that shall float no more –
but on oceans at night and in the valleys
richly remote, the courtyards of Venice;
louder far where the living work and piers
are patched for their pleasure and shops unshuttered –
shrill when the voices cease in clubs, the drummer
goes home and the dancers linger subdued.

II

The crosses tell us nothing of the minds
whose common negative is history,
nor what last thought kicked at the blunted nerves
of those who left no relics to record,
who lie unmarked in deserts of sand or sea.

O the cheated dead, uncounted, unseen
as the winds of the world cry out; for the words
that drove them left merging echoes behind,
the flimsy frontiers they died for are changed,
and, though the guns are draped, there is no peace.

Deòrsa Caimbeul Hay

Bisearta

Chi mi rè geàrd na h-oidhche
dreòs air chrith 'na fhroidhneas thall air fàire,
a' clapail le a sgiathaibh,
a' sgapadh 's a' ciaradh rionnagan na h-àird'ud.

Shaoileadh tu gun cluinnte,
ge cian, o 'bhuillsgein ochanaich no caoineadh,
ràn corruich no gàir fuatha,
comhart chon cuthaich uaidh no ulfhairt fhaolchon,
gun ruigeadh drannd an fhòirneirt
o'n fhùirneis òmair iomall fhéin an t-saoghail;
ach sud a' dol an leud e
ri oir an speur an tosdachd olc is aognaidh.

C' ainm nochd a th' orra,
na sràidean bochda anns an sgeith gach uinneag
a lasraichean 's a deatach,
a sradagan is sgreadail a luchd thuinidh,
is taigh air thaigh 'ga reubadh
am broinn a chéile am brùchdadh toit a' tuiteam?
Is có an nochd tha 'g atach
am Bàs a theachd gu grad 'nan cainntibh uile,
no a' spàirn measg chlach is shailthean
air bhàinidh a' gairm air cobhair, is nach cluinnear?
Cò an nochd a phàidheas
sean chìs àbhaisteach na fala cumant?

Uair dearg mar lod na h-àraich,
uair bàn mar ghile thràighte an eagail éitigh,
a' dìreadh 's uair a' teàrnadh,
a' sìneadh le sitheadh àrd 's a' call a mheudachd,
'a fannachadh car aitil
's ag at mar anail dhiabhail air dhéinead,
an t-Olc 'na chridhe 's 'na chuisle,
chì mi 'na bhuillean a' sìoladh 's a' leum e.
Tha 'n dreòs 'na oillt air fàire,
'na fhàinne ròis is òir am bun nan speuran,
a' breugnachadh 's ag àicheadh
le shoillse sèimhe àrsaidh àrd nan reultan.

George Campbell Hay

Bizerta

I see during the night guard
a blaze flickering, fringing the skyline over yonder,
beating with its wings
and scattering and dimming the stars of that airt.

You would think that there would be heard
from its midst, though far away, wailing and lamentation,
the roar of rage and the yell of hate,
the barking of the dogs from it or the howling of wolves,
that the snarl of violence would reach
from yon amber furnace the very edge of the world;
but yonder it spreads
along the rim of the sky in evil ghastly silence.

What is their name tonight,
the poor streets where every window spews
its flame and smoke,
its sparks and the screaming of its inmates,
while house upon house is rent
and collapses in a gust of smoke?
And who tonight are beseeching
Death to come quickly in all their tongues,
or are struggling among stones and beams,
crying in frenzy for help, and are not heard?
Who tonight is paying
the old accustomed tax of common blood?

Now red like a battlefield puddle,
now pale like the drained whiteness of foul fear,
climbing and sinking,
reaching and darting up and shrinking in size,
growing faint for a moment
and swelling like the breath of a devil in intensity,
I see Evil as a pulse
and a heart declining and leaping in throbs.
The blaze, a horror on the skyline,
a ring of rose and gold at the foot of the sky,
belies and denies
with its light the ancient high tranquillity of the stars.

Gwenyth Hayes

This Italy

I had not seen the earth so tender green
For two long dusty years:
Only I knew nostalgia too keen
Where sands of Egypt stretched
In utter desolation to the line
Of merging sand and sky . . . .
Until at length with bridled hopes we came
Upon this little land
So like the sea-girt shores of home it seemed
That head and heart and eyes had spanned
The continents between:
Not all a tourist's paradise man made –
Her tired cities knew
Such poverty and want and grim disease
The Nile is heir unto.
And yet there lay the land her soul had tilled
Throughout the stricken years –
The gnarled and roughened hands of peasant folk
Who understood not wars,
But from reluctant sod, with sweat and tears,
Coaxed the sour-wine grape,
And wove a patterned patchwork from the soil.

This, nature's garnering,
The iron rape of war cannot despoil.
The stalwart casas and the ramparts lie
A helpless heap of rubble,
But still the twisted olive drops its fruit
Upon the terraced hill,
And calm, deep-barrelled oxen bear the yoke
Of wooden plough and mill.

Robin Ivy

Soldiers at Capracotta. Apennines.

Snow and the snow
And the snow in the street
Nothing moved only snow
Massed in mounds over doors
Over panes frosted white
Where no eyes stared out bleak
On the snow in the street
On the silence that froze
On our lips on our breath.
Capracotta was sunk
In white death.

So we broke through the doors
Into rooms lined with books
Chopped up chairs and lit fires
Sat warm in their glow
To stare through the panes
At the face of the snow
Whose light filled the walls
Where cold chilled our bones
Where brightness warmed blood,
Dazzled eyes that had searched
Over plains through black mud.

For the snow and the snow
Froze bodies froze minds
No losses or gains
In this white silent world
Of houses where mouths were
Stopped up without eyes
Without ears and the roof
Of the skeleton
Church all blown up,
Madonna awry
With maimed arms outstretched

A starlit sky and shadows below
Huddled close round a fire
Keeping vigil for warmth.

Not a sound from the guns
Too high too remote
Lost Capracotta
In folds of the snow
You brought war to a stop;
And we lived for ourselves, by ourselves
For a time in the glow
Of the snow and the ice
Broke fingers that toppled from eaves;
Locked up and buried the ghosts
With the carpet of leaves
And the autumn rains and the stench
And filth of the plain,
The gangrened corpse and the agonised groan
Of the guns and the scream
Of pain of the shells.

Capracotta
Beauty in death
That came here by stealth
And we shared in your stillness
Your brightness your glory
That brought us a peace,
Madonna with arms released,
Till the rains came
And the vision melted
And we left you
Capracotta
To be an old story
Haloed among ragged peaks.

Sean Jennett

Mahoney

Then Mahoney, standing in the surf,
the convoy hanging in the misty sea
and landing forces moving up the beach,
dropped down his arms, and said
I wait, O God, I wait,
and these were his last words of common speech.

Christ in the shallows of the water walked
or in the sweaty hollow of his palm
appeared and spoke to his reluctant bone
or moved about the chambers of his skull,
the scourger of the temple, with a whip;
and in his heart also the lash had been.

So Mahoney stood and let his rifle fall
into the sea, where lug-worms claimed it, and
the servant tide; and heard his captain shout,
but did not move; and felt the weight of wheels
and tracks across the cortex of his brain;
but did not certainly hear the single shot.

Wife, children, parents, weep for him, who now
dead with the grey crabs and the starfish rests
where surges heap on him the slow and secret sand.
Yet even in the valleys of the sea
the dead can feel the libel, and Mahoney
in his stripped skull is tortured by a lie.

Peter Kneebone

See Naples

No motion and no future.
The only now of which one is aware
is the open tomb's delayed exposure.
Behind a crescent tourist pamphlet,
flashy sea–reflection, lies the split.
Behind the exquisite mosaic
the tenement.
Behind the orange grove
the sewer.
Behind the warm smile
the sickness.

. . . Street–corner Midas whose touch turns to dross,
his cult is the Sterling, the market his Mass.
. . . She parodies sex and her grossness blurred
in a mask, hollow–eyed, she seeks the reward.
. . . With threadbare eagerness, trembling hands
grope in the crowd for what they can find.
. . . The theme spills gratingly from barrel organs
(the present primitive – once charming pagan);
the faultless notes are faltering and jerk,
the thick-lipped tenor now a sensuous bark.
From their cracked and peeling cardboard casing
the apprehensive notes are rising
along the gutter to a final ceiling
of dust and heat and fear and wailing.

Uys Krige

Midwinter

Gone are the mountains, gone Il Gran Sasso, every peak, every
   cliff and outcrop, gaunt and black, craggy hard
swallowed by the mist;
and gone the fresh little mole mounds, no sooner heaped up than
   beaded with frost, here in the prison yard
no bigger than my fist.

Gone too the country-roads like rods of ebony that cut these
   fields of snow into strict squares of black and white,
rigid rectangles;
and gone the tiny tracks of snails that looped themselves round a
   clean cobblestone shining as beautiful and bright
as jingling bangles,
spooring the gutter's edge, crisscrossing the mess-kitchen steps,
   sparkling even in this crude half light
with the sheen of spangles.
And from the eaves the long, sharp-pointed icicle – winter's
   dagger with hilt and shaft silver-chased – stabbing the sight
no longer dangles.

We have come to the dead-end of all our days, all our nights:
   these four blank walls a drab red brown by day, pitch black by
   night. There is no turning
backward or forward from this.
This is our life, our death-in-life: this gloom, this ghostly pallor
   above each cot at noon, this cold at day's meridian, as cold as
   ice but burning, burning
even as war's embrace, the blazing battle's bitter kiss.

Through the chinks, the cracks in the wide wooden door, the
   shattered window, the mist seeps. Its wisps cluster, drift and veer
above each wooden bed.
The floor is of cement. There is no stove or fire. In two long
   rows we lie freezing under our blankets. In this grey
   whiteness lingering around us, drooping, drear,
from which all speech, all sound has fled,

no one speaks. All the old battles, desert scraps, dogfights,
   crashes on the desert's deck, swimming around in the cold,
   dark Med before the slow red dawn, all the heroism and
   gallantry, all the cowardice and the horror and the fear,
nothing, nothing has been left unsaid.

We have come to the end of all our small talk, our tether, our
   high hopes, ambitions. We have exhausted even the
   bickerings, the stupid quarrels, the sneer, the snarl. We have
   foregone all that we loved, cherished, held most dear
and all our books are read.

Prisoner of War Camp, No. 78, Italy

Ronald Lewin

Remembering Zion

Aloof as ghosts from the fireside world we cherished
And only in our daydreams revenants
We drain a brief and honeymoon delight
From the Remembered.

A tinsel trinket on a chain of brass,
A nibbled photograph, a threadbare letter
In the renewal of our milestone moments
Are Sesames sufficient.

And Memory, like some merciful reagent,
Planes from the past the bitter and the haggard,
Condensing into clear and rosy crystal
All we have treasured.

At night, at ease, even in the heart of tension,
Sudden as shells the revelation kindles:
Like liberty-men, to lost unhoped-for Edens
We take our furlough.

Observation Post, Enfidaville, 1943.

Edward Linstead

On The Troop-Deck

I yesterday met a savant
Head-down from a hammock hanging
– Headlong, slipping and helpless
Till someone, terrified, caught him.
But a savant, for when we talk
Of philosophic matters
With a calm insight he speaks
(Hurriedly briskly ticks
On his tanned wrist his nineteenth
Or twentieth birthday wrist-watch).

– Forehead wise, unlined
– Face studying the sea,
Watching beyond the rail
Our uneasy prospect
– Face fair and open
You survey our noon horizon
And all those failing waves
– These temporary truths.

Fate – prepare immediately
The upper and the nether,
Or break with a dabbing thumb
The backs of these young beings
Who speak, think, listen,
Grow too diversified
– Grind them safely back
To homogeneous dust.

Off Senegal, 1943

Lawrie Little

Sentry Duty, 7.15 a.m.

Morning grins in mud
But is too late
To mark the sleepy guard perform;
And wolfish, sulky dogs
Drowse now and ruminate
Like wrinkled logs
Which house gross, burning bees
Droning in furry hate
Before they swarm.

One fellah's eyes
Are cunning as a rabbit's,
Twitching wise:
He watches the soldiers at their making war
Who trundle in their khaki orbits,
Showing no black surprise.
They have interminable habits
And tell shifty lies
To miss the thought of their drab limits.

And under the feline velour of the skies
They sprinkle English catcalls,
Hum broken jazz,
And break the wet mud of a fellah's wall.
Grovelling round the few goods that he has,
For which he crawls.

Souk el Khemis, Christmas 1942

John Manifold

Defensive Position

Cupping her chin and lying there, the Bren
Watches us make her bed the way a queen
Might watch her slaves. The eyes of a machine,
Like those of certain women, now and then

Put an unsettling influence on men,
Making them suddenly feel how they are seen:
Full of too many purposes, hung between
Impulse and impulse like a child of ten.

The careless challenge, issued so offhanded,
Seems like to go unanswered by default –
A strong position, small but not commanded
By other heights, compels direct assault.

The gunner twitches, and unreprimanded
Eases two tensions, running home the bolt.

Ration Party

Across the mud the line drags on and on;
Tread slithers, foothold fails, all ardours vanish,
Rain falls; the barking N.C.O.s admonish
The universe more than the lagging man.

Something like an infinity of men
Plods up the slope; the file will never finish,
For all their toil serves only to replenish
Stores for tomorrow's labours to begin.

Absurd to think that Liberty, the splendid
Nude of our dreams, the intercessory saint
For us to judgment, needs to be defended

By sick fatigue-men brimming with complaint
And misery, who bear till all is ended
Every imaginable pattern of constraint.

Kevin McHale

Com-bloody-parisons

*Butman, founder of Melbourne, is quoted as saying, as he looked at the
Yarra Yarra river: 'This is the place for a village.'*

If you stand beside the Tiber
Where it splashes on the rocks
You can feel the ancient history
Come soaking through your socks
But I'm no man to give a damn
For others' rape and pillage
The bloody muddy Yarra is
The place I'd build my 'village'.

Have you seen the Colosseum
Where the plebs would get a treat
Watching hungry bloody Christians
Being given lions to eat?
But for me the Melbourne Cricket Ground
Is calling calling calling
With all those blokes from Pommieland
Their bloody wickets falling.

The plains of bloody Lombardy
We're led to understand
Are famous for their poplar trees
So tall and straight and grand
That's dinkum for the Ities
The tree for me, old chum,
A dirty great big sticky
Aussie eucalyptus gum.

There's quite a lot of beautiful
Ragazzas here in Rome
Attractive till they start to talk
Just like the birds at home
I dunno what they're saying
And I do not bloody care
I guess a sheila is a sheila
Any bloody where.

Colin McIntyre

Motor Transport Officer

Pyatt had something to do with horses.
No, that's not what I mean,
   wipe that smirk off your face.
I mean that in Civvy Street he had
   something to do with horses.
Not as a Trainer, you know, but in
   the buying and selling line.
A horse-chandler, or something.

We didn't have any horses in The Regiment,
   though we had some mules with us in Greece.
So we made him our Motor Transport Officer,
   as he was a Captain, and none of the other
   companies wanted him, not being a Gent.

He made a damn good transport officer, actually.
'Not afraid to get his head under the bonnet,'
   the Colonel always said.
And he could nurse a three-tonner back on the road,
   like a horse with an injured fetlock.

He didn't like the fighting much, and when shells
   fell, managed to be back with 'B' Echelon;
   and he drank too much.

But I wouldn't have wished his end, on man or beast.
Slewed a 15-hundredweight across the road, into a wall
　　when he came upon a sudden roadblock.
Trapped in the cab, when the bastard truck caught fire.

Well, they shoot horses, don't they?

Spike Milligan

The Soldiers At Lauro

Young are our dead
Like babies they lie
The wombs they blest once
Not healed dry
And yet – too soon
Into each space
A cold earth falls
On colder face.
Quite still they lie
These fresh-cut reeds
Clutched in earth
Like winter seeds
But they will not bloom
When called by spring
To burst with leaf
And blossoming
They sleep on
In silent dust
As crosses rot
And helmets rust.

Italy, January 1943.

N.T. Morris

Sicilian Town: August 1943

What was your crime, you little mountain town?
Why is that mother picking through those stones?
The entrails of the church stare to the sky;
The Military Police say: 'Out of Bounds,'

'No halting on the Road': the people stare
Blank-eyed and vacant, hollow-eyed and numb.
You do not seem to hate us: we are they
Who blew your town to dust with shell and bomb.

'Water not drinkable': 'One Way Street';
The road machine runts rubble from the track.
Was this a house, home of two lovers' joys,
Reduced by chemists' blast to pristine rock?

The moody mountain frowns, aloof, detached.
What was your crime, you little mountain town?
Just that you lay upon the Armies' route;
Two tracks met here by whim in ancient time.

A.F. Noble

When The Heat Is On

When the molten lead of the sun o'er head
gives aid to the scorching cordite fumes
and the heat from the spout
as the bullets flash out
withers the oleander blooms.

When the barrel's red–hot your adrenalin shot
and mortars mangle the olive trees
and your mind's in a maze
with the heat and the haze
and expelled empties burn your knees.

When the sweat of your mate (as you wait your fate)
runs off his chin and his nose
and oils the piece of rag
for 'Stoppage, new mag'
which you shout as the frenzy grows

and the clickety–clack of the piston draw back
stops. And his life stops too
and the buzz in your head
says the gun has gone dead
and you know that it's up to you. . .

That's when sweating stops. Your temperature drops
and as the hour–glass drains off sand
it isn't your brain
or your courage, or pain
that helps you to make a stand

But a dead hand seen on a filled magazine
(you've never yet done without it)
and as his soul flies out
with the rounds, up the spout
He'll be in at the kill do not doubt it.

Crete, May 28th 1941.

Harold V.S. Page

Epitaph

A fallen hero of our race
Lies buried here, and none beside
His parents, also commonplace,
Remembers clearly how he died.

Resplendent in a purple suit
He took his place when life was sweet,
And learnt his noblest attribute,
The art of spitting in the street.

The army took him clad and trained,
Produced a soldier from the dross,
Sent him to battle, then ordained,
His one award, a wooden cross.

Comfort ye, mourners at a humble grave,
Who weeps for Hector now? The great
Share their conclusion with the slave,
And just as soon disintegrate.

Sicily, 1943

M. Rawlinson

Mediterranean Song

There's some who say the Medi-
Terranean air is heady;
While others, who have stayed there
Are very much afraid there's
A lot more to be said
About the highly vaunted Med.

For instance there's malaria
In the Mare Nostrum area;
And pox in many a guise
Small and cow and otherwise
Can easily be caught
Doing things you didn't ought.

Then there's flies and fleas and
Lice and crabs, that tease and
Make themselves a pest
Always hanging around the test-
Icles; playing hide and seek
In the ballroom, so to speak.

And many more afflictions
That cause a lot of restrictions;
The brothers 'dyer' and 'gonner'
Are active winter and summer.
And dysentery's a damned in-
Convenience notwithstanding.

So I think that you'll agree,
That those who say the sea
Is nearly always blue,
(Which is nearly always true)
Are deliberately misleading
The folks who judge by reading
That the Med for sure and certain
Is the place to do some flirting.
But you and I know better,
And you can bet an old French letter-
Box, that when this war is over
I'll count myself in clover
As long as I've a bed,
And am nowhere near the Med.

Henry Reed

The Place and the Person

The place not worth describing, but like every empty place.
So much like other empty places, you yourself
Must paint its picture, who have your own such places,
Which lie, their whitening eyes turned upwards to the sky,
On the remoter side of a continent.
Under a burning sun. Their streets and hovels
Have lost all memory, and their harbours rot.
Paint it, and vary it as you like, but only
Always paint this: the solitary figure,
Who lies or squats or sits, facing the sun,
Now in bewilderment or a vacant calm,
In filthy rags, the ancient garb of exiles,
The casual mixture of others' memories,
Legacy or theft; and the mind perplexed and eroded.
In such a one, at the edge of his world, desire
Is buried or burned in lust, and love is banished
Beyond the creeping jungle; in the noontime heat,
Since even these can be lost, they are far away.
You will know all this, and can paint it as suits you best,
But paint alone the central figure faithfully;
His surroundings do not matter: they are yours or mine,
The walls perhaps with greying notices
Of the bygone sales of heifers, or the concourse
Of a troupe of vanished singers, singing there,
The carrion birds shuffling upon the roof,
The empty expanse of ocean confronting him,
The harbour steps, the empty sands below,
And the movement of water on the harbour bar.
And from the emptiness, still mute but moving,
Emerge the dancers who will not be still.
Nearest at hand two scuffling figures, who
Saunter a little and scuffle again and dance,
Or lie on the paving-stones and yawn at each other,
A daily ritual; if not with them, with others.
This is a dance, with ritual and celebration.

Others join in its windings as the day
Passes through noon and afternoon and evening
And wave on wave of heat and sunlight fall,
Illuminating and transfixing, and at last
The dreadful pattern of their lives disclosing.
From out of rocks and paths they come, the dancers:
One who walks solitary and shuns the gaze
Of the scuffling pair, now languid in the heat,
Until, withdrawn, he looks about and secretly
Seizing a dead shark's jawbone out of air,
Makes it a trap with stones and vegetation
For yet another who walks on the level beaches.
They congregate, beseeching or resentful,
Till the empty place is crowded with silent ghosts,
They are intangible, but he is one with them,
As with their proud, vindictive admonitions,
And sensual taunts, and gestures of possession,
They separate, part, return, link arms again,
Familiarly, yet not with reconcilement.
And, one with them, he cannot turn away,
Or forget in the motions of song and prayer and dance
The great dried fountains of their sombre eyes.

Fed on such visions, how shall a man recover
Between the dancing dream and the dream of departure?
For the dancers go, and their silent song and prayer
Go with them; and the ship goes from the harbour,
Vanishes in sea, or drowns in air, but goes.
The waves of noon can barely reach the shore,
And the jungle approaches always a little nearer.
This is the captive. And paint him as you will.
These are my images. The place not worth describing.

R.M. Roberts

Italian Road

Down the road they came,
The women of Italy.
The children, and the old,
Old men of memories.
Stumbling with their torn feet
On this broken road;
And we watched in silence
From the high turrets
Of our brutal armour.
Slowly they passed
Weary with children,
And the faltering footsteps of age.
Burdened with shock
And their pitiful bundles.
Treasured salvaged hopes
Of the home-makers.
These women of Italy
Powdered with dust,
Heavy with fear and fatigue
Trail past.
Only their eyes raised briefly
To the sun – and us,
From out of the sweat, mud and pain
Speak mutely, of the beauty,
The gentleness that must have been.
In them is no hate
Yet must we avert our gaze
Lest our pride be dry in our mouths
And the sweetness of our dreams
Be bloodied by their wounded feet.
And as they pass in the bitter dust
Of trucks and noise of distant guns
Our column moves
As the advance grinds on.

We leave them
These weary women of Italy
Lost in the harsh world of men
And our hearts grow a little tired
A little old.

N. Robinson

P.O.W. Camp, Italy

We stare across the wire
at the close of empty days
to where the wheatlands glisten
and the haughty cattle gaze;

To where the ploughman turns
his horse at the broken wall –
but the visions that meet our eyes
mean nothing to us at all.

For we live in a shadowland
like the audience at a show
while the play upon the stage
is the world we used to know.

Vernon Scannell

Eidolon Parade

A grey wind prowls across the lake of stone,
The flag flicks like a summer horse's tail,
The brass voice of the bugle climbs and clings
High before it crumbles, falls and fades.
C.S.M. Hardy, back from Salerno Beach,

Glitters with sea salt, winkles nest in his eyes,
But his voice grinds loud as ever as he calls
The Nominal Roll: Corporal Mick McGuire
Has returned from Alamein, each orifice
Is clogged with sand; but tonight he will appear
Once more at the Church Hall, battle-dress pressed
And patent leather highlights on his feet;
And when the lights are dimmed, the last waltz makes
Its passionate interrogation: *Who's*
Taking You Home Tonight? who but McGuire,
Although his terrible kiss will taste of sand
Gritting on shocked teeth, and his cold cheek
Will seem to her a stony reprimand.
And while the Corporal tangoes, Private Bain,
A bunch of quarrels hanging from each wrist,
Will sluice his guts with twenty black-and-tans;
But he stands still now, sober, at attention
With that small company paraded there
Waiting for inspection: Dodger Rae,
Equipment scruffy and an idle bootlace,
Is put on an eternal two-five-two;
Spike Liston, gaunt as a Belsen boy or saint
Still rages for more grub; Bull Evans broods
On all the thighs he'll never lie between
Or lie about, his pack and pouches stuffed
With fantasies and condoms; Les King, who crooned
Like Bing, is back from Mareth where he lay,
The tunes mislaid, gargling with his blood.
His songs are out of date. And there are others
Whose faces, though familiar, fade and blur.
The bugle publishes another cry.
Two more commands explode; butts and boots
Crash and ring; another echoing shout
And, by the left, they start to march away.
The steady tramping dims into a mist.
The stone ground stretches in its vacancy;
One final flick of flag, the mist comes down,
And silence stuns with its enormous weight,
And there is nothing left to do but sleep.

Walking Wounded

A mammoth morning moved grey flanks and groaned.
In the rusty hedges pale rags of mist hung;
The gruel of mud and leaves in the mauled lane
Smelled sweet, like blood. Birds had died or flown,
Their green and silent attics sprouting now
With branches of leafed steel, hiding round eyes
And ripe grenades ready to drop and burst.
In the ditch at the cross-roads the fallen rider lay
Hugging his dead machine and did not stir
At crunch of mortar, tantrum of a Bren
Answering a Spandau's manic jabber.
Then into sight the ambulance came,
Stumbling and churning past the broken farm,
The amputated sign-post and smashed trees,
Slow wagonloads of bandaged cries, square trucks
That rolled on ominous wheels, vehicles
Made mythopoeic by their mortal freight
And crimson crosses on the dirty white.
This grave procession passed, though, for a while,
The grinding of their engines could be heard,
A dark noise on the pallor of the morning,
Dark as dried blood; and then it faded, died.
The road was empty, but it seemed to wait –
Like a stage which knows the cast is in the wings –
Wait for a different traffic to appear.
The mist still hung in snags from dripping thorns;
Absent-minded guns still sighed and thumped.
And then they came, the walking wounded,
Straggling the road like convicts loosely chained,
Dragging at ankles exhaustion and despair.
Their heads were weighted down by last night's lead,
And eyes still drank the dark. They trailed the night
Along the morning road. Some limped on sticks;
Others wore rough dressings, splints and slings;
A few had turbanned heads, the dirty cloth
Brown-badged with blood. A humble brotherhood,
Not one was suffering from a lethal hurt,
They were not magnified by noble wounds,

There was no splendour in that company.
And yet, remembering after eighteen years,
In the heart's throat a sour sadness stirs;
Imagination pauses and returns
To see them walking still, but multiplied
In thousands now. And when heroic corpses
Turn slowly in their decorated sleep
And every ambulance has disappeared
The walking wounded still trudge down that lane,
And when recalled they must bear arms again.

Bernard Spencer

Salonika June 1940

My end of Europe is at war. For this
My lamp-launched giant shadow seems to fall
Like a bad thought upon this ground at peace,
Being a shadow of the shadow of a war.
What difference if I wish good luck to these foreigners, my hosts?
   Talking with my friends stand ghosts.

Specially the lives that here in the crook of this bay
At the paws of its lionish hills are lived as I know;
The dancing, the bathing, the order of the market, and as day
Cools into night, boys playing in the square;
Island boats and lemon-peel tang and the timeless café crowd,
And the outcry of dice on wood:

I would shut the whole if I could out of harm's way
As one shuts a holiday photo away in a desk,
Or shuts one's eyes. But not by this brilliant bay,
Nor in Hampstead now where leaves are green,
Any more exists a word or a lock which gunfire may not break,
Or a love whose range it may not take.

Douglas Street

Cassino Revisted

This place did catch a vast pox from off the Moon;
Crater and wrinkle all are here,
And we are travellers from another Time;
This place still keeps its own infected counsel;
The most thin atmospheres of loneliness and fear
Still make a heavy labour for the heart;
Yet tribes, I know, lived here, those loved and clumsy tribes
That men call regiments; one tribe would start
The day with telling of its beads; the men of one
Would talk of killings with the knives, and rum;
Yet others talked of the clean unchronicled Antipodes,
Of pasture and a blue haze of trees;
Some had left their private silken skies behind,
Folded neatly with the storemen, out of mind;
And all read letters smelling of the mules,
And talked of two myth-planets, Rome and Home;
For battle cries they used shy word – 'Perhaps' or 'Fairly soon'.

John Strick

Vineyard Reverie

A lemon-coloured house, lying
    Cross-wise upon the rising slopes;
Vine-green, wine-red, always
    A column of sweet smoke
Rising, rising, and the broad
    Blue water of the Southern sea.

Who came here, and why, and when?
   Whose voice calling in the vineyard?
Where are those who lived here?
   What memory have they carried
Into the dim land whence
   They are departed?

The Germans were here, grey-faced,
   Grim-helmeted, their guns
Remain behind the balustrade, round
   The corner of the road.
A thick, black-barrelled tube
   Lurks in the alley-way.

The beach is attractive, opalescent water,
   And the cold, clear virility
Of the mountain stream,
   Piles of 'S' mines, plates
And tapes – the strange silence
   Of deserted fortifications – unused.

Blood has sunk into soil,
   This year the new wine
Stamped under boot, is richer.
   Children gaze with saucer eyes,
'Sicilia bara' – jump and run
   Playing dive-bombers in the glittering sun.

Yes now, look now!
   There is a house standing.
Yes, this was Messina,
   Stone on stone –
They say it was
A large and prosperous city.

Sicily, 1943

John Warry

Athens – January 1945 (Extract)

The columns of the Parthenon infringe
Cloudy horizons, interrupt grey skies,
Not hewn of old from marble it would seem
But wrought of incandescent fantasies
In northern gloom, unhappy schoolboy's dream.
The columns of the Parthenon recall
A faded map suspended on a wall
Of pink and white distemper, peeled in places,
Near crucial dates and algebraic scrawl,
Rebellious hair and shoes with wandering laces.
The columns of the Parthenon are seen
At 7 a.m. by artificial light
With last night's learning mumbled from between
Diffident lips, strangely illuminate
The shreds of marmalade on thumb-marked pages
With lunar brilliance. Boys of different ages
Pose in the pediment or file beneath
When the bell calls them from a tumbled bed
By way of bath-rooms, cocoa and currant-bread
To blinkered panes made steamy by their breath.

Gold-tinted columns on a rock survey
The trams that go to Ambelókepi
(I spell the name as spoken). You may see
In those dim taverns just across the way
Barrels. You pay – at least you used to pay –
Some thirty drachmas for a hundred drachms.
And so you sit and listen to the trams.
So Pete and Bill and Bert and I sat there.
I don't think any of us were aware
Of grave gold-tinted columns on a rock. . .
In memory's bleak portico I find
A few last snowflakes shaken from the wind,
A meagre chicken pecking on the floor,
And crooked alleys paved with cobble-stones

Perceptible through the declining door.
What a strange smell! They're digging up the bones
And other rank appurtenance of those
Who dreamed that brave new worlds might rise from war
And have not yet had time to decompose,
For here we bury folk just where they lie,
Scratch names in pencil, guessing who they were,
Till time's found to exhume, identify,
And with due ceremony re-inter.

. . . .

    Through cobwebs to a disenchanted eye
Next morning drags Ilissus the dry ditch
Beyond a rusty apron of barbed wire
And scattered rounds of ammunition which
Bored sentries of a ragged army fling
At rats or cats or any moving thing
That scavenges that mouth of broken teeth.
Ilissus? No. It was not truth I heard –
That Socrates in literary mood
Came here to fable love. For that occurred
At tea-time once, when leafless trees revealed
The frosty surface of a football field.

Victor West

Drumhead

Four trestle tables in the sand
covered with issue blankets taken
from the tented hospital . . . The forms
pushed back, as though in hasty decision,
standing a solitary still-life
group in early morning sun.

The scene rises before me
and I people it in my mind.

Here, the President of the Court Martial
with the powder-puff pink
visage of his rank in contrast
to the dusty sunburn of the mountain
troop and the young parachutist Major.
On the other side, standing in casual
conversation, three officers like
three scabrous Graces.
But no grace here;
only short shrift to the accused
whose only crime that they are Greek.
A last, eloquent plea, translated
badly by the *dolmetscher;*
the Cretan in the white shirt
throws an arm around the youth
and flings a last, imploring gesture
for the old man, standing knees half-bent
by age in his black vraka.
But no pity here
for the 'Defending Officer'
has put his papers away and shrugs
off his defence with apologetic brevity.
Impassive, grey like sea-bleached
breakwater timbers – and with as much feeling,
the stolid guards stand close by,
starred with the pressed-tin edelweiss
like dead starfish. Down on the beach
wait the idle firing squad
ready for the verdict:
'Three more Greek bandits shot
for committing unspeakable atrocities'. . :

The scene has unfolded itself
and the figures vanish before my eyes. . .
only the horror remains
and that I cannot paint:
Four trestle tables in the sand.

29th May, 1941 'The Galatos Cage',
formerly 7th British Tented Hospital, Calibes, Crete.

Alan White

Monastery Hill (Cassino)

Away from the temptation of the town,
in disapproval of the valley's vice,
the monastery crowns the hill,
austere and celibate,
its isolation only pierced
by a deterrent, winding road.
Now its tranquil vespers are supplanted
by the wailing agony of *nebelwerfers*[1],
and its inmates are the paratrooper
and the panzergrenadier,
who finger bandoliers of ball and tracer,
the rosaries of their fanaticism.

Even in mountain mist, night gloom
or fog of smoke-shells
still the monastery persists,
an outline lit occasionally by flares.
Below there sprawls Cassino,
hiding its rubble carcase
underneath a winding sheet of smoke,
and in among the ruined maze
the infantry play hide-and-seek.

Hidden in the olive-grove
and on the forward slope of our own sector,
we observe. . .
and are observed ourselves.
In our student minds we strive to find
a means to break this deadlock
in a difficult campaign,
to burst the lock-gates
that will lead to Rome.

[1]Smoke-shell mortar

We wonder too if monks will ever
resurrect the spirit of the monastery,
or if it will be forbidden them,
forever branded as an evil monument,
a bastion, fêted by historians,
and once a valuable accomplice
in the art of war.

Overseas

Here is the airgraph's destination,
nucleus of the guardian thoughts
from those at home who think of us.
This is the country which we might so easily
have visited as tourists,
but with a camera rather than a pistol,
rubbing on the thigh.
Here is where we must forget
the numb bewilderment of separation,
and begin to learn
appreciation of new things,
such as the elegant ellipse
of Spitfire wings,
tilting and glinting in the sun.
Here the ties of tenderness
are stronger and delve back
into a precious past.
Here upon the battlefield,
the pawn on war's gigantic chessboard
can become a queen.
But with each coming night
a simpler thought prevails,
when soldiers make their bivouacs
into a fragile, private shell
tuned in across the waves
to England and their vivid home.

German P.O.W. Camp

Here where the flies are thickest,
and the jagged strands of wire
enclose with coil and palisade
is a zoo grotesque,
where trained, potential killers
are without their fangs
and pace the cage in twos and threes,
dragging boredom with each step.
On the ground, baked hard as teak,
the motley bivouacs are strewn,
ground-sheet, silken parachute,
torn canvas, dusty blanket,
anything that serves
as parasol and parapluie.
Observe the prisoners,
blond arrogance of hair,
the athlete in their stance,
and hear their marching songs,
drum-like in cadence
and as mellow maudlin
as the feel of wine,
making an outlaw flag
wave in the heart,
hysteria its nationality.
These traits in time of war,
when all virility is at high price,
almost compel an urge to fraternise.
But then an inner voice recalls –
Dachau, the death, despair and darkness,
Rotterdam, rased flat by bombs,
Paris, festering with pompous uniforms
and the malignant swastika,
and England's scars.
In a trice I have become
the gaoler once again,
confident with hate
and quick to penalise.

                                        Tunisia.

Lyall Wilkes

Troopship: 1942

You remember, coming over,
the stained oak lounge of the troopship,
with its many elaborate pillars
evoking strength
to reassure the timid –
(all hollow) –
and how on the small round tables
they put down their books –
Thorne Smith, and Horler, and Peter Cheyney –
to gossip and to drink,
drowning unease. . . .

And how for hours they played cards and joked in the saloon,
and went up for air and ragged on deck,
and as the days went by and the sun grew warm
parties were planned and talk grew animated
so strolling round the deck at night
you tripped on Li-Los and heard giggles from the poop,
for though everyone was a leader of some sort
everyone was also human.

When the topees and the khaki drill appeared,
after the first self-consciousness,
in the growing grim clipped speech,
you sensed the straining
which
behind the mask
so nearly wore them down.
Now
even the drinks
changed their names,
and it was about this time,
nearing Sierra Leone,
A.T.S. officers
began badgering
the steward
when they would see
the first
nigger.

Anonymous

The D-Day Dodgers

We are the D–Day Dodgers out in Italy,
Always drinking Vino, always on the spree.
8th Army skyvers and the Yanks,
6th Armoured Div and all their tanks.
For we are the D–Day Dodgers, the lads that D–Day dodged.

We landed at Salerno, a holiday with pay,
Jerry brought the band down to cheer us on our way.
We all sung the songs and the beer was free.
We kissed all the girls in Napoli.
For we are the D–Day Dodgers.

The Volturno and Cassino were taken in our stride
We didn't have to fight there. We just went for the ride.
Anzio and Sangro were all forlorn.
We did not do a thing from dusk to dawn.
For we are the D–Day Dodgers.

On our way to Florence we had a lovely time.
We ran a bus to Rimini through the Gothic line.
All the winter sports amid the snow.
Then we went bathing in the Po.
For we are the D–Day Dodgers.

Once we had a blue light that we were going home
Back to dear old Blighty never more to roam.
Then somebody said in France you'll fight.
We said never mind we'll just sit tight,
The windy D–Day Dodgers in sunny Italy.

Now Lady Astor get a load of this.
Don't stand on a platform and talk a load of piss.
You're the nation's sweetheart, the nation's pride
But your lovely mouth is far too wide
For we are the D–Day Dodgers in sunny Italy.

If you look around the mountains, through the mud and rain
You'll find battered crosses, some which bear no name.
Heart break, toil and suffering gone
The boys beneath just slumber on
For they were the D-Day Dodgers.

So listen all you people, over land and foam
Even though we've parted, our hearts are close to home.
When we return we hope you'll say
'You did your little bit, though far away
All of the D-Day Dodgers out in Italy.'

The last verse to be sung with vino on your lips and tears in your eyes.

'When they call us D-Day Dodgers – which D-Day do they mean,
old man?'

Anonymous

Ballad of Anzio

When the M.G.s stop their chatter
And the cannons stop their roar
And you're back in dear old Blighty
In your favourite pub once more;
When the small talk is all over
And the war tales start to flow,
You can stop the lot by telling
Of the fight at Anzio.

Let them bum about the desert,
Let them talk about Dunkirk,
Let them brag about the jungles
Where the Japanese did lurk.
Let them boast about their campaign
And their medals till they're red:
You can put the lot to silence
When you mention – the beachhead.

You can tell of Anzio Archie
And the Factory, where the Huns
Used to ask us out to breakfast
As they rubbed against our guns.
You can talk of night patrolling
They know nothing of at home
And can tell them that you learned it
On the beachhead – south of Rome.
You can tell them how the Heinies
Tried to break us with attacks,
Using tanks, bombs and flamethrowers
And how we flung them back.
You can tell them how we took it
And dished it out as well.
How we thought it was a picnic
And Tedeschi thought it hell.

And when the tale is finished
And going time is near
Just fill your pipes again, lads,
And finish up your beer.
Then order up another pint
And drink before you go
To the boys that fought beside you
On the beach at Anzio.

Anonymous

The Highland Division's Farewell To Sicily

I

The pipie is dozie, the pipie is fey,
He wullnae come roon for his vino the day.
The sky ower Messina is unco an' grey
And a' the bricht chaulmers are eerie.

Then fare weel ye banks o' Sicily
Fare ye weel ye valley an' shaw.
There's nae Jock will mourn the kyles o' ye
Puir bliddy bastards are weary.

And fare weel ye banks o' Sicily
Fare ye weel ye valley an' shaw.
There's nae hame can smoor the wiles o' ye
Puir bliddy bastards are weary.

Then doon the stair and line the waterside
Wait your turn, the ferry's awa.
Then doon the stair and line the waterside
A' the bricht chaulmers are eerie.

The drummie is polisht, the drummie is braw
He cannae be seen for his webbin ava.
He's beezed himsel up for a photo an' a'
Tae leave wi his Lola, his dearie.

Then fare weel ye dives o' Sicily
(Fare ye weel ye shieling an' ha')
And fare weel ye byres and bothies
whaur kind signorinas were cheerie.

And fare weel ye dives o' Sicily
(Fare ye weel ye shieling an' ha')
We'll a' mind shebeens and bothies
Whaur Jock made a date wi' his dearie.

Then tune the pipes and drub the tenor drum
(Leave your kit this side o' the wa')
Then tune the pipes and drub the tenor drum –
A' the bricht chaulmers are eerie.

(Tune: 'Farewell to the Creeks,' a Gordon Pipe March.)

Air

John Bayliss

Reported Missing

With broken wing they limped across the sky
caught in late sunlight, with their gunner dead,
one engine gone, – the type was out-of-date, –
blood on the fuselage turning brown from red:

knew it was finished, looking at the sea
which shone back patterns in kaleidoscope
knew that their shadow would meet them by the way,
close and catch at them, drown their single hope:

sat in this tattered scarecrow of the sky
hearing it cough, the great plane catching
now the first dark clouds upon her wing-base, –
patching the great tear in evening mockery.

So two men waited, saw the third dead face,
and wondered when the wind would let them die.

O.C. Chave

There are no Frontiers in the Sky

There are no frontiers in the sky,
The clouds exact
No custom dues; the long, bright lanes of sun
Ask not the parentage of those who fly.

What care the winds the colour of a face
Or does the night
Play jealous with her stars unless she knows
The status of an airman's dwelling-place?

This infinite upon whose little rim
Man dares to crawl
Assesses not his politics or creed
But with indifference slays or succours him.

David Stafford Clark

Casualty

'Easy boys; leave it to the doc . . .'
'Afraid he's pretty bad, doc; we've not heard
A word from him since just before we bombed . . .'
Hands under his arms and knees
Lift him down gently; unplug his intercomm.
And disconnect his oxygen.
Now guide his shoulders and dislodge his feet
From the wrecked turret;
So lay him down, and look at him.

'Much you can do?'
     'No – I'm afraid he's dead,
Has been for hours – ' 'Oh. Well, I'm sorry – '
                  'Yes,
Probably never knew what hit him.'
But in the torchlight you can see
His face is frozen:
Cannon shells pumped into his side
From neck to knee. Skin white like rigid lard,
Eyes glazed, with frosted lashes,
Flying suit crusted with red chalk
That was his blood . . .
          Such is the cold
In a smashed turret open to the wind
Torn at that height and speed through icy darkness.

Yesterday
I heard someone complain
'Last night the bombers in procession
Kept me awake . . .'

March 1944

Molly Corbally

. . . *Ad Astra*

I took my leave of the earth and men,
And soared aloft to the lonely sky,
Thro' the gathering dark, to the silent stars,
And the whisper of Angels passing by.

I heard the beat of the Angels' wings,
In the silent watch of the starlit night.
I felt His touch, and I heard His Voice.
I, Man, communed with the Infinite.

Far below lies a burnt-out wreck,
Soft, the strains of the bugles sound.
The Ensign flutters a last salute
As another pilot is laid to ground.

Men are sighing, and women weep.
Ah! foolish friends, do not grieve for me,
For I heard God call in the silent night,
And flew on, into Eternity.

Herbert Corby

Officers' Wives

Vicious as missionaries, assured of right,
they bring their glim of culture to the night
of backward England: generous as gods
they benefit by example these poor clods
who live their lives in only rural ways:
– they bring to them the vacuum of their days.
See one, the loud-mouthed wearer of a fur,
purse her dyed lips and call the town to her,
deign to stride the cobbled market-place
with bold predatory eye, with ravished face;
haughty in style, she many times had been
flattered by likeness to the brazen queen,
and would not, if inducement too held awe,
be slow to overlook the marriage law.
Child-like, she must be noticed, laugh or cry
she craves the attention of the public eye,
and when she dines, will raise her voice just loud
enough to reach the suburbs of the crowd,
including in her converse intimate
false confidences of the truly great.
Larger than sense, her wit will make her ring
with self-esteem: she jokes of queen and king,
and though none other smiles, her grimaces
dazzle the quiet room's patient emptiness.
Incongruous in the fields, she strides among
the unimpressed droll cows, scorn on her tongue
should any dare to talk without her nod.
She would be kind, if she were only God!
Her public voice, a red crusader, stalks
all men: she tries conversion as she talks,
demanding – for her vision of the right –
homage and honour – these her great delight.
Sneering in windows of the normal shops
at the grey merchandise, she always stops

to view her long legs in the flattered glass,
and yawn aloud and wish the day would pass
into the equal emptiness of dark.
She strides like doom the inoffensive park
abhors the gnats' exaggerated haste,
and cries the ornamental gardens not her taste.
She has no taste. The war that made her man
pompous, saluted, promoted her in vain,
and though she shouts and laughs for all to hear,
she'd be more natural drawing up the beer.

Or see this other, expecting humble thanks,
condescend to notice other ranks,
compute their payment with a stately leer,
aided by her officer, a cashier,
who has his hour fortnightly, when he pays
the notes out with a self-deceiving ease.
All are the same to her, alike as apes,
though some are slightly dirtier, and wear tapes,
who honour the uniform she walks beside
with perfunctory salute: or turn aside.

Or this one, who, though her evenings are
drudged in service at the canteen bar,
merely permits this charity, lest she
works usefully in shop or factory:
vinegar-voiced, her moment of sublime
achievement is attained at closing-time.
– she lifts the cups like Florence Nightingale,
and hands them to the sergeant's wife to swill,
and leaves her working, puts on airs, and greets
the manager with a hope of extra sweets!

This is their effort in the total war,
to brag and think of self, and how they are
bothered by the frippery on a hat.
They are a race apart. Thank God for that!

No Trace

The scar has healed where late last summer died
the glittering Hampden,and tore the building down.
Only the garden did not suffer: wide
now are all the healing blossoms of the town,
and where she crashed and burned, and where they fell
tenacious grasses move in ebb and flow,
and none would look, for nothing there will tell
how men were killed down there a year ago.

E. Denyer Cox

Elegy

Clouds stippled against the blue band of sky;
    under the consciousness the drum-roll of guns.
Through the still night to feel the crush
    of presses beating shape from the white-hot metal;
To clasp the incandescent ore close to the body,
The limbs and heart forming part of the ingot,
To be tortured to cylinder-shape, to contain
    within one the toppling of a church,
    the ceasing to be of how many men,
Essence of hammer-blows, the bright blood
    leaping in the body, the tears and agony
    of men.
        He was my brother. I will kill
        the brothers of him who killed my brother.
The moon in the star-laden sky
    becomes the thin smile, as the hand moves
    the bomb-release, and others, compacted
    of bone and blood the same even, die below.
    The energy loosed shreds the flesh, and leaves
    the soul to fly bat-like in a night as black.

When quiet returns, a few gather beyond the town;
   a clock booms (why yet spared?)
   and crashes to the bubbling flames
   covering the shame of men.

P. Heath

We, The Bombers

We have no graceful form, no flashing shape
To flicker, fish-like, in the dome of the sky;
No famous whine of motor, glint of light
Proclaims us to the earthling's ear or eye.
Darkly we go, unseen, by friends unsped,
Leaving the homely fields that are our own,
Up to the heights where sunset's early red
Changes to blackness. We are there alone.

No heat of battle warms our chilling blood;
No friendly soil beneath us if we fall;
Our only light the stars, whose fickle mood
Will lead them to desert us when we call.
Death down below or stealing through the dark
Awaits our coming with a silent grin.
Bellona's fireworks, curtained round our mark,
Form doors of fire through which we enter in.

Flame, smoke and noise surround us for a while;
A shuddered jerk – the load goes screaming down;
Cold hands and feet move levers for escape;
A chain of fire bespatters through the town.
Back to the darkness, friendly now, we speed
To count our wounds and set a course for home,
Speaking to Base, attentive to our need,
Watching for that far friendly line of foam.

Hour upon hour the long-drawn journey runs;
Fighters and searchlights still our road proclaim.
Salt-eyed, we watch the heavens for the Huns,
Weary, we dodge the heaven-splitting flame.
Then, with no certain vict'ry to impart,
Out of the dawn we drop from frosty height,
Welcomed alone by those who saw us start
And watched and waited for us through the night.

January, 1942.

Written after being snubbed by a WAAF in a Fighter Mess,
who enjoyed the glamour.

Thomas Rahilley Hodgson

Searchlights over Berlin

Their silver scalpels probe the wound of night
seeking our doom, a death
to death. And now
no highflung phrase, no braggart
gesture of the hand or jaw
can still the double fear. Who fly
ten thousand feet above in the shrill dark
are linked with those who cower
under earth to hear, vague as sea
upon an inland wind, the murmur
which is, for some
eternity, for some
an ending.
And he is rising mad who searches here
for meaning.

Stuart Hoskins

Polish Airman

*(Tribute to survivor of Battle of Britain, who later crashed over
Manston, Kent, June 1944.)*

No kin had he,
Unknown from the next bed to me.
A language bar
Did little for esprit-de-Corps.

I only know
Our Squadron W.O.
Bore best blue, kit away,
Borrowed the chaplain from 253,
Marshalled with Highland thoroughness
Grumbling mourners from the Sergeants' Mess.
'Fall in, the strangers!'

Over that grave
A sloppy squad
Ragged salvo gave.
Two fields away
A mild old horse.
Peewits quavered, altered course
As echoes, rolling, died.
There was small human gesture made.
Back in the cosy Mess
We drank his death.

Redmond Macdonogh

Heil Hamburg, Forty One

Height is just ten thousand feet. The night
Lit dimly by stars, is solemn, quiet, still.
My sergeant in the nose, his target map a sorry, crumpled mess,
His bombsight checked, his figures proved and double proved,
I sniff. The smell of fear is in this craft, it clings.
We wait the tracking guns below to find us.

Now into the glare – ahead the searchlights probe, then group,
And in their mingling hold a victim, their moth,
The guns are on him now: we watch the killing
In that bright slaughterhouse where we shall be
Two minutes hence. I check the time and wait.
And there he goes! He burns, he falls, he spins,
And still he drops, and still we look and pray for 'chutes –
But none, he's gone. There will be no prisoners to feed.
God rest them all. And now . . . it's us in the crucible:
We start survival drill. I turn full five to starboard,
Two hundred up, then port for ten. Down again, five more,
No constant course to aid the murd'rous guns below,
No rest, no peace, no hiding place, naught our human skill our
   aid.
And then the last of it – and us? – the straight run in on target.
The hoarse non–actor's voice from nose and lung and heart –
'Bombs gone'. Lightened, the aircraft leaps, I turn then,
Diving to port, a vertical steep turn. We enter cloud, glad
   shelter,
A thundrous crack, blue flames along the wing-edge, we drop,
   rise.
The static deafens: my cockney aimer drives away my terror
'Cumulus, skipper, currents vertical, course two seventy for
   home'
Home . . . happy word, land we left three hours since.

While in Hamburg they rake the cinders of the dead from one
   small plane.

                              In a Bristol Blenheim, Autumn 1941.

To Germany, Three Nights A Week

The little airbus jogs us round the rim
Of 'drome, to bombers radially aligned.
Its faint blue lights illumine aircrew eyes,
Strained, old beyond their years:
No talking now, no boasting.
We have, if we survive this night,
Two days of peace, of boozing, lethe and love.
I sign
The Blenheim is maintained and fuel fed.
We clamber in, we strap, I switch.
The batteries connect, the engines hum.
Off/on magnetos, all is well, the chocks
Are slid away, and we await the start.

Near Maastricht now: my gunner shouts
'Fighter with lights on, Skip, the starboard bow'.
A tyro he ; I turn to look but see
No enemy with 'lights on'. Then he fires
A hundred rounds at Venus, low ensconced.
I muse. If stared at, stars *do* seem to move. . . .

I think back. At home, the ground crews waiting,
Thaw cold, skilled hands on tiny spirit stoves.
No glamour here, those fitters, riggers, all
Who keep the planes aloft, who light with joy
When their own plane, own crew are back with them,
Anxious, stricken, when theirs is overdue.

We bomb, come home and end
In the debriefing room, all smiles and mugs of tea.
The stories mount to epics, lies abound,
Are checked, debunked. We count the missing dead.
The eyes are young now, thankfully, we know
We have, each of us, two more days of life.
To Germany, three nights a week.

Epitaph for Johnny Brown

A daylight raid, an instant, probing thing,
When planes went in, God helped(?) at fifty feet,
Watching the nearing pylons loom.
I led a sortie thus, nine of us, three times three,
A yard apart, more frightened than we knew,
And number two, on right, dear John, was you.
God rest you, Johnny, a shell removed your crew,
From starboard, three souls by blast heavensent.
Then Station Commander, warrior manqué, said
'Redmond, tonight, tell his widow ...... how it went'.
I braced my coward's shaken self, frightened,
Told him 'You tell her, sir, it's not my job'.
That evening to the inn, and there she was,
Small, beautiful and brave, anxious,
I heard 'My husband's late, Redmond,'
And funked it, muttering,
'He was with us when we left'.
We had a drink, we kissed, then I walked back to camp.
I wouldn't tell her, Johnny; let them do it.
They don't fly.

John Pudney

For Johnny [1]

Do not despair
For Johnny-head-in-air;
He sleeps as sound
As Johnny underground.

[1] Written on the back of an envelope
in the London Blitz.

Fetch out no shroud
For Johnny-in-the-cloud;
And keep your tears
For him in after years.

Better by far
For Johnny-the-bright-star,
To keep your head,
And see his children fed.

The New Story

Let the cold fire break out in happy men,
Their blade the reasoning edge, their bomb the fury,
Outblast the understanding, force sudden,
Deliberate as surgery.

The gun within my hand all fear shall stun.
The bombing eye shall look for peace not glory.
Be there no news of honour being won
But the beginning of a new story.

The fire, in man instinct, now coldly flares
Kindled from gutted earth, the modest room
Open to skies, from love spent unawares
And little figures mustering for doom.

Limply the broadcast words balloon on air,
Stale as the comic jokes: now gunfire only
Is real: not the brief landscapes which must tear
The lonely from the lonely.

Combat Report

'Just then I saw the bloody Hun'
You saw the Hun? You, light and easy,
Carving the soundless daylight. 'I was breezy
When I saw that Hun.' Oh wonder
Pattern of stress, of nerve poise, flyer,
Overtaking time. 'He came out under
Nine-tenths cloud, but I was higher.'
Did Michelangelo aspire,
Painting the laughing cumulus, to ride
The majesty of air. 'He was a trier
I'll give him that, the Hun.' So you convert
Ultimate sky to air speed, drift and cover;
Sure with the tricky tools of God and lover.
'I let him have a sharp four-second squirt,
Closing to fifty yards. He went on fire.'
Your deadly petals painted, you exert
A simple stature. Man–high, without pride,
You pick your way through heaven and the dirt.
'He burnt out in the air; that's how the poor sod died.'

Anthony Richardson

Kit and Effects

'Reported missing. . . .' So they closed his room,
Packed up his kit, according to 'King's Regs.'
His batman grumbled at the extra work,
Being a new chap, one of those square pegs
In a round hole. (He'd been a grocer once
In civvy street and owned a little joint
On the first corner.) . . .

                    The officer in charge
Made out the inventories, point by point –
Four shirts, six collars and nine pairs of socks,
Two uniforms complete, some flying kit,
Brushes and comb, shaving gear and shoes –
(He tried a jumper on, which didn't fit!)
There was dirty washing, too, which was a bore,
Being certain to get lost in the delay,
A squash racket with two strings gone, and a cap
That, like himself, had seen a better day.
Then there were letters, beginning 'Darling Dick',
Photos and snapshots all of the same girl,
With a pale eager face and fluffy hair. . . .
This business put your brain-box in a whirl,
Sorting each item out. And then Main Stores
Hadn't sufficient packing cases left
To hold the residue. . . .
                    Oh! Hell!

'Such odd impersonal things now. . . . Darling, do you remember?
Oh! do you remember that day when we shopped together?
And you laughed, because I said I was proud to have a pilot husband!
Laughing . . . can you remember? Why did we laugh?
Can you hear me, now. . . . Can anyone hear me? . . .'

                    The chest of drawers
Was empty at last and then the wardrobe cleared,
And the washing stand made tidy. So the place
Was fit for a newcomer. That job was done –
And satisfaction on the batman's face.
The Adjutant rang up and said: 'Good show!
Thanks for taking Dick's effects in hand.
He was a cracking type. Oh! by the by,
His wife's been on the blower, I understand,
She wants his wings – the ones on his best blue.
Just cut them off and post them. That's the trick.'

With everything nailed down and locked and strapped!
The batman said: 'Unpack! That's pretty thick!'

'I wouldn't have troubled you . . . but to wait so long. . . .
Something that was his . . . so personal . . . he wore it just above his
    heart. . : .
For memory's sake, you see . . . and it's all so difficult being so
    alone. . . .'

The Equipment Officer issued them a set
Of brand-new pilot's wings. They picked and rolled
Stitches and cloth, rubbed in a little dirt
To give the thing a look being old.

'I can't thank you enough . . . and you have so much to do. . . .
I shall always think of your great kindness. When I think of him. . . .
Thinking of him. . . .always and always. . . .'

And, conscientious to the last degree,
The batman posted them immediately.

Address to the Mother of a Dead Observer

Madam, this war is scarcely of my making –
Why pick on me? I'm sorry about Jack.
There was a gunner and a pilot, too,
Who won't come back. . . .

I had to bring the news. It's just a part
Of an Adjutant's work. It breaks your heart?
Madam, I have no heart, I have none left –
So much bereft!

And can't you stop your wretched husband crying?
It's really rather trying.

That's right, sir. Pull yourself together, that's the 'gen' –
At least amongst men.
'Poor bloody men. . . .' My wife said that,
When war broke out.

Madam, I frankly cannot see the use
Of treating me to your abuse.
I didn't kill your son. I gave no order
Posting him across the final border.
I'm only here to see if I can help. . . .

Help? Stranger, what help could you give?
Can you make the dead live?

Once he grew within myself and lay
Wrapped in my body. Every night and day
He grew within me in that fast embrace,
Until at last I saw him, face to face,
And he was in my likeness and I, aflame,
Cried out to God: 'I glorify Thy Name.'
And now God snaps his fingers. . . .

Madam, I loved him too. . . .
                                You owe me yet
Two shillings for the wire I sent his wife,
But that, alone, I'm willing to forget.

Anonymous

The Gremlins

This is the tale of the Gremlins
Told by the P.R.U.[1]
At Benson, Mount Farm and St. Eval,
And believe it or not it's quite true.

When you're seven miles up in the heavens,
(That's a Hell of a lonely spot)
And it's fifty degrees below zero,
Which is not exactly too hot.

[1]P.R.U. Photo Reconnaissance Unit, flew unarmed planes at great speed.

When you're frozen blue like your Spitfire
And you're scared a Mosquito pink,
When you're hundreds of miles from nowhere
And there's nothing below you but drink.

It's then that you'll see the Gremlins,
Green and Gamboge and Gold,
Male and Female and Neuter,
Gremlins both young and old.

It's no use trying to dodge 'em:
The lessons you learned in the Link
Won't help you evade a Gremlin,
Though you boost and you dive and you jink.

White ones will waggle your wing-tips,
Male ones will muddle your maps,
Green ones will guzzle your glycol,
Females will flutter your flaps.

Pink ones will perch on your perspex,
And dance pirouettes on your prop.
There's a spherical middle-aged Gremlin,
That spins on your stick like a top.

They'll freeze up your camera shutters,
They'll bite through your aileron wires,
They'll break and they'll bend and they'll batter;
They'll insert toasting forks in your tyres.

This is the tale of the Gremlins,
Told by the P.R.U.
(P)retty (R)uddy (U)nlikely to many,
But fact none the less to the few.

Benson, c. 1941–42.

Sea

Charles Causley

Chief Petty Officer

He is older than the naval side of British History,
And sits
More permanent than the spider in the enormous wall.
His barefoot, coal-burning soul,
Expands, puffs like a toad, in the convict air
Of the Royal Naval Barracks at Devonport.

Here, in depôt, is his stone Nirvana:
More real than the opium-pipes,
The uninteresting relics of Edwardian foreign-commission.
And, from his thick stone box,
He surveys with a prehistoric eye the hostilities-only ratings.

He has the face of the dinosaur
That sometimes stares from old Victorian naval photographs:
That of some elderly lieutenant
With boots and a celluloid Crippen-collar,
Brass buttons and cruel ambitious eyes of almond.

He was probably made a Freemason in Hong Kong.
He has a son (on War Work) in the Dockyard,
And an appalling daughter
In the W.R.N.S.
He writes on your draft-chit,
Tobacco-permit or request-form
In a huge antique Borstal hand,
And pins notices on the board in the Chiefs' Mess
Requesting his messmates not to
Lay on the billiard table.
He is an anti-Semite, and has somewhat reactionary views,
And reads the pictures in the daily news.

And when you return from the nervous Pacific
Where the seas
Shift like sheets of plate-glass in the dazzling morning;
Or when you return
Browner than Alexander, from Malta,
Where you have leaned over the side, in harbour,
And seen in the clear water
The salmon-tins, wrecks and tiny explosions of crystal fish,
A whole war later
He will still be sitting under a purser's clock
Waiting for tot-time,
His narrow forehead ruffled by the Jutland wind.

Lizbeth David

Air Sea Rescue

Twenty-three hundred – and Skerries light is steady
Coming through the rain and the night:
MLs[1] are in harbour lined and silent lying ready
And Sparks is dozing in the light.

Telephone . . Duty Officer? . . . Telephone: Warning
Plane believed down in sea.
Broadcast. IMMEDIATE. Operator yawning
Switches on and reaches for the key.

'All British ships in area quoted
Keep a good lookout for plane . . .
All British ships . . . position to be noted . . .
Sending message through again. . .'

[1]Motor Launches, used as part of the coastal forces for patrols and for air-sea
rescue.

Enter Commander, magnificent and swearing,
Gentleman, vague to the hair,
Clutching the warm British sack[2] he's wearing
Over crimson Gent's Night Wear.

'Send this to SOUTHERN SPRAY – IMMEDIATE. No,
      cancel,
Send what I gave you before.'
The Duty Officer, distractedly wielding her pencil
Scribbles and smiles to the floor.

'Message coming in, Sir. Object sighted,
Believed rubber dinghy.' 'Go ahead –
Phone through to Valley and get some flares lighted – '
'One picked up, believed dead.'

Feet on the stairs, to the SDO and back again. .
Telephone . . . 'Anything new?'
Drifting Commander in his warm British sack again. . .
Messages. . . the long watch through.

O Five Double O – and Skerries light is steady
Coming through the rain once more.
MLs are in harbour lined and silent lying ready
And Sparks is scrubbing the floor.

[2]'Since I had never seen a duffel coat before, I described it as it seemed to me, a
cross between a sack and a British Warm.'

Sunday Watch (Extract)

Man is not lightly shaken from the ways
Formed in a thousand lifetimes – he outstays
One generation's battles, hates and haste.

Recall to mind the sometime treasured taste
Of native Sundays – forenoon interlaced
With lights and incense, evening half asleep
With Garth-air in the head and boots unbraced.

And though it is legitimate to kill
For seven days a week, we have our fill
By Saturday. The business on the air
On Sunday is approximately nil.

Cast off your stockings then and take a chair –
Sunday's not far away for those who care
To smell the rosbif at the Ward Room door
And note the tiddlys the ratings wear.

And when the time arrives to go ashore
Put on again the rain-wet shoes you wore
And crystallizing random globes of praise
Go up to church as you have gone before.

W.D. Dunkerley

Honour

Two empty syllables that we abuse,
To countenance the dirty tools we use.
The blood-soaked earth, the sweated people cry
'Oh take away our honour and we die.'

An oily lie, an empty silly threat,
Spewed up by politicians, who have met
Some situation with this easy word,
To stupefy their foolish herd.

And was it always so? Always a shield
For those who fought, but fighting meant to yield?
Always the trumpet with the tinny ring. . .
The tune the smoothest cheat knew how to sing?

I like to think that certain souls distressed
Upon this earth, in other worlds are blessed
By finding, to their new felicity,
That *honour* did not mean *publicity*.

Roy Fuller

Y.M.C.A. Writing-Room

A map of the world is on the wall: its lying
Order and compression shadow these bent heads.
Here we try to preserve communications;
The map mocks us with dangerous blues and reds.

Today my friends were drafted; they are about
To be exploded, to be scattered over
That coloured square which in reality
Is a series of scenes, is boredom, cover,

Nostalgia, labour, death. They will explore
Minutely particular deserts, seas and reefs,
Invest a thousand backcloths with their moods,
And all will carry, like a cancer, grief.

In England at this moment the skies contain
Ellipses of birds within their infinite planes;
At night the ragged patterns of the stars.
And distant trees are like the branching veins

Of an anatomical chart: as menacing
As pistols the levelled twigs present their buds.
They have exchanged for this illusion of danger
The ordeal of walking in the sacred wood.

The season cannot warm them nor art console.
These words are false as the returning spring,
From which this March history has made subtraction:
The spirit has gone and left the marble thing.

Royal Naval Air Station

The piano, hollow and sentimental, plays,
And outside, falling in a moonlit haze,
The rain is endless as the empty days.

Here in the mess, on beds, on benches, fall
The blue serge limbs in shapes fantastical:
The photographs of girls are on the wall.

And the songs of the minute walk into our ears;
Behind the easy words are difficult tears:
The pain which stabs is dragged out over years.

A ghost has made uneasy every bed.
You are not you without me and *The dead
Only are pleased to be alone* it said.

And hearing it silently the living cry
To be again themselves, or sleeping try
To dream it is impossible to die.

Norman Hampson

Foreign Commission

November's anger flays all northern seas
And whips great weals across the slaty waste,
The sheering bows fling wide the broken water
It tumbles off the focsles, bitter spray
Knifes by the lively bridges bursting through
And low hulls welter in the marbled water.

On cabin panelling the pictures hold
Their balance in a world swung all awry,
On the damp mess decks now the lisping water
Slides with the restless hours, the cable bangs
Its slow mad rhythm in the naval pipes
And close-packed hammocks jostle all the night.

From heaving tables spins the inky thread
Leading from Theseus through the maze of time
To inland homes where seas are images;
These faded photographs hold frozen truth,
Quick smile, blown hair, in lines map-accurate,
The contour skeleton of living land.

Through all the shapeless months these minds support
Fading perspectives with their wishful dreams,
Assurance grows appeal, their letters scream,
Their own alarm makes fact of all their fear,
The woman's boredom stares between the lines;
And then the silence and the anxious faces.

These are your heroes, whom tomorrow's dawn
May find half-frozen in an oily sea;
They have their memories, their friends who were,
They know the shapes of death and dare forget,
But slow corrosion rusts their lives away
And etches grief on brows that should be young.

There are no killers here, whom crusted pride
Armours against their own humanity,
Or bigot's eyes can blind to bloody hands;
The quiet counties are their pedigree
Whose honest living asks no easy answer
Nor moves the goal to meet their straying ways.
Look for no tragic actors great in stature,
Whose blazing hearts might kindle half a world,
These lives obscure, only their sorrows vast
Winds of humanity that sigh by night
Through all the peopled earth: the men who bear
A fate acceptance cannot make less real.

Assault Convoy

How quietly they push the flat sea from them,
Shadows against the night, that grow to meet us
And fade back slowly to our zig-zag rhythm –
The silent pattern dim destroyers weave.
The first light greets them friendly; pasteboard ships
Erect in lineless mists of sky and sea.
A low sun lingers on the well-known outlines
That take new beauty from this sombre war-paint;
Familiar names trail childish memories
Of peace-time ports and waving, gay departures.

Only at intervals the truth breaks on us
Like catspaws, ruffling these quiet waters.
Our future is unreal, a thing to read of
Later; a chapter in a history book.
We cannot see the beaches where the dead
Must fall before this waxing moon is full;
The tracer-vaulted sky, the gun's confusion,
Searchlights and shouted orders, sweating fumbling
As landing craft are lowered; the holocaust
Grenade and bayonet will build upon these beaches.

We are dead, numbed, atrophied, sunk in the swamps of war.
Each of those thousands is a life entire.
No skilful simile can hide their sheer humanity.
Across the narrowing seas our enemies wait,
Each man the centre of his darkening world;
Bound, as we are, by humanity's traces of sorrow
To anxious women, alone in the menacing night,
Where the rhythm of Europe is lost in their private fear
And El Dorado cannot staunch their grief.

Cecilia Jones

Shipbound

One day on a ship is much like another.
The ship moves, the waves hiss.
But the red cross is on fire and flames the lifeboats.
We watch the mast and sky.
The mast is still but the stars move.
Small sparks fly from the funnel and are lost.
The sea is black but the wake shines and is alive.

By day, the ship rolls and the sea is gray.
All things are lashed with rope, for fear they break.
The sky lurches, the sea heaves.
Many are sick and lie down,
Wishing for death, to be still again.
The sea mocks and rolls the ship,
Dashing us from side to side.
The wind howls and flings spray high;
We shut the portholes for fear of wet.
The air is thick, our heads reel.

Then the pall lifts, the sea shrinks
And becomes a friend.
The sun shines, sparkling on the tips of small waves.
The breeze is fresh: we are alive again.
We crave for warmth, and the sun is hot.
The sea is green and winks at us.
Men take away the ropes and cords.
Food is fresh in the mouth again,
Thirst can be quenched again.

One day drifts to another.
Time is not. Only the starred night
And freshblown day are true.
One day on a ship is much like another –
Ay me, why did we come to sea?

John Moore

Carrier off Norway

There was a snowstorm coming down from the north.
It wasn't dark, for it never really got dark,
But a ghostly twilight fell. And we stamped back and forth
On the bare windy flight-deck; then suddenly . . .

We heard the mutter of engines faint and afar
Above the sea's surge and the wind's slow sigh
And we stared till our eyes smarted, and 'There they are'
We cried, and counted the speck in the grey sky.

That was lit by the pearly gleam of the midnight sun;
We counted seven, and tried to make them eight,
But still there were seven, and when they had landed on
There were still seven, and we said 'Billy's late.'

A ship is a village, even a great ship,
and news travels as swiftly as the wind,
As it does in the village street from lip to lip
And sometimes, I think, even from mind to mind.

Men on the mess-decks, stokers, look-outs, crews
Of the guns, all talked of Bill, 'A hell of a bloke . . .
He was always the same. How bloody awful to lose
Billy, who always had a smile and a joke.'

For us on the deck it was worse, for still we listened;
He'd still got petrol, a few minutes to go.
Is that an engine's murmur? No, hell, it isn't,
Sea's surge, wind's sigh, whisper of driven snow.

And then – because a ship's like a village bereaved,
News like a postman going from door to door,
We heard that a signal from Billy had been received:
'Delayed by three Heinkels.' Nothing more.

'Delayed by three Heinkels'. We fell silent
Thinking the same thought, although nobody spoke
As we huddled together in the lee of the island:
'Billy always had a smile and a joke.'

And then the steady surge of the sea faltered,
And we felt the lurch and the list as the ship's head
Swung, helm over, hope over, course altered,
And we shrugged our shoulders and went to bed.

Kenneth Mould

Night Clothing

(The Gunnery Rating's Lament.)

Shall I muffle in a duffel or just shiver in a shirt?
Is the problem that confronts me when I hear the night alert
And have to go on deck to man an adjectival gun
In a manner that's far chillier for me than for the Hun.
But to dawdle over dressing would be treason, nothing less:
I'm too sleepy not to dawdle, and it's quicker not to dress,
So I usually compromise, and hurtle up on deck
With one sock and a tin hat on, and a jumper round my neck.
Very soon my vital organs are set solid with the cold,
And I stand like that for hours: now can you wonder I look old?
As my knees begin to rattle, and my skin to go all raw,
And my few remaining teeth to chatter wildly in my jaw,
I thank my stars I didn't have that after-supper shave;
If it wasn't for my tot I soon should totter to my grave;
As whizzbangs rush above my head, and bombs cascade around,
And every other second I can hear a whooshing sound,
If by chance you see me tremble, it is just the chill night air,
When I'm rigged in Navy blue I'm far too tough a guy to scare,
But in this ragbag outfit, and with nothing in my belly,
Can you wonder if my heart stops and my limbs all turn to jelly?

At last I stagger down below, and just drop off to sleep
When somebody reminds me I've a jetty watch to keep.
I find it's started raining, and proceed to get wet through,
And before I find my towel comes the signal to turn to.
So here's a word of warning to you silly little men
Who have insufficient wisdom to avoid the Royal N;
Though you have to do latrine fatigues, and act as Captain's
  runner,
For heaven's sake take my tip, and don't become an ack–ack
  gunner!
Look at me! I creak all over, and I'm dying with the 'flu,
Can you wonder I feel chokka? . . . . cad you. . . . .
        wudder. . . . . Atishoo!

Hugh Popham

Against the Lightning

A Poem from an Aircraft Carrier

One

Silver in this transfigured light
above a world lost, unawake,
in a before–dawn sleep and smoke,
with wings not as of earth below,
drab, dope–flaked, too nearly real,
but masters of sun and air we wheel.
Arran is dark, dark
all the shadowed Clyde;
the small ships steal
still–groping, heavy–eyed
up channel.
Only the gaunt and sea–girt sentinel
of Ailsa Craig
toply demands the sun.
Above the haze,

stabbing the cloth of night,
her summit steals the dawn.
Bank westward –
lost the twilight of Kintyre –
and, far below,
the small flat leaf that is the carrier.
Wake-white the sea streams aft,
bow-waves arc out,
the deck still dark and inhospitable.
How far our present
swift Olympian splendour
from the realities of speed and height.
We turn and spiral
down to the dark again,
down for a second dawn.

'Red Section – Line Astern.'
Ready for landing on
the hooks go down.
The wake a wide half-circle as she turns,
wind swings from beam to bow,
the flag streams flatly
from the signal boom.
Down wheels and flaps,
and number one goes in to land.
His speed drops off;
slowly over the curdling of the wake
like a small tired bird
he crawls in and lands.
We follow on
just as the tardy sun
lights the dead surface of the night-damp deck.
The early transformed hour
slips out of mind;
the beauty flung
above them murk of the night-shrouded world
and stolen from
the usual toil of the clock-captive day –
they have no being now.

Now one is skilled,
victim and master of the held machine,
a sorcerer's apprentice to the art.
The leap of heart
evoked beyond immediate thought and need
subsides into the shell of privacy,
remotely shared, unlinked
with the response and reflex of the mind.

Wheels and flaps down,
trimming, airscrew-pitch to fully fine.
Awareness only holds
the batsman's signals,
knowledge of the deck,
the nerves screwed up into one tautened string –
to know instinctively.
Too fast, get up a bit,
hold it at that –
the swift unguided movement of response:
over the round-down
cut the throttle back;
the hook engages:
glad of that sudden jerk
the nerves relax.
The hookmen from the nets release the wire,
crouching against the slipstream.
Taxi forward up the deck.

One more achievement in futility,
one more reward of aimless mastery –
to no known end –
    to no known end?

                    H.M.S. Illustrious, *July–October, 1943*

Alan Ross

Mess Deck

The bulkhead sweating, and under naked bulbs
Men writing letters, playing Ludo. The light
Cuts their arms off at the wrist, only the dice
Lives. Hammocks swing, nuzzling-in tight
Like foals into flanks of mares. Bare shoulders
Glisten with oil, tattoo-marks rippling their scales on
Mermaids or girls' thighs as dice are shaken, cards played.
We reach for sleep like a gas, randy for oblivion.
But, laid out on lockers, some get waylaid;
And lie stiff, running off films in the mind's dark-room.
The air soupy, yet still cold; a beam sea rattles
Cups smelling of stale tea, knocks over a broom.
The light is watery, like the light of the sea-bed;
Marooned in it, stealthy as fishes, we may even be dead.

Destroyers in the Arctic

Camouflaged, they detach lengths of sea and sky
When they move; offset, speed and direction are a lie.

Everything is grey anyway; ships, water, snow, faces.
Flanking the convoy, we rarely go through our paces:

But sometimes on tightening waves at night they wheel
Drawing white moons on strings from dripping keel.

Cold cases them, like ships in glass; they are formal,
Not real, except in adversity. Then, too, have to seem normal.

At dusk they intensify dusk, strung out, non-committal:
Waves spill from our wake, crêpe paper magnetized by
    gun-metal.

They breathe silence, less solid than ghosts, ruminative
As the Arctic breaks up on their sides and they sieve

Moisture into mess-decks. Heat is cold-lined there,
Where we wait for a torpedo and lack air.

Repetitive of each other, imitating the sea's lift and fall,
On the wings of the convoy they indicate rehearsal.

Merchantmen move sideways, with the gait of crustaceans,
Round whom like eels escorts take up their stations.

Landfall, Murmansk; but starboard now a lead-coloured
Island, Jan Mayen. Days identical, hoisted like sails, blurred.

Counters moved on an Admiralty map, snow like confetti
Covers the real us. We dream we are counterfeits tied to our
    jetty.

But cannot dream long; the sea curdles and sprawls,
Liverishly real, and merciless all else away from us falls.

J.H. Schofield

Ode to a Steam Fly

Oh loathsome and horrible prolific sextuped,
Often I wonder just what is your worth?
With your bloated winged body tinted its brownish red,
What your vocation save plaguing the earth?

You egg-laying horror, why of all places
Must you inhabit this miserable ship?
Eating my Keatings and then running races,
Treating as nectar my impotent Flit.

Antennae waving and cutting your caper,
So! You'd come scuttering across my bulkhead,
Just once too often see! – Smack goes my paper.
Filthy, repulsive brown cockroach, you're dead!

Snippet

In the blackout on the deck
Phillip puffed his cigarette.
Hermann in the submarine
Soon espied the tell–tale gleam.
The lone unanswered 'SSS'
Was epitaph to thoughtlessness.

Herbert Smith

Convoy 1943

(After an attack)

North of the convoy, escort craft
Eluded by a pinpoint killer
Under an endless sea listened,
With defiance fading gradually –
When of a sudden, contact made,
They became white-bowed and fleet;
Raised brief Everests of brine
To ransack an impervious sea
Where, submerged but breathing still
The enemy sought escape – to kill.

South, swept out to sea and certain death
One from a stricken ship called out:
'TAXI!' then, fading: 'Taxi! . . . Taxi! . . .'
Causing wonderment in seamen
Whose chill and tension made them *taste*
The metal of their weaponry.

Then hearts beneath their duffel coats
Cheered that victim-jester borne
On a bier of soft-clawed wave
That served the ocean's waiting grave.

His cortège now, the convoy saw
That seaman on his final voyage,
And below steel helmets, eyes
Casehardened but saddened now,
Vowed that if they survived,
First reaching war's last port of call,
Then paid-off life in age and bed,
Just as bravely they'd call out
From final voyage on Death's North Sea:
'TAXI!' then, fading: 'Taxi! . . . Taxi! . . .'

John Wedge

Still No Letter . . .

There's still no letter . . .
                              In my troubled mind
I seek a reason, and quickly reasons find,
Indeed they tumble in, to be discarded
Each as it comes. . . It could be that
You're very busy; missed the evening post;
Or else it's held up in the mail. A host
Of explanations. . . Yet that gnawing fear
O'errides them, still keeps dunning at me that
You just don't want to write. And vainly I
Attempt to thrust aside the thought; deny
It with your last note, and the one before.
But no. I must resign myself to wait
Until tomorrow, or the next day and
A day. Surely then I see your hand-
Writing and envelope. And life is sweet, until
A week or so, when . . .
                              Still no letter.

Convoy Episode

No sound save swishing sea is heard
Above the throb of engines. Ships
To starboard silently pursue
Their course; a single seagull dips
Astern, and dusk and the grey gloom
Steal ever closer from the dim
Horizon . . . . Mute, be-duffeled men
Stand grouped around their guns, as grim
As gravestones, peering eastward for
That shape which spells a welcome chance
Of action . . . Heroes? No – beneath
Each muffled frame a heart a-dance
And stomach sickly strained
With apprehensive tension.
                        Then . . .
'Aircraft in sight!' The air at once
Is full of sound, alive again,
The pom-poms pumping death, swift red
Tracked tracer tears the sky,
Staccato clatter marks the quick
Fed Bren; green beaded streams let fly
From other guns, ship shakes as shells
Are hurled from major armament –
Exhilarating cordite fumes
Escape as every charge is spent.
The Heinkel hesitates, then twists
And disappears beneath the swell . . .
A cheer. . .
           'Cease fire'. . .
                       A happy crew
Collects the case of every shell
Expended - souvenirs, as were
The boxing programmes years ago –
The thrill of victory the same
And joy of contest. Well they know
The penalty for aiming low.

Normandy to Berlin

Douglas Street

'Love Letters of the Dead'

A Commando Intelligence Briefing

'Go through the pockets of the enemy wounded,
Go through the pockets of the enemy dead –
There's a lot of good stuff to be found there –
That's of course if you've time', I said.
'Love letters are specially useful,
It's amazing what couples let slip –
Effects of our bombs for example,
The size and type of a ship.
These'll all give us bits of our jigsaw.
Any questions?' I asked as per rule-book;
A close-cropped sergeant from Glasgow,
With an obstinate jut to his jaw,
Got up, and at me he pointed;
Then very slowly he said:
'Do you think it right, well I don't,
For any bloody stranger to snitch
What's special and sacred and secret,
Love letters of the dead?'

Commando H.Q., December 1941

Kingsley Amis

Belgian Winter

The plains awkwardly revealed by history,
War in the wrong place, the usual day,
Stupid in the dignity of shot,
Blunt the ambitions, make all speak alone.
Martyrdom is a thing of cities, not
The country of the dull; the beautiful
And eloquent showily marked for death;
Unmoving faces are destined to live long.

From my window stretches the earth, containing wrecks:
The burrowing tank, the flat grave, the
Lorry with underside showing, like a dead rabbit.
The trees that smear all light into a mess;
World of one tone, stolid with fallen snow.
Here is the opaque ice, the humdrum winter,
The splintered houses suddenly come upon
Left over from wounds that pierced a different people.

But there are people here, unable to understand,
Randy for cigarettes, moving hands too
Jerky to move in love; their women matrons, their daughters
Frantically guarded or whores with lovely teeth;
The sons come from somewhere else, fair of skin;
The children have thick white socks and an English laugh,
Bearers of flowers, quiet and pointlessly clean,
Showing their parents up, not easily amused.

Behind is the city, a garnished London, a Paris
That has no idea how to live, of Chirico squares;
A feast of enemies, the stranger entertained
With opera and lesbian exhibitions,
Assurances of enjoyment and sameness; the pubs
Like railway buffets, bare and impersonal.
Smiles exclude the hypothesis of starving, but
The conqueror is advised to keep to the boulevards.

Then if history had a choice, he would point his cameras
Oh yes anywhere but here, any time but now;
But this is given us as the end of something
Important, something we must try to remember;
No music or kisses we want attend the fade-out,
Only a same sky or an embarrassing room,
Lust for something and a lust for no one,
Aloneness of crowds, infidelity, love's torture.

E.G.C. Beckwith

Innocence (28 July 1943)

We had had our bathe;
Down at the shallow end
A little girl, in a white rubber cap and a swim-suit,
Played with a friend.

Did she know who we were?
If she did I doubt if she cared;
Just a lot of men who talked in their own funny language
And joked and stared.

Father stood by,
Watching the two together,
In a long white raincoat – strange attire
For such lovely weather.

A drone in the sky
And, silver against the blue,
High, very high, like a cloud of moths, half a hundred
Aircraft flew.

Nothing so strange;
Pretty, they looked, so high
– When, right in their way, a pattern of little black smoke puffs
Flecked the sky.

'*Gott in Himmel!*'
'Look there, Charles! By the Powers –
'Pinch me in case I'm dreaming –
'Charlie, they're *ours!*'

'Can you see them, Vati?'
The child came out of the water;
But the man in the mackintosh set his teeth
As he gripped his daughter.

Over the hill
Out of sight now they were,
But the 'crump, crump–crump' of the big bombs bursting
Filled the air.

'Cassel has got it'.
The German thought of his friends
Caught in the crowded town on a July morning
When hell descends.

A whistle blew.
Out from the bath we went,
Hearts brim-full with the message of hope
That the day had sent.

Back in the pool
The children were at their play;
Their splashing and laughter were all we heard
As we went our way.

IXA/H Upper Camp, Schloss Spanenberg
(Housed 200 British POW Officers)

Night Bombers

You dined last night at Mildenhall
And you shall breakfast there
If kindly Fate shall bear you straight
Through the steel-splintered air;
Breakfast well-earned, your duty done,
Safe-landed from another run.

Forgive us if we think of you
We hear your engines' drone,
We hear the mutter of the guns
Long after you have gone.
Not in your hour of storm and stress
– But eating breakfast in the Mess.

Oflag VIB, Warburg, Westphalia

Michael Davis

Winter in Holland

Oh, it's nice to stroll in Holland
   On patrol beside the Maas,
While you watch each moving shadow
   And the lazy tracer pass.
You'll be freezing like the turnips
   Come the fading of the stars.

Then it's nice to lie in Holland
   In siesta half the day,
And beneath a mound of blankets
   Dream the winter hours away.
As the evening shadows lengthen
   Take your slumber while you may.

You can dream, when you're in Holland,
   Of a convoy heading west
To the land of rear-guard heroes
   With their battle-dresses pressed,
Where the canteen tea-cups tinkle
   And a soldier takes his rest.

But this hole beside a river
   Is the place I chance to be,
Like some lonely polar monster
   In a phone-equipped O.P.
As it thaws, the soil of Holland's
   Simply captivating me!

Haelen, Christmas 1944.

Melville Hardiment

Holed-Up Cyclops

Crawled through the cragged
chapfallen wheat towards
the burnt-out shell of a Churchill
tank both sides use as an O.P.

Armed with a Thompson Sub-machinegun
crawling through the sizzling sun
towards this eyeball to eyeball
confrontation with a little weasel
nazi sniper standing in his circular hole
with his hands in his pockets wanking.

So I got in a burst between his eyes
before he could shout 'Bingo!' And at once
a red bandanna flew across his forebrows
and down each side of his nose.

Old sagging holed–up Cyclops
pissing away his life
in a circular pit of doom
in a cornfield in Normandy.

Woods of La Londel,
D Day Plus 10

Poor Dead Panzer

Poor dead Panzer!
It must have cost you some
to crawl through this wheat
setting it alight,
into this ditch
where swollen flies
buzz round the stiff upturned legs
of a Uccello cart–horse:
And you must have hated the stench
of which you now stink too.

Dragging your torn shoulder
through the corn, an oily smudge
on your tunic sizzling, and clutching
to your chest this evil–looking
Schmeisser machine pistol I covet,
and which sure you must have treasured
to spin round it a frothy cocoon
of brain tissues and dried blood
oozing from that hole in your forehead?

Poor old Panzer!
You sought to protect it so,
did you not? And you felt less vulnerable
with it in your hand.
Now here I am – half jew
and victorious invader –
dispossessing you.

And as I take the butt
into my plough-hands
seeking the point of balance,
I catch a whiff of Bavarian
harvest fields and temporarily
drop it back beside you.

Epron Cross Roads,
D Day Plus 20

A Man of Few Words

Black eyed Corporal Farrell
was a man of few words other
than the usual anglo-saxons
sprinkled around barrackrooms
and camps. He had no words
for the ragged shrapnel slicing
through his knee-caps but
used his morphia and that was that.

We sat side by side in the sun,
for 'lightning never strikes twice
in the same place' I had said.
Side by side wishing the frank
sharp crack and slap of shrapnel
would cease and leave us be.

He might have dreamt of England
and some soft hospital bed. I don't
know, and we just waited. And then
a sniper's bullet holed his head.
He looked at me reproachfully and barked
'Fuck!'

Touffreville, D Day Plus 41

John Buxton Hilton

Armistice

Snuff the candles, day is done,
Foeman scattered,
Battle won;
Blood ridged mountains of this morning
Solaced, shade the tiring sun.

Field to furrow,
Speed your cart;
Caesar's rendered,
Played your part;
Now in deep nostalgic stillness
Seek the voices of your heart.

Duty called for,
Paid with zest;
Hatred nourished,
Fought your best;
Now the man who slew his brother,
Homes to peace, but knows no rest.

Berlin, 1945

Rest On Your Arms Reversed

The peace for which your comrades lived, you found:
Found all alone while they were seeking wild,
Tearing up hell for peace; true fortune's child,
You stumbled on your prize of secret ground.
Let them advance – you found your silent goal,
Untroubled by your name, your rank, your birth,
Uncalled on countless rolls; for you the Earth;
Uncried the broken prison of your soul.

Now let them cry you got their peace for them,
Let them take post to trumpet what you won;
Let them retire to live your gain undone –
You shall not tire of what dull days condemn.
When war-dreams fade, and fireside colonels fret,
Yours not to weep when humdrum men forget.

Berlin, Winter 1945

Belsen

Cast in pits
And strewn with common lime;
Their fault that God ill-chose
Their place and time.

Bergen-Belsen, April 1945

Valkenswaard Cemetery

These among others,
Uniformed, marble-faced, dressed-in-line, soul-mortgaged
  brothers,
Dream in their own unexpressive peculiar way
Of marching through thunder,
And strange laughing halts by the way,
And peace got for others.

Valkenswaard, Holland, Winter 1944

Geoffrey Holloway

Airborne Log

Caught that Douglas easy as a tube
(leaving, the platform's lower).
Doc with a red streak from his tin hat;
said it was bad manners to interrupt a bullet.
Over the Meuse more holes than deck.
One of the Yank aircrew knelt by the door
whipcracking .22, the cowboy.
After the Rhine, dropped.
Woke like a parrot cage, feeding time.
In the wood, worse than the 88's
or the Aunt Sally grins of the tree stuck,
wild flowers. Like home, incredible.
Felt like dysentery, held the stretcher
like a marathon runner grips.
On the way, bumped across Doc;
who'd said too much.

Jim Hovell

Landscape With Tanks

The tanks speed through the still, grey afternoon.
In drab villages straddling the road
shabby people cluster bewilderedly,
wave listlessly at the unmindful convoy.
If they raise a thin cheer, it goes unheard by the soldiers,
armour-cocooned, insulated by engine-roar, track-clatter
and their own thoughts from this winter landscape
and its sombre figures.

'Never knew about them before, did you, Corp?'
Trooper Boyce shouted to Corporal Stone,
standing beside him in an open turret.
'Knew about what?'
'Where we're going, I mean. These Ardennes,'
Boyce said and, remembering other battles,
ran the tip of his tongue over dry lips.

HQ 33 Armoured Brigade, Belgium, 1944.

Distant Destinations

Their battered wireless sets brought the news.
'It's over!' they called to one another,
grinned and shook hands.
Then they fell silent,
thinking of Saturday pints in cheerful locals,
quiet nights after work, dozing with the evening paper,
and, later, upstairs, the comforting presence
alongside in the double-bed.

But, already, in Adjutants' offices,
meticulously listed, were the rank, name and number
of those available for drafting
to distant and unimaginable destinations
where another enemy balefully awaited their coming.

When, later on, a former haberdasher,
whose name they barely knew,
answered 'yes' to the unthinkable question,
these men were not at the time
and were unlikely to be henceforth
among his critics.

HQ 33 Armoured Brigade, Germany 1945.

P.A. Hyatt

The Weeping Beeches of Sonnenberg

Ankle deep in old dead leafs
I strode among the stately beech trees
of this old battlefield,
Anguish in my heart.
I wept for long dead comrades,
I wept for the peace and silence
In these dark woods where trees,
like my soul, are scarred and pitted with old wounds.

The melancholy anguish I have carried these many years
Those boys I killed (shall I ever be forgiven?)
I see these boys every waking day,
the grey green uniforms,
their white marble, dead faces.
People say 'why do you grieve, they would have killed first'
Would that I had been killed first,
than bequeathed with a life of guilt.

Those questions I put to the trees,
they answer, 'Why do you grieve so?'
Did you not leave us shattered, torn and broken,
swathes of destruction left through us?
But look at us now, Look well my friend
for we are regrown and reborn,
Look closer, see we still carry scars.

Mute and silent I ponder this.
Closer I looked and noticed the trees too were weeping,
but not with my anguished weeping.
They wept for joy.
Small nodules each with a tear duct I noticed everywhere,
Each nodule a piece of shrapnel ejected and rejected.
As they rejected they wept for joy, reaching up to the sky
and joyfully rejecting the iron from the soul.

And so the trees have repaired, regrown,
Deep and lovely are the groves of weeping beeches of
   Sonnenberg.

4th Ind Para Brigade, 1st Airborne Division,
Arnhem/Oosterbeek 1944

Robin Ivy

S.E.P.
(Surrendered Enemy Personnel)

We've known each other, enemy, brother,
Tied in battle to the common danger:
We are the cattle, the constant reminder
That time has not conquered the tyrant, the slave.

We have shared secrets, close, undercover.
We've been backstairs, seen the refuse of life,
The ruffian in mufti, the resolute stranger
That lurks in the shadows for daughter and wife.

Yours is the tragedy, fearer, father,
With green faded coat and crease at the knees,
Defeated, dejected, number, neglected,
Pathetic in practice and nervous at ease.

Fear is your brother, unwanted lover,
Lost without, eager for, someone's order.
This is our modern man, plunderer, shooter,
Broken one, homeless one, fireside stranger.

F.E. Macé

The Padre[1]

Greenjackets
Eleventh Armoured Division
Charging black bull, badge of Mithras
Bridgehead breakout, Orne and Odon
Hill 112.
Out of battle for a refit
In a field at Bretteville l'Orgueilleuse
Service in few minutes, Communion after
Disperse on air attack.

Coming, brother?
Me? In Civvy Street I'm a dustman
Quipped the sergeant – childhood echo –
Jesus wants you for a sunbeam
Clouds they parted and a voice said:
In no wise will I cast him out.

Unwashed, unshaven
All hands soiled, including padre's
Oil and petrol
Blood, earth and sweat, et cet.
Surplice dirty, torn and crumpled
Sleepless eyes and slurring speech
Military Cross and death hid future
Pulpit bonnet, altar bumper
Wine long finished
Wafers halved, then quartered, crumbled. . .
Carry on to the Amen.

Time and water – wash and shave
Take a pickaxe and a spade
Unto God's most gracious mercy
Go bury now our youthful dead.

[1]The padre is identified as the Rev. H.J. (Jeff) L. Taylor, M.C. CF. He was awarded the MC for saving the lives of two severely wounded men during intense enemy action.

Belsen

(St Matthew 25:39)

A prisoner I in Belsen
Cruelty, forced labour
Starvation and gas chamber
In Forty-five came Typhus
In Forty-five at daybreak
Encircling British armour
And Green Jackets
Came Freedom
And the armoured division raced on.

Came then guts and compassion
Food, warmth and DDT
Pioneer and policeman
Retribution and rule of law
Skill of doctors and nurses
Shrouds and burial parties
Prayers of priest and padre
For the living and the dead
And the armoured division raced on.[1]

[1] F. Coy (8th Bn The Rifle Brigade 11th Armoured Division) crossed the Leine and Aller rivers and on April 15th, after a journey through some most difficult wooded country, led the battalion to Belsen Concentration Camp. This had been declared a neutral area before they arrived because of typhus, so it was a bloodless liberation.

Alexander McKee

The Question

Perhaps I killed a man to-day,
  I cannot tell: I do not know,
But bare three hundred yards away,
  Where weeping willows grow,

Fell sudden silence on the heels
   Of my last shot, whose echoes rang
Along the Rhine. A silence steals
   Across the river, save the bang
Of distant, screaming shell;
   The tapping of the Spandau
Comes no more; brief quiet fell
   Where weeping willows grow.

Perhaps I killed a man to-day,
   The secret's hid, forever laid
Among those willows o'er the way;
   Here, beneath the quiet shade
Of a heeled, abandoned tank,
   I fired across the river,
   Made water ripples shiver,
     And perhaps I killed a man
Upon that distant bank.

Who am I to play at fate,
To aim, and fire, and arbitrate
'Tween life and death; not knowing hate,
   To send with sad, departing whine
   Irrevocable death across the Rhine.
The willows answer not. The scent
Of clover lingered while I went
   Between the fields where ruins stand;
   Dead horses lie along the land,
   Who died, and did not understand
Why this should be; no more may I
Explain why any man should die.
And still I fired; and wonder why.

Nijmegen, April 1945.

Maple Leaf Down

Normandy, focus of the world in summer,
All eyes, all thoughts upon you,
And a million men locked up in Calvados.
Your roads like deserts, deep in dust,
Dust that cloaked the fields and the blue
And rose-entwined meandering
Of trellis-work upon your cottages of stone.
A summer blue with skies, in Normandy,
And white with cumulus and dust,
And black with smoke of battle.
Like serpents, the armies crawled up from the sea,
And writhed upon your roads;
The vast armada lay, two-score mile of ships,
About your burning beaches, and the spires
Of Courseulles and Arromanches
Were but prelude to the guns of Caen,
Of Villers Bocage, and the heights before Falaise.

All that is gone: down corridors of memory
I see the bullet-marks on white-clad walls,
And stone churches standing in the hills,
The windings of the Seulles and of the Orne,
The perfumed blue of Norman night,
And the stars, ragged in the trees.

All that is gone: buried at the end of all the years,
Beneath the weight of other memory.
But if I go back so far in time
That the Rhineland plain shall fade,
And the jagged towers of Arnhem,
The bleak and wintry Maas, and Antwerp
In her vale of pain; and stride down the years –

Past Ghent in autumn, and Calais
Standing at the last gate of summer,
By Abbeville and Beauvais, across the Seine,
I shall come at last to you. Again
You shall be mistress of my dreams,
The end, as once you were the beginning,
The gateway to Europe, of the path that leads us home.

Brussels, May 1945.

John A. Ottewell

'Evrecy', July 1944

Men of the 'Black Flash', 'Sospan' and 'Dragon',
Wading through 'bayonet' wheat, knee-high and wet,
Mortars and 'eighty-eights' playing their 'overtures'
Spandaus and Schmeissers are waiting and 'set'. . .

Up to that hill enshrouded in mortar smoke,
Tellermines, 'S' mines, a'mushroom the slope,
'Tiger' tanks, 'panzerfausts' blasting our 'carriers'. . .
'Air burst' exploding like 'bubbles of soap'. . .

Now cross the singing Guighe into the alder wood,
Remnants of companies merged to platoon,
Screams for the stretchers with 'Mother' and 'Jesus!!',
'Steady old son . . . we'll have you out soon'!!

Men of the 'Black Flash', 'Sospan' and 'Dragon'
Limping it back . . . all haggard and pale,
Two hundred dead for a handful of prisoners,
Just one consolation . . . 'They've brought up the Mail'!!!

Michael Riviere

Eichstatt, 1943

Well, Riviere's dead. Muffle a smallish drum,
Beat it in a small way, let us be apt and just.
Small stir kept step with him and can see him home
Very well. The firing party? Simplest
To brief some children for a pop–gun squad.
Art (though he wrote some poems) seems none the worse.
He was in one battle, but unfortunately on the side
That lost. Once managed to ride round a steeple-chase course
(Unplaced). Riviere is dead. Look moderate solemn,
Walk moderate slow behind his seven-foot corpse
Who was a half-cock, pull-punch, moderate fellow,
And symbol of so much and vain expense
For years carried pints and gallons of blood about
To manure this casual, stone-sprouting plot.

Oflag Night Piece, Colditz

('The poor man's wealth, the prisoner's release' – Sir Philip Sidney)

There, where the swifts flicker along the wall
And the last light catches, there in the high schloss
(How the town grows dark) all's made impregnable.
They bless each window with a double cross
Of iron; weave close banks of wire and train
Machine guns down on them; and look – at the first star
Floodlight the startled darkness back again . . .
All for three hundred prisoners of war.
Yet now past them and the watch they keep,
Unheard, invisible, in ones and pairs.
In groups, in companies – alarms are dumb,
A sentry loiters, a blind searchlight stares –
Unchallenged as their memories of home
The vanishing prisoners escape to sleep.

Alan Rook

Bombed City

Walk with me to the silent city
walk with me in the fainting street
where the tramlines of evening
wind around the houses.

The churches lay the sorrow
of their bricks across the pavement
and houses no longer
cut the sky with swords.

Tendrils of silence
have bound the broken faces
the lens of day has caught
the overthrow of houses.

What fury here! what pain of living!
What monuments! what pitiless
enduring violin sounds
the white act of dying.

Woman lies with
city to her breast
crushed by the towers
and pain of mortar.

Child lies with
tourniquet of fear
and on his lips
the milk of death.

Inverted image of his city
reflected in the eye of man
his sorrow turns
and writhes like snakes.

Walk with me to the silent city
walk with me in the fainting street
let the knife of seeing
purify your strength.

Larry Rowdon

Counterpoint

A covey of small brown birds
circumvent this field
creating a certain frame
as the scenes come back
with the old confusions.

The land was adorned in sunlight
and the swathes of summer hay
so carefully sheaved
led up to the burning tank
in its final destruction.

But for the grip of each other's arms
through the tumult of explosions
one might have become deranged.
We are still under that sky
separated only by silence.

Divertimento

One still feels cause to rage
against the errors made by war
remembering conversations
that sparked the winter evenings,
for at that time we honestly believed
that God was on our side,
longed then for some recognition

of actions that were made –
which seldom came
or came too late.
while the earth turned
and changes arrived
oh, far too swift,
sometimes like lightning,
until one could not comprehend
amidst the plenitudes of anger
such reasons for indifference,
and this unbroken blaze
of disillusionment
rose from the ashes
of our own consistent failures
making it seem that we alone
betrayed humanity.

P.M.B. Savage

For a Friend

I shall miss him for the private jokes
    And the familiar reactions,
    For the common background of memories,
    The smoothed edges of silence,
    And all the special small things.
And I shall miss him in the things that we did together,
    In the tastes he so subtly shared
    Or argued with understanding,
    And in the places where we went,
    Though I try to avoid them.
But much, much more than even for those things,
    I shall miss him for the long counter-coloured pattern of
        purposes
    That is dead without him.
Even in the broad afternoon, sometimes I shall miss him.

Schstätt 1944

Sydney Taylor

Collaborator?

She raised a glass ablaze with light,
and, as she drank,
I heard the night grow hushed.

She rang so true to pattern,
that I stared around,
amazed to find no heads upon the ground!

Gerry Wells

Jones

A man from a haunted land of men.
Dark, secretive and oblique, he fought
without comment, without rancour
as his blood had always fought
against the English and rock and rain;
against hunger and isolation.

He was a bad enemy; he knew
the land, was a part of it. It showed him
the panzer hidden hull-down and waiting,
and unerringly where snipers had to be.
He saw everything. Sometimes he sang
a language we did not understand,

but his guns spoke a common truth.
It was humiliation for him to miss.
He seldom missed: it was the shepherd
stamping on a cornered rat, a gibbeting
of carrion under sharp skylines; it was
something private, natural and uncorrupt.

In the Rhineland was a farm we stopped at
where a mare was foaling. It was wrong,
too early, and she tensed by gunfire,
was wounded, wild and white in her eye.
Then Jones forgot about airbursts and guns,
left his tank and worked to get the foal.

All night he worked by lantern,
the German with him, in the shattered
barn we slept in. At first light we checked
firing circuits, warmed engines; the mare
was dead, her foal breached and half-born
lay on the trampled straw,

and Jones, bloody to the elbows,
stood by himself in silence. The
peasant from harsh mountains, far in
the fatlands of an enemy, raged
at the other war he was born to –
a familiar he had thought to forget.

South-East Asia and the Pacific

Tom Beaumont

Range Discipline at Rawalpindi

Boldly and unhurriedly
The Sun
Dissolves like the Cheshire Cat
Into an Infinity of Colour.
Cattle
Plod wearily homewards
In a melody of tinklings.
Man-made music
Lingers mournfully
In the stillness.
Only Camels
Creeping,
Silently disdainful
Of their masters,
As conscious as the Sun
Of the simplicity of Everything,
And the purple silhouette
Of the Himalayan foothills
Prevent a sensational confusion
Between the Punjab and Stoke Poges.

And here am I,
Worried and Unhappy
Because of my Ignorance
Of Range Discipline.

23 November 1941

Steven Bracher

14th Army

Men say the echoes that the gun-fire woke
Round Palu peaks and Pegu sleep once more
And by that weary Irrawaddy shore
Only the fishermen sends up his smoke,
Far-seen and lonely on the silent stream
Where death was once the substance, life the dream.

The stir and rumour of ten thousand men
Moved in those forests once, and shook the leaves,
Sudden and secret, as the hot wind breathes
Tossing the jungle, and is still again.
Silence has taken all. The runways fade,
The jungle marches where our camps were made.

.   .   .   .

Beneath the monsoon cloud-wrack and the rain
The steaming valleys of the Kabaw sleep,
And all the jungles of the Chindwin keep
Their savage silence rendered back again.

Clive Branson

Untitled

Millions of years old – over the whole
Hangs the universe like a dome
Pillared on mountains, that fade into their own height,
Breaking through dense jungle shade to white,
And higher yet into the burning night,
Star-spluttering and belching darkness.
   Over the whole spread a silent vastness
   So still, the silence recoiled on itself
   And broke to pieces in a myriad whispers –
   A mountain stream worming its way to the sea –
   The hushed shifting of sand before the breakers,
   Heard from miles beyond the forest's edge –
   Insects' wings brushing the breathless air –
   A leaf falling on leaves and the drip of dew,
   Then through the night the howl of homeless dogs
   To hurl the stillness back into no noise.
   When from the hills, not seen till touching the trees,
   Morning, like a flock of flamingoes, wings
   To settle in the branches and spread across the fields.

G.A.G. Brooke

Home Thoughts From Abroad, 9th May 1945

*(Written on VE Day in a carrier of the British Pacific Fleet, with no
end in sight to the war against Japan. A bogey was an unidentified
aircraft, presumed hostile.)*

No more the voice of plane and gun,
　　The war (in Europe)'s over now,
Away the blackout's ugly pall –
　　Have music, dancing, petrol; show
That five long years have not at all
　　Drained England dry of fun.

Time to rejoice O you who burned;
　　So clear the beaches, light the streets
Fill air-raid shelters with the earth
　　of new-hewn gardens, spread clean sheets
For welcome warriors, whose mirth
　　Is truly and well earned.

As travellers from the wind and rain
　　Take rest awhile, your strife is done,
Then settle down to work in peace,
　　Build the home as you beat the Hun.
Let faith and charity increase
　　And hope spring high again

And let the milk of kindness flow,
　　What, did you say, was that?
Bogies – several – twenty – low?
　　Hi! That's MY tin hat!

Paul Buddee

Relativity

It's funny how the older blokes
  Of forty years and more
Found themselves much younger
  When Australia went to war.
The toothless boys of thirty nine
  And bald heads, thirty five,
All found a splendid youthfulness
  And zest of being alive.
While, at the other end of it,
  Some kids of fifteen years,
Had lost their birth certificates,
  And were eighteen – it appears.

I remember in our billets once
  We swopped our army age
And hoary heads of fifty six
  Skipped many a yearly page.
They turned then to our youngest lad,
  A beardless boy named Snow,
And said 'Now what's your age young chap?
  We'd really like to know.'

To which, with humour, Snow replied,
  'It's hard to calculate –
To use my own arithmetic
  Or to take your discount rate.
Me army age is eighteen years
  But doing what you're doing,
To tell the truth I'm not born yet
  And pa and ma's still wooing.'

Douglas Cole

Fragments

Those hands that held you in the dark
Are held now by a Tiger shark,
The lips that kissed your tender brow
Are looking more like mincemeat now,
The arms that held your slender waist
Are valued now by a fish's taste,
And legs that ran to meet you dear
Are providing a shark with a meal, I fear,
This head that charmed your hazel eyes
Deep in his hungry belly lies.
While bit by bit I disappear,
Remember I died for love my dear.

South Pacific, August 1945

John Durnford

Lying Awake At Night

When men die here I am afraid –
Death takes no ceremonial leave
With horse and foot, in a parade
Acceptable to those that grieve,
The silver, and the glossy plumes,
The solemn uniforms, slow tread
Of soldiery, the stifled drums
That make one doubt a man were dead;
Here only the owls betray the grave,
Only the yews are evidence
Of what rich marrow ever gave
Their roots strange sustenance.

When men die here I am afraid –
Too much lies buried deep, too deep
The ancient soil is over-laid
With blood, too many armies sleep
In the same ground unaware;
Too many times the hideous priests
Hallowed their sacrifices where
These thickets stand; too many feasts
Were held on these high places, since
Obliterated by the rain;
Too often has a Burman prince
Slaughtered his heroes in this plain.

When men die here I am afraid –
The night is motionless and still,
Each minute afterwards is made
More silent by the cricket's shrill
Interruption. Sleepless lie
The listeners. Wild dogs keen
In the shuttered village, the whole sky
Shakes with the pinions and obscene
Gloating of vultures, and no moon
Discloses to the frightened skies
The obscure agonies so soon
Changed into birth before our eyes. . . .

But I believe each death conceives
And bears new children, and a store
Of great fertility derives
From every grave. For into them
Only untraceable remains
Without reality or name
Are ever lowered. Who maintains
With any certainty indeed
Anything but that a kindly spade
Turns over soil for ever made
More fertile by another seed?

Chungkai, December 1943

Prisoner of War Mail

Here in my hand your letters lie,
So unfamiliar-looking, signs
I imagined altered, yet the same,
Their typed undeviating lines
Betraying nothing; grief and pain,
Laughter and love alike conform
To postal regulations, stain
Of the often-hidden tears,
And all the heart's unbroken storm
Are absent from the printed page,
Only the shape of 'o' and 'a',
Like letters of a by-gone age
Bright with illumination, may
Suggest the hand, imply the whole.

R.V. Gibson

Police Report

Reported: One o'clock, Track Eight,
   Woman, near-naked, lying flat
Had been dead five hours.

Lightly she lay as a fallen cone
   On the cold stone.

Item: one corpse, weight sixty pounds.
(Why will they trespass in private grounds?)
   Cause of death, hunger.

Back to the chawls where low life eddies
   To wait for bodies.

Effects: one hobble-stick, value nil,
(It cannot pay for her funeral.)
   Guide, witness, mourner
   To one performer.

O! the level paddy,
The water and the buffalo;
See, she lies dead, my scarecrow
Guarding the light-green paddy
On the black stone.

India

George T. Gillespie

Sleeping

I used to sleep in a green room
full of second-hand books and Dürer's etchings.
I had a desk full of papers and manuscripts.
At that time I owned many clothes
to perform athletic feats and other activities.
In that room were all the sproutings of my being.
I was Faust. I was a professor of evolution.
I was a poet and a budding etymologist.

Now I sleep in a forty-pounder.
All my life is clipped away,
until all that remains of my character
will pack up in a tin box and bedding-roll.
I have a picture of my sweetheart on a board.
I have a watch, a notebook, and a pencil.
I carry out my duties correctly
and get drunk or go to the pictures.

Perhaps, when the necessary lopping of my mind
has ended and the grim battle is fought out,
I shall be allowed to sprout again;
but let it not be deformed or doubled
like the lost limbs of newts and frogs.

Ranchi, Burma, October 1942

Bernard Gutteridge

The Enemy Dead

The dead are always searched.
It's not a man, the blood-soaked
Mess of rice and flesh and bones
Whose pockets you flip open;
And these belongings are only
The counterpart to scattered ball
Or the abandoned rifle.

Yet later the man lives.
His postcard of a light blue
Donkey and sandy minarets
Reveals a man at last.
'Object – the panther mountains!
Two – a tired soldier of Kiku!
Three – my sister the bamboo sigh!

Then again the man dies.
And only what he has seen
And felt, loved and feared
Stays as a hill, a soldier, a girl:
Are printed in the skeleton
Whose white bones divide and float away
Like nervous birds in the sky.

Namkwin Pul

Each soldier as he passes looks at their breasts
Laced tightly in childlike bodices (in Northern Burma, the full
Breasts of the Indian women are unfashionable),
    And lets his glance run

Over the swaying hips to their hard ugly feet.
They come to our small market with eggs for salt.
Yesterday there was one girl dressed in crimson
    Who lolled with a whore's walk

And plucked a flower with a sharp pull and jerk
So that her breast came free from her clothes –
As she intended – and at the soldiers' whistle
   Pretended to be shy.

But most are prim as they follow their bullock carts
And crossing the Namkwin Pul avert their eyes
For standing in the pink sunset that glides
   Along the kine grass spears

Knee high in the water the soldiers soap their thighs
And crack their bawdy jokes, brown to the waist.
And gleaming white bottoms – a hundred of them –
   Shock the Burmese lasses.

Patrol: Buonomary

Beyond the white dust flushed by the carriers
A scene of mangrove and sea:
Ten small figures running stumbling over the hill,
Our bullets yelping after like harriers
Keen on a kill.

And that was all the enemy's resistance.
The pot–bellied children fondled
Tommy-guns and brens; brought bananas; stared.
The chalk road gashed into the distance,
The sea glared.

The men swam idly all the afternoon,
Beech leaves on the brilliant water;
The tide dropped; stems of the mangroves shiny and seal black
Lifted tight green sheaves from the lagoon;
The horizon went slack

With orange sunset slipping into the sea.
Sentries were detailed and posted.
Night followed the shadows, snakes of fire leapt
Where the men smoked and brewed their tea,
Gossiped and slept.

And in the policeman's house I slowly sipped
The poisonous rhum with some alarm;
Admired a photo of de Gaulle, laboured: '*Oui,
Paris avec les Boches, Madame,
Ce n'est pas Paris.*'

R.C.M. Howard

The Voyage Back

It was the time of voyaging back. It was the time, now, at last.
We had come to the end of the days and nights we went
   patrolling
The wastes of ocean. We'll not retrace our wake, all that is past:
The salt-bleached struggling ship, the frozen spray in the
   rigging,
Like filigree icing, and the sight of seamen's wind-scored faces
As they hump the shells, with blue-red hands, to the taut,
   whitened,
Intractable single-whip tackle while the ship plunges and races,
Shudders and slips to the slash of the waves, and the stomach
   feels tightened
In a gritted, queasy contraction, and the smell from the galley
Swims in the head, and the staler stench of tobacco smoke stains
Fingers and mouth. To watch no more for the green break of
   light that stilly
Creeps out of the spume to etch again the twisted convoy lanes,
And later the stretched off stragglers hove up from the pallid
   mouth
Of a snoring dawn. To feel, to know, to touch this no more,
To say it is done, for a few years at least, makes the heart want to
   shout
With the joy of relief for the flesh that was flayed by the raw
Wracking winds from the south and the west. Praise God, it was
   the last, last time;
We were just about at the end of the rope, waking or sleeping,
We dreamed of the plunge and the rise and the endless wind and
   the rime

Of the needling frost that ate its way into eyes and ears and
   brain.
No wonder I saw a young seaman his face puckered and
   weeping
As we ran in the lee of the land back to port and he felt the rain
Falling quietly down from a sky that stood still, out of a peace
That spelled home, gentleness, love. His tears were only the
   tears of release.

Far East, August 1945

Alun Lewis

The Sentry

I have begun to die.
For now at last I know
That there is no escape
From Night. Not any dream
Nor breathless images of sleep
Touch my bat's-eyes. I hang
Leathery-arid from the hidden roof
Of Night, and sleeplessly
I watch within Sleep's province.
I have left
The lovely bodies of the boy and girl
Deep in each other's placid arms;
And I have left
The beautiful lanes of sleep
That barefoot lovers follow to this last
Cold shore of thought I guard.
I have begun to die
And the guns' implacable silence
Is my black interim, my youth and age,
In the flower of fury, the folded poppy,
Night.

The Jungle (Extract)

In mole-blue indolence the sun
Plays idly on the stagnant pool
In whose grey bed black swollen leaf
Holds Autumn rotting like an unfrocked priest.
The crocodile slides from the ochre sand
And drives the great translucent fish
Under the boughs across the running gravel.
Windfalls of brittle mast crunch as we come
To quench more than our thirst – our selves –
Beneath this bamboo bridge, this mantled pool
Where sleep exudes a sinister content
As though all strength of mind and limb must pass
And all fidelities and doubts dissolve,
The weighted world a bubble in each head,
The warm pacts of the flesh betrayed
By the nonchalance of a laugh,
The green indifference of this sleep.

Grey monkeys gibber, ignorant and wise.
We are the ghosts, and they the denizens;
We are like them anonymous, unknown,
Avoiding what is human, near,
Skirting the villages, the paddy fields
Where boys sit timelessly to scare the crows
On bamboo platforms raised above their lives.

A trackless wilderness divides
Joy from its cause, the motive from the act:
The killing arm uncurls, strokes the soft moss;
The distant world is an obituary,
We do not hear the tappings of its dread.
The act sustains; there is no consequence.
Only aloneness, swinging slowly
Down the cold orbit of an older world
Than any they predicted in the schools,
Stirs the cold forest with a starry wind,
And sudden as the flashing of a sword
The dream exalts the bowed and golden head

And time is swept with a great turbulence,
The old temptation to remould the world.

The bamboos creak like an uneasy house;
The night is shrill with crickets, cold with space.
And if the mute pads on the sand should lift
Annihilating paws and strike us down
Then would some unimportant death resound
With the imprisoned music of the soul?
And we become the world we could not change?
Or does the will's long struggle end
With the last kindness of a foe or friend?

Edward Lowbury

The Soldier

Try to divide heaven from earth – there's darkness;
    Try to divide body from soul – there's death;
Take a man's reason from his lips – there's madness;
    Give him your own to chew – there's waste of breath.
Give him cold water when he dies of hunger,
    Give him to eat when he is dying of thirst
And say 'What are you carping at?' – there's anger,
    There's hate, loneliness – but that's not the worst:
We know, we're detailed to do tasks of grandeur –
    Perhaps we'll do them, if we're scared enough;
And not unthankful for the wild adventure;
    Yes, and we know the enemy is rough:
But we are men who struggle for their lives
Against division from their sons and wives.

J.F. McGregor

Rice

We swallow with joy most incredible tales
And it's hardly a wonder we got off the rails

Illusions are shattered in less than a trice
When somebody mentions that bloody word –
          RICE
We scramble in muck-heaps, for brushes and pails,
Our life is an ill-fated scramble for nails,

Our senior officers wrangle in vain
With the Nips who have nothing to show but disdain

But no matter how heavily loaded the dice
The fruit of *defeat* is undoubtedly –
          RICE
We seize what we can evey day through the wire
And the troops got the best from the 'ladies for hire'

Some Colonels and Majors and Subalterns, too,
Reverse the procedure we see at the zoo

And some live on memories prior to the blitz
Of epicurean repasts held at the Ritz

But whether our manners are nasty or nice
It's a quid to a farthing – the answer is
          RICE
We've no blankets, nor clothes and we sleep on the floor,
We have scarcely a window to close and no door,

And a problem most weighty for someone to solve
Is how to maintain some hygienic resolve,

But who gives a hoot for the menace of lice
As long as those . . . . keep giving us
                    RICE

Shamshoipo POW Camp, Thailand,
March 1942

Eugene D. Morgan

A Prisoner Dies . . . .

Where Night, like a negro slut
Hangs over the attap hut,
Here, with Night for witness and the oil lamp prying
Gunner Boncourt is about his dying –
With the rags of that pallid grace
On his Spanish hidalgo's face,
Here he lies
Under a malice of flies.
When the old year's hours were running
He was about his gunning,
Under yesterday's lost suns
Once he fed the great guns
And served to their bellies the meal
Of thunderbolts cramped in steel
– That was his look of pride
As he died.

Bind the arms that are brilliant with blue
Ships and whales in tattoo,
Bind the poor fallen chin
And the cheeks crumpled in
And the lips that will never more shape to a word or a grin;

Let us pray for his soul,
The thin flame swept from its blackened bowl,
Let his comrades welcome him down the years,
The crossbowmen, the arbalesters,

Crusaders sweating at a mangonel,
A Roundhead poised with his petronel,
Do their spirits wait
As behind him clangs the gate?
In the black of Night's gut
Do their spirits press round the bamboo hut,
Poise, as his moments fade,
The men of his trade
To lead the voyager to
Stranger lands than he knew,
And the servant of the gun
Out of the sun?

W.A. Murray

The Desolate Market

Sergeant Godwin advancing through the dust
At first light in the desolate market
Placed his men. After some play with mortars
They withdrew,
Leaving the sergeant in an empty shop
(It was the Indian's who dealt in rice).
A Rajput armoured car tried the same trick
As the sun rose, found a mine
Which knocked a corner off Sam Jimmy's stall
(Sam Jimmy père the shoe-maker).
The rest outflanked the place. About noon
The flies got busy, and the market-place
Buzzed with sunlit emptiness.
At dusk the Japs came back; our gunners dropped
The odd round on them all night long,
Added four corpses and one dying man
To the desolate market's customers:
Two dead in the silk shop, and two
In the open square by the broken armoured car:
The dying man shared Sergeant Godwin's room.

At dawn the Japs left for the hills
Across the river, and Sergeant Godwin's men
Through the dust came back again.
Godwin's corporal
Having deloused the place of booby traps,
Buried the Sergeant, burned his bed-fellow,
And set up quarters in the Indian's stall
Saying
'1111789 Godwin, married, two kids both boys
Believed in the advance of Man
Died for political justice, so he thought,
In a rice-dealer's shop, Toungoo.
All such ideals are false and end in this,
The flies' buzz and the maggots' crawl.
A clean-living Jacobin, nothing of him
But doth change, into something rich and strange,
A new decoction of decay, below the hot earth.
The hot earth of this Burmese square
Walled with darkness roofed with brass
Is the earth of all the world
Earth of a market place where life's a coin
Expendable and base,
How many did he kill before he died?
What rate was his exchange?
Blessed are they who do evil and do it not
Their kind shall inherit the earth,
The desolate earth.'

Beyond the river, up in the olive hills,
Six yellow men tugged at a worn-out gun,
Into the soft hillside dug its steel trail
Fired their last rounds, wrecked the piece
And off into the shadow of the trees,
Shambled on rag-bound feet,
Down to the plain came the shells, whining
Over the river, the temples, the town,
At random killing or not.
In the market the rice-dealer's stall
Gaped roofless at sunset.

His Lieutenant said
'2221830 Byron, single, numerous affairs,
But revenu du tout, had ancestors
And a post-war, depressive attitude.
Plus ça change and all that.' Quite right too.
What did *He* fight for though? He didn't
Like the blood and guts, et cetera.
What brought him to the market-place
Who didn't come to trade for the new world,
Always on sale for some?
'Wrong attitude to history' he said
'The Nazis have', or, 'that fellow Wagner!'
And 'I like Chopin'.
He loved his version of the old. It dies with him.
The living left, to cross a bamboo bridge
Crazily tilted on the sliding river.
The market lay deserted in the sun
The unburied stank, the blow-flies bred
A tuktu called from the tamarind tree
By the gate. Towards dark, from the jungle
Out came Joseph, a Eurasian boy,
He had betrayed his sister to a Jap.
Been local Judas to a friend or two
At the well they found him. One wiped his dah
And said 'He chose the winning side, a choice
Hard to make twice, although he tried.'
They went to deal with others such.
Joseph was buried, with his head,
By a Madrasi transport company.
After a month the rains came, suddenly,
And the old market steamed and splashed
Wrecked and deserted. A new square was built
Not far away; and Joseph's friends
Fell out about the winning side again.
Joseph was dead, no use to hate him now.
So the new market will be just the old
Removed some yards in space or time
A temporary structure in Toungoo,
New York, or Moscow, where men sell
New lives for the old prices once again.

Vernon Powell

Mr and Mrs Mosquito

Looking for a bare arm—
    Or a leg will do:
Landing very softly,
    Biting me or you.
If it's 'Mr' feeding,
    Well, you'll be alright:
Only when it's 'Mrs'
    Need you get a fright!

Ivor Roberts-Jones

Battalion H.Q. Burma

Dante imagined it thus, and Doré reading
Saw eye to eye with him. The signallers crouch
In their dark holes tense as the wires that reach
For the tilted pole. Watch the torsos swing
In the hot pit as the dust peels like petals
Of thin ruin from the cliff face, and when
The guns shout in the narrow valleys, a little
More shifts, like a girl arranging her dress,
At the start of the party waiting for the young men.

There in the black tunnels, like red blood
The lines hang from the telephones, and the heat
   Grins, palpable, commanding, like a foreman stood
Astride his ditches. See where the colonel sits
In his Dante-cum-Doré inferno, apart,
Gesturing like a fastidious actor, correct
And cool with his veined hands.
                      A small part,
No lifting of heavy words to the gilded darkness,
But charming, and in a quiet way, almost perfect.

Roger Rothwell

A Prayer For Food

You know, Lord, how one has to strive
At Shamshoipo to keep alive,
And how there isn't much to eat
Save rice and greens at Argyle Street.
It's not much fun, when dinner comes,
To find it's boiled cyrsanthemums;
Nor can I stick at any price
Those soft white maggots in my rice
Nor yet the little hard black weevils,
The lumps of grit and other evils.

I know, Lord, that I shouldn't grumble,
And please don't think that I'm not humble
When I most thankfully recall
My luck to be alive at all.
But Lord, I think that even you
Would soon get tired of daicon stew.
So what I really want to say
Is; if we don't soon go away
From Shamshoipo and Argyle Street
Then, please Lord, could we have some meat?
A luscious, fragrant heaped-up plateful.
And also, Lord, we would be grateful
If You could grant a loving boon
And send some Red Cross parcels soon.

Another Prayer For Food

Lord, I have asked you once before
To send more food into the store.
To send us something really nice –
Not just chrysanthemums and rice.
I asked for meat and lard (or ghi)
And parcels from the B.R.C.[1]
But that was several weeks ago
And nothing has been sent, you know.

It may be that you didn't hear
Or else because good food is dear –

Though, if you shopped at our 'canteen',
You'd know what prices really mean.
You know, Lord, that we're on our uppers
With only rice 'bas' for our suppers;
And that many through this process
Have got this avitaminosis
And some pellagra too, and very
Many have got beri-beri,
While others that I have in mind
Have gone stone-deaf and nearly blind.

I tell you, Lord, there's hundreds who
Would sell their souls for Irish Stew.
I'm sure you've done it for the best
To see how we should stand the test;
But don't you think we've stuck it well
Through two years' pretty average hell –
As far as food's concerned at least –
I don't count thiamine or yeast,
For what we need to cure our ills
Is solid food, not drugs and pills.

[1]British Red Cross

A Yorkshire ham, a dozen eggs,
Would cure the aching in our legs
And chunks of beef are better far
Than pills of Wakamoto are
To drive our aches and pains away.
So please Lord, send without delay
Some meat and bread and eggs and cheese
And, if You really want to please,
A crate or two of Guinness stout
To fill our scrawny muscles out.

Bowen Road Hospital POW Camp

John Charles Sharp

The Night-Walker's Complaint

When in the star-gemmed sky the lunar lamp
Is lifted high, and all the sleep-wrapped camp
Is swathed in mud and quiet: then with a start
I hear Joe's snore and Jonah's fart,
And as I toss and turn I feel a pain –
An urgent warning to get up again.

In pitch-black haste I seek beneath the board
Where awkward boot with tangled lace is stored.
Its perverse partner shuns my groping hand,
While griping grips me like a band
Or iron, till finally thus hasty shod
I strive to stumble o'er the slippery sod.

O'er boot and shoe, o'er body, bed and bucket
I gain the door, with many a stifled 'dash it'.
I straightway slide into a muddy lane
And scarce avoid a tumble in the drain.
On through the mud with many a clumsy caper
– And then return, because I've brought no paper.

At last I reach the shelter of the jakes
And pick my way through other men's mistakes.
In Stygian darkness scarce have I time to tear
Th'obstructive pants from off my bursting rear.
In haste I squat – but little comfort gain
From thund'rous gusts of watery wind, and so to bed again.

Envoi

O Nippon, are the pains of prison camp so few
That you must lavishly add diarrhoea too?

Banpong POW Camp, Thailand, June 1942

John Sibly

I shall come limping back to you

I shall come limping back to you
On a couple of sticks when this war is through
The leg with the wound is smashed inside
With a few odd bumps and lumps in its hide;
It will carry me still though a trifle short
The doctor said in his last report.
I shall have to wear a special boot –
A good enough fate for a second loot!
And tutelary voices call
Lucky to have a leg at all!
Luck – you're lucky to be alive,
A subaltern's lucky to survive,
To be alive and draw his pay,
And eat his rations every day,
To be safe and moderately sound
When most of his pals are underground.
And so if I come to you
Short of an inch of leg or two,
I won't complain and you won't complain
If I come limping home again.

Burma, 1942

John Smith

Private Mathy's teeth

When I asked for Private Mathy
In his tent, they yelled, 'Not 'ere!
In the cookhouse, or the shithouse,
Or the beer-line gettin' beer!'
So I thanked them all for nothing,
And I hurried off to look
For my quarry, getting nowhere,
Till I found the Sergeant Cook. . . .

Said that 'wallah', 'Private Mathy?
No, I think he's seen the light,
And it's on the cards you'll find him
Singing hymns with Padre White.'
So I thanked the Sergeant Cookie,
And I hurried off to find
Any singing or reciting
Of the Bible-banging kind. . . .

'Private Alexander Mathy?
No, my son, this is a shock!
How I wish he were among us,
But he's down at Kukum Dock.'
So I thanked the gentle padre,
And away I went once more,
Down the coral road that led me
To the shipping by the shore. . . .

Said a Yankee on the 'Wharton',
'Well it's none o' my concern,
But yer buddy's gone up topside,
An' he's fishing off the stern.'
So I thanked the Yank artificer,
And climbed three steps at once,
Up the gangway of the liner,
Almost winded for the nonce. . . .

When at last I found the Private,
With a scowl he said to me,
'You can tell the blasted Colonel
That I won't be in to tea!'
But I soon aroused his interest,
When I told him I had come,
To inform him he could broadcast
His own message home to 'Mum'. . . .

'Private Alexander Mathy?
Are you sure you've got it right?
Hang on, corporal – just a jiffy,
I could swear I've got a bite!'
So I hung on to a stanchion,
While he nearly flattened me,
With a salvo of three sneezes –
'A – a – choo! A – cha! A – chee!'. . . .

'Three for luck!' exclaimed the Private.
'That's the sign a letter's due;
But a fourth one would encourage
Somethin' better into view!'
So I waited, little knowing
Misadventure would result,
And he'd lose his lower denture
From the fourth and final jolt!. . . .

Stammered Mathy, gaunt and gummy,
'Now I've lost me bottom pwate,
An' it's somewhere in the bwiny
Wiff the fish I nearwy ate!'
But I had to leave him cursing,
While I hastened to report
To the 'wallah' who recorded
Soldiers' messages in short. . . .

Said that tongue-in-cheek lieutenant,
'Lost his artificial plate?
Go and see the unit armourer –
He'll bring him up to date!'

But I wouldn't be a target
For this kind of persiflage,
And I left the young 'two-pipper',
Ere he put me on a charge. . . .

'Private Alexander Mathy?
Let the bludger rant and rail!
For I see the dwindling beer-line,
And I'm off to join its tail!'

Next day. . . . Same time. . . .

Said the Yankee on the 'Wharton',
'Sure the self-same bitch's son
Has just gone aboard this minute,
An' he's fishing, ten to one.'
So I thanked the chewing Yankee,
And I hurried off once more,
With my message of salvation
From the Island's Dental Corps. . . .

'Private Mathy,' I informed him,
'Divvy-Sigs. have put them wise –
There's a 'stiffy' up in Vella
With a denture just your size!'
But the Private gave no answer,
Or intelligible sign:
He was much too busy watching
The behaviour of his line. . . .

Said that eager beaver, Mathy,
'Take it 'teady, boy – a bite!
Yeah, it weally is a nibble,
An' te line is dettin' tight!'
So, expectantly, I watched it
Till it left the sea beneath,
With its catch all hooked securely –
Ruddy Private Mathy's teeth!

Pacific, 1945

Leslie Spooner

Burma: Reflections (Extract)

A thought for the days that are gone now,
Of the long marches over the plain,
Banana leaves stretched out above you
To ward off the soaking night rain.
Bed down in a clammy wet blanket
And drag at a fag to keep sane.

The chota monsoon has arrived now,
For it is the turn of the year,
The turkey and plum duff's behind you
And so is the last can of beer,
Naught left but the meagre rum ration
To keep out the cold – and the fear.

Stretch out your legs in the blanket,
Stretch them and try to get warm,
Put your Sten gun snug down beside you
To keep it from coming to harm,
So it's clean and ready for workin'
In case of a sudden alarm.

Do not consider the leeches
Or the ticks that are burrowing deep
Or the sores where your pack straps have chafed you
But settle and try to get sleep,
For it's up and away in the morning
And the tracks now are rugged and steep.

But after a sleep of exhaustion
It's time to get up and stand to –
A couple of biscuits with jam on
And a mess can full of hot brew
With plenty of sugar and tinned milk
For the chances to brew up are few.

And it's on with your kit and away then
In Indian file down the track
With three hundred rounds in your pouches
And 'K' rations stuffed in your pack.
Two 36's stuck in your belt top
And seventy-five pounds on your back.

With stick in your hand you're a-treckin'
The mountains are looming up high,
Sweat rash 'neath your pack is a-stingin'
As the sun climbs up high in the sky,
And as the first stint is completed
You sink on your pack with a sigh.

Light up a fag for a minute,
A swig from your bottle and then
It's up on your feet and get weavin'
The column is off once again.
So hitch up your pack and your harness
And pick up your stick and your Sten.

You stumble across the brown river
And hold up your kit o'er the flood,
You wallow out up the far bank there
And sink to your waist in thick mud.
Your boots get full of fat leeches
Filling their gut with your blood.

Scramble along up the hillside
With bamboo to left and to right,
Struggle with heart nigh on burstin'
To keep the next man there in sight,
And crave for the moment of restin'
And the chance to bed down for the night.

This is the spot we've been seekin'
Although it's not marked on the map,
There's lots to be found on the ground all around
To prove it's well known to the Jap,
And given a little good fortune
We'll soon turn it into a trap.

Then it's off with your kit and get diggin'
And dig it as deep as you will,
For the troops of the Son of Heaven
May soon be climbin' the hill,
And then 'twill be someone's last moment
As they 'Banzai' in for the kill.

The Bren gun is out on the flank there,
The pins are half out of the Mills,
But the sun is beginning to sink now
And soon will be back o' the hills,
And a weary long wait is before you
Throughout the damp night with its chills.

Baboons are a-barkin' behind you,
Far off is the howl of a dog,
You find yourself bathed now in moonlight
Now shrouded in silvery fog,
A rattle of bamboo beside you
As up comes your share of the grog.

And this is the time for the thinkin'
For mentally roamin' away,
With one eye cocked for a movement in front
Whilst your thoughts are permitted to stray
To those who are waiting across the wide world
For an early reunion day.

That day now has come and departed,
Other days by the thousand have gone,
And what to you was a lifetime
Has shrunk as the years have rolled on
To one or two words in the history
Of how the Far East war was won.

So a thought for the days that are gone now
And the lives that went with them too,
Of the silent graves up on the hillside
With the crosses made out of bamboo,
For there lies the Forgotten Army,
Forgotten by all but a few.

G. Stewart-Peter

Organisation: GHQ Delhi

Too much paper in dust-laden piles,
Too many typewriters clicking away
Too many large and over-full files
Too short a night so too long a day.

Too many teacups on table and floor
Too many visitors tramping around
Too many servants behind every door
Eyes ever open and ears to the ground.

Too much time from Army to Corps
From Div. to Brigade too far away
Fighting battalions training for war
Get all the paper but short on the pay.

Thought

Man is born free
But everywhere he is in queues.

C.L. Wilkner

The General[1]

I saw the general standing,
Part of a group but, somehow, quite away,
Gazing silently as the army straggled
Dispiritedly. It was late in the day.

Studebakers passed with engines grinding.
Tired men stared stolidly ahead,
Peering out from sleep-encrusted eyes,
Non-seeing as the wide-eyed dead.

The rain, the very first we'd had
This monsoon, had turned the dry
And choking dust to mud.
Lowering clouds enveloped all the sky.

The general made as if to walk away,
Paused a moment, then looked back again.
To me there came, in that brief gesture,
An aura of unutterable pain.

[1] The general was Wavell whom I saw standing by the roadside watching the remnants of the Burma Army coming over the Chin Hills into the Imphal plain.

The Charger[1]

That noble head outstretched upon the ground,
Damp with froth and sweat around.
An effort now and then to rise;
A look from liquid trusting eyes,
Wide open as with mild surprise;
A rasping breath, the one and only sound.

With craven hand I stroke your mane,
As oft before but now the pain
Is more than I can tell.
For you who served so faithfully and well,
I must pass through my private hell,
And put a three-eight bullet in your brain.

[1] I have had to shoot two chargers and a large number of mules, some because of wounds but mostly because of disease. I always find it a hateful duty.

Anonymous: 'F.H.T.T.'

Lines to the Censor

I wonder what it's like to be a Censor,
And daily read what other people write.
Are they always hunting for the latest story
Or for 'purple patches' loving swains indite?
Or do they deftly track the nimble rumour
With blue-black pencil sharpened for the fray
Or hunt for codes elusive and ingenious
With charge-sheets ready placed in grim array?
I can't help feeling life would be much brighter
For them – yes, and for us, I rather think
If one could write exactly what one wished to;
But then it might just drive them all to drink.

I mean, how nice to know just what the Army
Was thinking re allowances and pay
Or whether some new man who'd been appointed
Was quite the sort of bloke to win the day.
To know just what it thinks about its Air Mail
Which takes from three to four months for the trip.
Does the Censor's office keep it quietly pending
Or is it wafted here by sailing ship?

To learn how much we like to read in 'Victory'
That when we send our girl some local wear
She's now to sacrifice her clothing coupons
('more blessed 'tis to give than to receive!')
But then of course the soldier's wife's so wealthy
Compared with any poor civilian's spouse
That she can well be taxed and docked of coupons
When plutocratic husband sends a blouse!
Well – here's to all those bright 'blue-pencilled' censors
And may they never read between my lines
Or I've a sneaking feeling in my marrow
They'd put me where the Sappers put the mines!

India

Anonymous: 'K'

Jungle Night

The man with the green cigarette strolls down the path
Waving it in the air in conversation.
The man with the tiny anvil strikes it softly like a bell –
Tink-tink; tink-tink.
The man with the dark blue cloak goes quietly by.
There goes the man with the green cigarette again.

They are not really there. You know quite well
They are not there.
Then one of them whistles softly
You finger the trigger of your Bren.
Half fearing, half-desiring the sudden hell
Pressure will loose.
You listen –
Nothing –
Then

The man with the green cigarette strolls by again
Waving it in the air.
Down comes the dew,
Drip-drip: drip-drip.
The man with the tiny silver anvil
Strikes twice; strikes twice
Softly passes the man with the cloak of blue.

Fireflies.
Bell birds
Shadows
Japanese.

15 June '45

Martin Bell

Three Days: The War Ends

A pleasant way to finish the war off
At the convalescent Depot at Salerno,
Scrounging, on the Education Staff –
Run Quiz, Tombola, Brains' Trust in the N.A.A.F.I.,
Give left-wing lectures on the post-war world.
Plenty of cheap, good spirits in the Sergeants' Mess,
And sea and time enough to swim off hangovers.

Armistice, Italy, was a fine day.
We were awed and excited, suddenly free.
Finito Tedesci. Finito Boum Boum. And no fear now
To be sent up through squalid transit-camps
To front-line mountains, snow and mud and bang.
Sang the RED FLAG again, several times this time –
Alex had brought it off before Montgomery–
And a muscular Glaswegian R.S.M.
Thumped on the bar and glinted through black brows:
'It's victorry for the lads. I'm glad. I'm glad
It's victorry for the worrkers back at home'
We left the mess and went swimming, drunk in the moonlight.

V.E. Day[1] was a different matter, stale.
Started drinking in the morning, went on all day,
We'd expected this so long, and O.K. this was it,
We were rancid with expectation.
And Churchill wireless-spoke, fatigued. What was it?
Submarine bases, Ireland? What about demobilisation?
And a red-cap sergeant, who nobody trusted,
Lay groaning under a table: 'Four bleeding years!
Churchill! Four bastard years and a half!.
Churchill! etc., etc ., etc.,'
True but tedious, we thought.

Next day got up with brass-sick mouth.
We went about our duties, sullenly.

V.J. Day[2] I spent in Halifax, Yorks.,
Wilfred Pickles' home-town, R.E. Depot.
They had the gall to get us on parade
For a major to tell us the war was over.
It wasn't we weren't pleased the new invention
Had finally finished things off. And no fear now etc.
But there wasn't much celebration, there wasn't much beer in
    the town,
And the locals wouldn't have a lot to do with us.
They'd had time to get used to soldiers, all through the war.

[1]VE Day – Victory in Europe, 8 May 1945
[2]VJ Day – Victory over Japan, 14 August 1945

Edward Lowbury

August 10th, 1945 –
The Day After

Who will be next to break this terrible silence,
While the doom of war still shivers over these
Unwilling either to die or to be defeated, –
In the agony of death still torn, contorted,
Torn between saving face and body, both
Mutilated almost beyond recognition?
The face fights on long after
The body's overwhelmed and hacked to pieces.
Every scar of it's their fault; yet I am dumb;
In the blind eyes of pity the good and the evil
Are equals when they're gasping in the sand,
Helpless. The reality so blinds
Our senses that it seems less than a dream,
Yet we shall live to say 'Twice in a lifetime
We saw such nakedness that shame
Itself could not look on, and of all the feelings,
Hate, anger, justice, vengeance, violence, –
Horror alone remained, its organ voice
Searching us with a sickening clarity.'
And now the word comes in of those two cities
With all their living burden
Blown to the wind by power
Unused except by God at the creation, –
Atomised in the flash of an eye.
Who else but God or the instrument of God
Has power to pass such sentence?
Here the road forks, to survival or extinction,
And I hold my tongue through the awful silence,
For if God had nothing to do with it,
Extinction is the least price man can pay.

Biographies

The editors have compiled basic biographies of the poets in this collection, where the information was available.

Drummond ALLISON: Born 1921, Caterham, Surrey. Bishop's Stortford and Queen's College, Oxford. Sandhurst, 1942. East Surrey Regiment. North Africa and Italy. Killed in action on the Garigliano, Italy, 2 December, 1943.

Brian ALLWOOD: Born 1920. Joined RAF 1941, sent to North Africa. Mentioned in despatches. Killed in Italy 30 June, 1944, buried at Caserta.

'ALMENDRO': Denis Saunders, South African Air Force, poet and joint founder of *Oasis* in Cairo, 1942. Served later in Italy. Today homoeopathic doctor, Ferndale, Johannesburg, South Africa.

Kingsley AMIS: Born 1922. City of London School, and St John's College, Oxford. Royal Corps of Signals, North-West Europe. Poet, author and critic.

Donald BAIN: Born 1922, Liverpool. King's College, Cambridge. Royal Artillery and Gordon Highlanders. Invalided before the end of the war. Acting career. Co-editor of *Oxford and Cambridge Writing*, 1942.

Hugh BARTY-KING: Born in London in 1914, the son of a Scots doctor who was a chest specialist. Commissioned Royal Corps of Signals with special interest in wireless. Author of several industrial histories. Lives in Ticehurst, East Sussex.

Stephanie BATSTONE: Wren, visual signaller at Oban, Scotland, and later in Northern Ireland. Post-war, medical social worker.

John BAYLISS: Born 1919, Gloucestershire. Latymer Upper and St Catharine's College, Cambridge. Flight Lieutenant in RAF. Co-editor of *New Road, 1943–44*, with Alex Comfort. In publishing and Civil Service after the war.

Tom BEAUMONT: S. Yorks/Notts family. Sapper Royal Engineers 1939, when qualified as a solicitor. Commissioned, Indian Army in Sudan, India and Burma. Post-war, legal aspects of Town and Country Planning.

Ted BECKWITH: Captain, Sherwood Foresters, taken prisoner in Norway. Edited *The Quill* in PWO camps. Post-war, Hon. Colonel of the Regiment.

Martin BELL: Born 1918. Taunton School and University College, Southampton. Royal Engineers. After the war taught for the LCC. Gregory Fellow at Leeds University from 1967 to 1969 and later Department of Fine Arts at Leeds Polytechnic. Died 1978.

D. Van Den BOGAERDE: Born 1921. University College School and Allen Glen's School. Queen's Royal Regiment. Served in Europe and in the Far East. Better known as film actor Dirk Bogarde.

Winifred BOILEAU: Born 1900. Joined Auxiliary Territorial Service (Women's Branch of the Army) in 1938, commissioned 1940. Anti-Aircraft Regt at Hackney in the Blitz, then Mixed Searchlights at Chatham. Maiden name was Mudie (of Library fame). Married Colonel Digby Boileau (Royal Army Service Corps/Staff); one son, Lieutenant-Colonel Peter Boileau (QDG) retd. Died 1979.

Basil G. BONALLACK: Born 1907. Mill Hill School and Clare College, Cambridge. Engineer. Honourable Artillery Company 92nd Field Regiment Royal Artillery. British Expeditionary Force (Rearguard Dunkirk). Sicily. D-Day. Italy. Germany. 'Dunkirk' poem, from which we publish an extract, was begun in France 1940 and completed on the Anzio beach-head three years later.

David BOURNE: Born 1921, Meopham, Kent. Cranbrook. Pilot Officer, Royal Air Force Volunteer Reserve. Left 140 poems. Shot down 5 September, 1941.

Clive BRANSON (Royal Armoured Corps): Born 1907, in India. Educated Bedford and Slade School of Art. Fought in Spain, eight months in a prison camp. Exhibitor at the Royal Academy. Killed on the Arakan front, 15 February, 1944.

John Cromer BRAUN OBE (also John Cromer): Major, Served Middle East. Co-founder of the Salamander Society with Keith Bullen. Post-war: legal profession, magistrate, City Councillor, Portsmouth. Secretary Advertising Standards Authority and head of Consumer Protection EEC.

G.A.G. BROOKE: Son of a Naval Officer, Lieutenant-Commander Brooke, DSC, RN, lives in Sussex and works for Racal Marine. His war, recounted in *Alarm Starboard*, included being sunk in *Prince of Wales*, escape from Singapore in a Malay boat, Malta and Russian convoys and being 'kamikazed' off Japan. Represented Great Britain in the 1948 Olympics.

Jocelyn BROOKE: Born, Sandgate, Kent. Bedales and Worcester College, Oxford. Royal Army Medical Corps North Africa and Italy. Died 1966.

J.E. BROOKES: Private with 2/5 Bn Australian Infantry Force (AIF). Served 1940–5. Worked his passage from Liverpool to Australia pre-war landing with 2/6. On outbreak of war walked from Broken Hill to Melbourne to enlist. Today living at Galhampton, Yeovil, Somerset.

Paul Edgar BUDDEE: Born 1913, Australia. Teacher and writer of children's fiction.

W.H. BURT: Lieutenant in 51st Highland Reconnaissance Regt., when he wrote 'Stane Jock'. Killed in Germany shortly before end of the War.

John BUXTON: Born 1912, in Cheshire. Malvern and New College, Oxford. No. 1 Independent Company. A pre-war poet, taken prisoner in Norway, 1940, interned in Oflag VII.

Roy CAMPBELL: Born 1901, South Africa. Durban High School. Pre-war poet; lived in France, Portugal and Spain. Fought in Spain – on Franco's side. North and East Africa as Sergeant, King's African Rifles, until invalided 1944. Died in motor accident 1957.

Norman CAMERON MBE: Born 1905. India. Fettes and Oriel College, Oxford. An advertising copywriter before the war, and poet. Political intelligence and propaganda during the war. Died 1953.

Michael CARVER: Field Marshal, Lord. Middle East GSO 1, 7th Armoured Div at El Alamein. Commanded 4th Armoured Brigade 1944–7. Author of *El Alamein*, *Tobruk*, *Second to None*, *Seven Ages of the British Army*.

Charles CAUSLEY: Born 1917, Cornwall. Horwell Grammar School and Peterborough Training College. Navy 1940–6, mostly with Communications Orkneys, Atlantic, Gibraltar. Teacher, poet and broadcaster. BBC 1953–6.

Elsie CAWSER: Born 1915, Staffordshire. Dairy Laboratory worker in war and in voluntary organizations. Lives at Doveridge, Derbyshire.

Louis CHALLONER: Born 1911, Blackpool. Educated Preston and University College, Southampton. 2 RHA (25 pounders), Western Desert to Algiers. Headmaster post-war. Archivist, Salamander Oasis Trust.

Robert Laver CHALONER: Born 1916. Jesus College, Oxford: Lieutenant in Royal Artillery, then Captain, Medium Artillery. Caen to Hamburg.

O.C. CHAVE: Born 1912. Flight Lieutenant. Shot down 1943.

David STAFFORD CLARK, DPM, FRCP, FRC Psych.: Born 1916. Felsted School and University of London. Guy's Hospital. War service 1939–45 RAFVR. Medical parachutist. Twice mentioned in despatches.

William CLARK: Regular soldier in Dorset Regiment and RAMC. BEF France and Belgium, evacuated Dunkirk 1940. First published poem accepted by George Orwell in *Tribune*. Orderly Room Sergeant HQ 3rd Corps. 'Military Cemetery' written when visiting the Menin Gate (World War One) at Ypres, May, 1940.

Les CLEVELAND: 2 New Zealand Expeditionary Force, 25th Battalion, Pacific, then Egypt and Italian campaign, where wounded. Published poet, *The Iron Hands*. Reader in Political Science at Victoria University, Wellington, New Zealand.

George E. COCKER: Born Liverpool 1921. Flight-Lieutenant, Air Gunnery Officer. Enlisted December 1939. 31 operations with 218 Wellington Squadron 1941. Took part in 1000 Bomber Raids, 1942. Air Gunnery Instructor, Middle East. Post-war Head of Adult Education Centre. Retired. Lives in Deal, Kent.

Douglas Arthur COLE: Born 1926, London. St Olaves and St Saviours Grammar and Latimer Upper School. Public Relations Manager and Journalist (*Daily Telegraph*). Writer in the Royal Navy 1943–6.

Henry COMPTON: Born 1909, Coventry. Journalist. Intelligence Corps, North Africa, Sicily, France and Germany. Edited Bournville Works Magazine. Lecturer in Communication College of Advanced Technology, University of Aston.

G. HASLETT CONNOR: Born Warrenpoint, N. Ireland 1919. Campbell College and Queen's University, Belfast. Captain Royal Army Medical Corps (RAMC) 1943–6. Doctor, GP, Harrow.

Robert CONQUEST: Born 1917, Malvern. Winchester and Magdalen College, Oxford. Served in Bulgaria and the Ukraine. In Diplomatic Service after war. Poet, literary journalist, and writer on Russian affairs.

Molly CORBALLY, SRN, Territorial Army Nursing Service: Called up January 1940. Egypt, four years service at 19th General Field Hospital, Bitter Lakes, nursing battle casualties (ours, allies and enemy's) – and working with the eminent surgeon Lieutenant-Colonel Professor Ian Aird. Post-war, nursing children and the elderly.

Herbert CORBY: Born 1911, London. RAF Armourer in a bomber squadron. Foreign Service post-war. 'Officers Wives' poem stems from the RAF (Fighter and Bomber) practice of having wives living near station in certain cases.

Joy CORFIELD: Born 1925, Manchester. Joined ATS 1944 at Guildford. Special Wireless Operator, then driver in Germany. Married 1947. Disabled by polio 1950.

Timothy CORSELLIS: Born 1921. Winchester College. In ARP during London Blitz. 2nd Officer in the Air Transport Auxiliary.

Michael CROFT, OBE: Born 1922, Oswestry. Burnage Grammar School. Royal Air Force 1940–1, Royal Navy 1942–6. Professional actor after the war, then Keble College Oxford. Taught at Alleyn's School 1950–5. Founded the National Youth Theatre in 1956.

N.J. CRUICKSHANK: ATS Driver 1941–45, staff cars, lorries, trucks and ambulances, Norfolk. Book of verse, *In the Tower's Shadow*, received the Rockefeller Award.

Ralph Nixon CURREY: Born 1907, South Africa. Kingswood and Wadham College, Oxford. Schoolmaster before the war. Royal Artillery and Army Educational Corps, posted to India 1943.

Lizbeth DAVID: Born 1923, Wales. Joined Wrens 1942, W/T Operator. Commissioned Third Officer WRNS 1943. Cypher Officer on staff of NCSO Belfast, C-in-C Portsmouth (Fort Southwick) and C-in-C East Indies (Colombo). St Hugh's College, Oxford, MA (Theology); in industry and Government Service until retirement 1983.

Dan DAVIN, MBE: Born New Zealand. Rhodes Scholar, Fellow Balliol College, Oxford. Platoon Commander 23rd NZ, Battalion in Greece, wounded in Crete 1941, Intelligence. Official NZ historian Crete campaign. Served at Cassino, Intelligence representative in the Joint Control Commission until end of war. Oxford Academic Publisher. Short story writer and novelist.

Michael DAVIS: History teacher. Private in 2nd Battalion, Glasgow Highlanders. Sergeant in Intelligence Corps, Germany. Lives near Leatherhead, Surrey.

Paul DEHN: Born 1912. Shrewsbury and Brasenose College, Oxford. Major in Intelligence Corps, instructor with Special Operations Executive. Post-war script-writer, librettist and film critic.

Erik de MAUNY: Born 1920, London. French and English parents. Educated New Zealand, Victoria University College, Wellington:

School of Slavonic and East European Studies, University of London. Pre-war journalist in New Zealand, 1940–5, served with NZ Expeditionary Force in Pacific, Middle East and Italy. BBC Foreign correspondent for seventeen years. Novelist. Living in Normandy.

C.P.S. DENHOLM-YOUNG, Colonel, OBE, FCIS: Commanded the Signal Regt of the 51st Highland Division. Post-war returned to accountancy; now genealogist.

Keith DOUGLAS: Born 1920. Captain, Royal Armoured Corps. Professional soldier and poet, independent-minded, he disobeyed orders to take tank into action at El Alamein, wounded; made final revision of his poems and arranged for the revenues to go to his mother, before leaving for Normany, June 1944, where he was killed 9 June, 1944. The poems were handed by him to Tambimuttu, Editions Poetry London, from whom the Trust has taken the poet's version in contrast to others who have revised the poetry years later.

W.D. DUNKERLEY: Lieutenant-Commander Dunkerley joined submarines on 26 August, 1929, and *Thames* was his third command after *H.43* and *Tuna*. Believed *Thames* sunk from an explosion from its own torpedoes when chasing the battleship *Gneisenau*, 1940.

John DURNFORD: Born West Country. Sherborne and Trinity Hall Cambridge. Royal Artillery. Commissioned December 1940, India and Malayan Campaign, 1941–2. Captured at the fall of Singapore in February 1942 with 11th India Division. Lives at Box, Wilts.

Lawrence DURRELL: Born 1912. Darjeeling College of St Joseph; St Edmund's School, Canterbury. Foreign Service Press Officer, Athens, Cairo and Alexandria. Director of British Council Institute Kalamalu, Greece and Cordoba, Argentine. Novelist and poet living in Provence, France.

D. EVERETT: Born 1911. Bodmin, Cornwall. Joined Midland Bank in 1928. RAMC 1940, with 57th and 82nd General Hospitals, Egypt, Palestine, Cyprus, Western Desert. Returned to bank after war to become Manager until retirement in 1970.

Gavin EWART: Born 1916. Wellington and Christ's College, Cambridge. In advertising and literary work before the war. Officer RA, North Africa, Italy. Today poet and critic.

Ian FLETCHER: Born 1920, London. Served in Middle East, including Sudan. Poetry includes: *Orisons, Picaresque & Metaphysical and Motets* and *Twenty One Poems*. Professor of English, Arizona University, formerly, Reading University.

Keith FOOTTIT: Born 1922, India. Wellington School. Trained in the United States; Flying Officer; Halifax bombers. Shot down over Magdeburg, 21 January, 1944.

G.S. FRASER: Born 1915. MA St Andrews, trainee journalist *Aberdeen Press & Journal*. Warrant Officer Class 2, Army Middle East, Ministry of Information. Post-war, lectured in Japan and Leicester University. Helped found The Salamander Oasis Trust. Died 1980.

Alan FREEDMAN: London Editor *Manchester Evening News* and former chairman of the Newspaper Conference. Served in RAF Intelligence, Middle East Forces, later posted to Air Attaché's Office, British Embassy, Ankara.

Roy Broadbent FULLER, CBE: St Paul's School. Ordinary Seaman 1941. 'Service discipline made my verse more precise'. 1942 East Africa. 1943 Fleet Air Arm. Left Navy 1946. Professor of Poetry 1968–73 at Oxford University. Governor of BBC 1972–3—80. In 1970 awarded Queen's Gold Medal for poetry.

Brian GALLIE, DSC: Captain, Royal Navy, served in Mediterranean. Died in Portugal in 1982.

Robert GARIOCH: Edinburgh University. Served in Middle East, captured when Tobruk fell 1942. Post-war schoolmaster, Hayes, Kent and Edinburgh. Garioch wrote in Lallans or the 'doric' of Lowland Scots. Recognized as one of the major poets of the Scots Rennaissance.

John GAWSWORTH: Born 1912, London. Merchant Taylors' School. Part of Neo–Georgian movement of the late 1930s. RAF, served in North Africa, Italy, and India, known in the services as Sergeant T.I.F. Armstrong.

Ronald V. GIBSON: Caius College, Cambridge. Joined Army 1941, served Royal Indian Army Service Corps until August 1944.

Reg. T. GILCHRIST: Infantry, torpedoed in cruiser on way out to Malta: assault landing in Sicily and Italy: Brigade Intelligence Officer in North-West Europe.

George GILLESPIE: Born 1917, Toronto, Ontario.'King's College, London. Commissioned into the Border Regiment 1940. Service in France, Belgium and South-East Asia. Twice wounded and mentioned in despatches. Captain. September 1945–6 interpreter officer POW Camp, Brough-on-Sands. Served with the Foreign Office, German Section; Control Officer in Local Government and Admin, Berlin and Schleswig-Holstein. Professor of German (University of Wales).

Tony GOLDSMITH: Poet and writer before enlisting: Lieutenant, Royal Artillery, killed at Longstop, North Africa, 22 April, 1943. Inspired Spike Milligan, who served in his battery.

E.F. GOSLING: Lieutenant Colonel, Yeomanry Regiment, Middle East.

Alec GRANT: RAF, North Africa, Italy and Yugoslavia.

Grace GRIFFITHS (née Lane): Born 1921, Devon. Crediton High School. Joined ATS (Royal Signals, Special Y Section) 1942. Stationed at Shenley, Herts and Harrogate. Demobbed 1946. Librarian Teignmouth Branch, Devon County Library and Area Children's Schools' Librarian, South Devon.

Bernard GUTTERIDGE: Born 1916, Southampton. Cranleigh School. Hampshire Regiment. Served in Combined Ops and with 36 Div. in Burma (with Alun Lewis), reaching rank of Major.

John HACKETT: General, Sir. GSO1 Raiding Forces, Middle East. Commander-in-Chief British Army of the Rhine 1966–8. Visiting Professor in Classics, King's College, London. Publications include *I Was a Stranger* and (jtly) *The Third World War*.

Michael HAMBURGER: Born 1924, Berlin. Westminster and Christ Church, Oxford. Army 1943–7. University lecturer and translator.

Norman HAMPSON: Born 1922, Manchester Grammar School, and University College, Oxford. Ordinary seaman in HMS *Carnation*, Sub-Lieutenant in HMS *Easton* in Eastern Med., escorting convoys. Liaison with Free French and landing in South of France. Professor of History, York University.

Melville HARDIMENT: Regular Army Sergeant with 2nd East Yorks Regiment, landing in Normandy on D-Day to be wounded at Toufreville, east of Caen, 41 days later.

George Campbell HAY: Born 1915, Tarbest, Argyll. Edinburgh and Oxford. Served in Middle East. Wrote poetry in several languages but chiefly in Scots Gaelic(acquired in childhood). In 1983 won the Comunn Gaidhealach's prize for the best Gaelic book (*Mokhtar is Dughall*). Died March 1984.

Gwenyth HAYES (née Evans): Middle East, First New Zealand VADs (Voluntary Aid Detachment) January 1942, private secretary to commanding officers of 2nd New Zealand General Hospital at Kantara on the canal, Egypt; then 2nd New Zealand Div. in Italy. Twice mentioned in despatches.

P. HEATH: Commissioned, ex-Cranwell, 1929. 25 Fighter Squadron, Fleet Air Arm. 1932–3. China Station and RAF Selentar. HMS *Eagle*. Bomber Command, 1940–4, HQ 2 Group, 99 Squadron, Waterbeach and 2 Officer's Training Unit (OTU) as Chief Instructor. Air Ministry 1945–7. CO Airborne Forces Experimental Unit, HQ Maintenance Command, Air Ministry. Retired 1954.

Hamish HENDERSON: Born 1919, Blairgowrie, Perthshire. Dulwich College and Downing College, Cambridge. Intelligence Officer, Alamein. 51st Highland Div., Libya, Tunisia and Sicily. Mentioned in despatches. At Anzio. Liaison with Italian partisans. Research Fellow in School of Scottish Studies.

John BUXTON HILTON: Born 1921, Buxton. Cambridge University. Beds & Herts and Royal Norfolk, 1941–2. Royal Artillery 1943 (Gunner). I Corps, 1943–6 (Sergeant – despatches). Language teacher, then Headmaster, Chorley Grammar School. HM Inspector of Schools. Now full-time crime novelist.

T.R. HODGSON: Born 1915. Poet at 17. RAF, shot down May, 1941.

Quintin HOGG: Born 1909. Viscount Hailsham of St Marylebone, CH, FRS, Lord Chancellor. President Oxford Union. Rifle Brigade, Middle East. Poems published under title *The Devil's Own Story*.

G. HOLLOWAY: Born Birmingham 1918. Educated Alsop High School, Liverpool. Royal Army Medical Corps, 225 Parachute Field Ambulance, 6 Airborne Div., N.W. Europe. Post-war, Social worker in Cumbria. Now retired.

F.A. HORN: Born 1906, Bradford. Bradford College of Art. Advertising Art Director. Royal Army Ordnance Corps. Organized Publicity Department at Chilwell. Typography specialist. Wrote *Lettering and Work*. Died 1975.

Stuart HOSKINS: Warrant Officer. Navigator in Beaufighters (143 Squadron). Main missions, Dutch Coast shipping strikes, reccees, Biscay patrols and Post D-Day E boat attacks. Member of the Goldfish Club, having survived a ditching in the North Sea.

Jim HOVELL: Joined 61st Training Regiment Royal Armoured Corps, March, 1942. Commissioned, 155 RAC and Yorkshire Hussars. North-West Europe 1944. Liaison Officer HQ 33 Independent Armoured Brigade and later HQ 22 Armoured Brigade. Post-war in advertising and public relations.

R.C.M. HOWARD: Journalist *Sunday Chronicle* before war. 'The Voyage Back' written in Far East, August 1945, while serving in Royal Navy.

Phil HYATT: Military Medal, 4th Ind. Parachute Squadron RE, 1st Airborne Division, North-West Europe, Arnhem/Oosterbruck 1944. Died 1983, Perth, Western Australia.

Robin IVY: Lance-Corporal served North Africa, Sicily, Italy, Austria.

John JARMAIN: Captain 51st Highland Div., anti-tank unit. Chiefly Western Desert, but killed in Normandy, 26 June, 1944. The night before he worked through the records of his unit, assessing each man. Like Keith Douglas, foresaw his own end. Against advice he went on a recce into St Honorine la Chardonnerette to be killed by a German mortar bomb.

Sean JENNETT: Served Middle East. Post-war typographer, Oxford University Press.

C.A. JONES (now Hutchinson): Born 1919, Manchester. Joined QAIMNS (Queen Alexandra's Imperial Military Nursing Service Reserve) February, 1944. Nursed on hospital ship, Italy, Sicily, Greece, N. Africa. Later India. Demobbed December 1946. Plastic surgery nursing 26 years; where met husband, one of Sir Archibald MacIndoe's aircrew patients at Queen Victoria Hospital, East Grinstead.

Eric Douglas JORDAN: Born 1913. King Edward VI School, Birmingham and Wadham College, Oxford; teacher of Classics. Commissioned Royal Artillery, mobile Light Anti-Aircraft Battery, Middle East. Seconded as a Staff Officer to HQ Paiforce (Persia and Iraq Command) at Teheran, Kermanshah, Basra and Baghdad.

Sidney KEYES: Born 1922. Tonbridge School and Queen's College, Oxford. Lieutenant in Queens Own West Kent. Captured on patrol in N. Africa and died 19 April, 1943.

Uys KRIGE: War correspondent Egypt and Abyssinia. South Africa's leading poet World War Two, POW Camp No. 78 Italy.

L.K. LAWLER: Middle East and Palestine. Former BBC executive, living at Henley-on-Thames, Oxon.

Patricia LEDWARD: Born 1920. Driver with AA Unit, ATS. Edited *Poems of This War* with Colin Strang for Cambridge University Press in 1942.

Ronald LEWIN CBE: Royal Artillery North Africa and North-West Europe. Wounded, mentioned in despatches. BBC 1956–64, Head of Home Service 1957-64. Gold Medallist, Royal United Service Inst. Military historian, books include official biography of Field Marshal Lord Slim, Commander of 14th Army, SEAC. Died 1984.

Alun LEWIS: Born 1915, Aberdare. Cowbridge Grammar School and University College, Aberystwyth. Schoolteacher before war. Wrote short stories of the war as well as poetry. Entered Army as Sapper in the Royal Engineers, commissioned in the infantry. India 1943. Killed 5 March 1944, on the Arakan front.

Jack LINDSAY: Born 1900 at Melbourne. University of Brisbane. Royal Signals. Settled in Essex. Author.

Edward LINSTEAD: City of London School. Went into advertising, working for an Australian Company. Served in Sierra Leone, West African Electrical and Mechanical Engineers. Wrote travel book on Sierra Leone. Won four literary competition prizes.

Lawrie LITTLE: Born 1921, London. Alleyn's School. Served North Africa, Italy, Austria. Wrote novel, *Dear Boys*. Concerned with Caxton Trust, an educational charity, based in Pimlico.

Edward LOWBURY: Born 1913. St Paul's School, and University College, Oxford. Newdigate Prize 1934. Specialist in Pathology. Served RAMC 1943–7.

Redmond MACDONOGH: Born 1915. St Aloysius College, Highgate, and London University. Commissioned 1937. Served as pilot in No. 21 and 101 Squadrons. BBC works include *Nevada Pastoral* and *Plot on the Moon*, both directed by Gielgud.

François Édouard MACÉ: Born London 1909 with dual French nationality. Reed's School 1919. Stock Exchange clerk 1925. TA 1939, 2nd London Rifle Brigade (8th Rifle Brigade – 11th Armoured Div.). L/Cpl, Normandy 1944.

Sorley MACLEAN: Born 1911, Isle of Raasay. Edinburgh University. School teacher at Portree, Skye. Signals Corps in the Desert; wounded at Alamein. After war taught at Boroughmuir, Edinburgh, then Plockton, Western Ross, as headmaster (1956). Now living in Braes, Skye.

H.B. MALLALIEU: Born 1914, New Jersey, United States. Journalist before the war. Commissioned in a Light Anti-Aircraft unit (Royal Artillery). Served in the Mediterranean and Italy.

John Streeter MANIFOLD: Born 1915. Australian. Geelong Grammar School and Jesus College, Cambridge. British Army in West Africa and Europe. In 1949 returned to Queensland, Australia.

Geoffrey MATTHEWS: Born 1920. Kingswood School, Bath, and Corpus Christi College, Oxford. Royal Signals, Middle East. Lectured at Finald and Leeds University. Since 1972, Reader at Reading University.

Neil McCULLUM: Lieutenant in 8th Army, Alamein, Libya, Tunisia and Malta.

Dennis McHARRIE, OBE: Wing Commander RAF, posted to 38 Bomber Squadron, Middle East, 1942, as a Flight-Lieutenant, moving to Barce near Benghazi. Now lives at Blackpool, Lancs.

Colin McINTYRE: Black Watch, Company Commander, Lovat Scouts. Journalist.

Alexander McKEE, OBE, FRGS: Discoverer of the *Mary Rose*: Schoolboy hobby aviation and flew solo at the age of 15. Served with London Scottish and the Gordon Highlanders; Normandy July 1944 with HQ of 1st Canadian Army. Later writer and producer of radio documentary programmes; awarded best British radio features script 1969. Lives in Hayling Island, Portsmouth.

J.G. MEDDEMMEN (pen-name of J.G. BARKER): Oasis poet, cousin of George Meddemmen, artist. Conscripted into army 'and marriage' in 1940. Sapper, Royal Engineers, Middle East. Post-war, British Rail shipping.

Spike MILLIGAN: Born 1918, India. Bombardier, Royal Artillery, North Africa and Italy. Film actor, radio and TV comedian and script writer, including the Goon Show. Wrote *Monty, His Part in my Victory* and sequels.

James MONAHAN: Pre-war on staff of *Manchester Guardian*. Served as officer with Combined Operations.

John MOORE: Born 1907, Tewkesbury, Glos. Malvern College. Correspondent on the Republican side during the Spanish Civil War. Fleet Air Arm Pilot, World War Two. Lieutenant-Commander RNVR. Naval Beach Commando on D-Day. Wrote *Escort Carrier v The Fleet Air Arm*.

Norman T. MORRIS: Born 1912, Cheshire. Lancaster Royal Grammar School. Teacher. Enlisted September 1940, 50th Royal Tank Regt., Western Desert, Sicily, Italy and Greece. Post-war, headmaster for thirty years, including school at Elephant and Castle, London. College lecturer and examiner.

William E. MORRIS: NZEF in Western Desert and Italy. NCO on railway lines to run military stock in Desert Construction Unit, June 1940 (12th Railway Survey Company). Member of International Poetry organizations. Tagore Institute and New Zealand and Poetry Society. Poems translated into Hindi and Russian.

Kenneth MOULD: Pre-war on staff of Official Solicitor. Enlisted Navy as a telegraphist, commissioned 1944 as Signal Officers home waters, later in Belgium.

W.A.MURRAY: Tactical HQ staff of 90th India Division as G3 Intelligence Burma 1944. Professor of English, University of Lancaster.

A.F. NOBLE: Royal Sussex Regt, North Africa, September 1939 to August 1940. Joined No. 50 (ME) Commando; raids on Dodecanese Islands, (Kasos, Casterlorizzo). Fought with Commando unit in rearguard on Crete. Captured after last ship had left. Eight days in closed cattle truck, Salonika to Berlin.

G.C. NORMAN: Territorial Army 1939 and served in France, Egypt, North Africa and Italy. Returned to Barclays Bank to become Manager. Died, Pyrford, Surrey.

John Albert OTTEWELL: Born 20 June 1925, Brecon, South Wales. Brecon Secondary School. Home Guard 1941–3. Joined Royal Welsh Fusiliers 1943 (Fusilier) to 1945. Normandy June 1944; France, Belgium, Holland – 53 (Welsh) Infantry Div., 7th Bn. RWF. Script writer and broadcaster.

Harold V.S. PAGE: Born 1916. France 1940. Western Desert 1941. Paiforce/East India 1942. Invasion Sicily 1943. Germany 1945. West Yorkshire Regiment and RASC. Staff Sergeant. Post-war bank manager.

Kenneth W. PARKHURST, Rev., MBE, HCF: Born Brighton. Trained for Baptist Ministry Regent's Park College. Army Chaplain. After Dunkirk 1st Bn Royal Welsh Fusiliers and India and Burma with the 14th Army.

H. POPHAM: Born 1920, Yeovil, Somerset. Cambridge University. Royal Navy Fleet Air Arm pilot.

Enoch POWELL, MBE: Born 1912. King Edward's, Birmingham, and Trinity College, Cambridge. Professor of Greek pre-war. Rose from Private to Brigadier. GHQ, MEF.

Vernon POWELL: Royal Engineers 1942–6. 910 India Works Section. CRE 120 Works (India). Airfield construction (contract and works Surveyor) – India through to Burma and finally Singapore. Commendation from Lord Mountbatten when demobbed WO 2, in 1946.

F.T. PRINCE: Born 1912. Balliol College and Princeton University, USA. Kimberley, South Africa. Captain, Intelligence Corps MEF. Post-war Professor of English at Southampton University and Boston, USA.

John PUDNEY: Born 1909. Gresham School, Holt, Norfolk. *News Chronicle* 1937–40. RAF Squadron Leader, 1940–5. Book Critic, *Daily Express*, 1947–9; Wrote 'For Johnny' on back of envelope during London air raid 1941. Official Historian on Battle of Malta. Died 1977.

M. RAWLINSON: with Royal Tank Reg., Western Desert, 8th Army.

Henry REED: Born 1914, Birmingham University. Journalist and writer before the war. Called up in the Army, 1941, Royal Army Ordnance Corps, but released to work at the Foreign Office. Radio writer after the war.

Anthony RICHARDSON: Flight Lieutenant, RAFVR.

Michael RIVIERE: Commissioned in the Sherwood Rangers Yeomanry. Taken prisoner in Crete 1 June 1941; after escaping in 1943 with sixty other British Officers from Eichstatt in Bavaria, sent to Colditz (Oflag IV C). Mentioned in despatches.

R.M. ROBERTS: Born 1909. Royal Signals in Western Desert and Italy. Post-war built up furniture and clothing store in Burnley, Lancs.

Newman ROBINSON: Served with South African Medical Corps (L/Cpl), taken POW, Western Desert. Wrote reminiscences *In the Bag* (Macmillan SA 1975).

Alan ROOK: Born 1909. Uppingham and Oxford. Royal Artillery, Dunkirk, Major, with 6th AA Division. Later invalided out. Editor of the Oxford Magazine *Kingdom Come* with Henry Treece.

John ROPES, OBE: Served in Western Desert. Brigadier at GHQ Cairo; put on entertainments for the troops.

Alan ROSS: Born 1922. Haileybury and St John's College, Oxford. Royal Navy, the Arctic and North Seas. Intelligence Officer with destroyer flotillas. Naval Staff, Western Germany, 1945–6. Post-war, British Council and then journalism. Editor, *London Magazine*.

Roger ROTHWELL: Lieutenant 1st Battalion Middlesex Regiment. POW of the Japanese in Hong Kong from Christmas Day 1941 until August 1945. Poem written in prison camp hospital, where admitted with malaria and dysentery January 1944.

Larry ROWDON: Born Canada. Served with Royal Regiment of Canada, 2nd Division Canadian Army. Landed at Normandy beach and wounded near Caen.

Alf SAMSON: Served Middle East, artist and writer. Post-war, advertising.

P.M.B. SAVAGE: Born 1916. Westminster and Christ Church, Oxford. Commissioned South Staffs Regiment (5th member of family in that Regiment). Cypher HQ Crete. Captain 1941. POW 1941–5. Headmaster post-war.

Christopher SCAIFE: Evacuated Tobruk as casualty June 1941, then Ministry of Information, Middle East. Spring 1945, Educational Adviser, Government of Iraq. September 1947, British Council's Visiting Professor of English, American University, Beirut. 1957, Permanent staff of University. Chairman Department of English to 1963. October 1968 retired. Professor Emeritus. 1977, elected a Fellow of Royal Society of Literature. Retired to Arezzo, Italy.

Vernon SCANNELL: Born 1922. Queen's Park School, Aylesbury and Leeds University. Won Northern Universities Boxing Championships at three weights. Gordon Highlanders. 51st Highland Division from Alamein to Tunis, Sicily and Normandy. Poet, novelist and critic.

Francis SCARFE: Born 1911. Durham University and Fitzwilliam House, Cambridge. University lecturer before war. Served in the Orkneys and Faroes and reached the rank of Lieutenant-Colonel RAOC and Army Educational Corps. Director of British Institute in Paris.

J.H. SCHOFIELD: Merchant Navy Radio Officer in ships varying from a troop transporter to an Admiralty salvage vessel.

Victor SELWYN: Journalist and researcher; wrote *Handbook on Map Reading & Navigation, Middle East*. With David Burk (pre-war *Daily Mirror* and now *Bild*, Hamburg), met Denis Saunders at the 'Music for All' Services Club, Cairo, 1942, from where Oasis was launched. Manages Salamander Oasis Trust. Lives Brighton.

J.C. SHARP: Signalman Royal Corps of Signals. POW Banpong Camp, Thailand, June, 1942.

John SIBLY: Born 1926, Gloucester. Cambridge University. 2nd Lieutenant 1st Bn the Gloucestershire Regiment (28th) Burma Campaign of 1942. Wounded. Taught in East Africa and England.

Charles SMITH: 2nd NZ Div. HQ Defence Platoon, Egypt, then G 'runner' in Greece and Crete. Evacuated by destroyer *Napier* to Western Desert, then Italy and Trieste. Lives in Whangarei, New Zealand.

Herbert SMITH: On Royal Naval destroyers in North Atlantic and 'E-Boat Alley', LST (Landing Ship Tanks) Far East, including Indonesia after the war. Wrote novels and short stories.

John SMITH: 24th Field Ambulance, New Zealand Forces in the Philippines. Member of the unit concert party Guadal Canal and Green Island where established hospital. Back in New Zealand acting head-master of city school.

Kenneth SMITH: Lieutenant RNVR, served first as signalman in the cruiser *Aurora*. Later in minesweepers including clearing Italian stretch from Leghorn to the French boundary.

Bernard SPENCER: Born 1911. Marlborough and Oxford. British Council, Greece and Middle East. Died 1963, Vienna.

Richard SPENDER: Born 1921, Hereford. King Edward VI School, Stratford-on-Avon. Won scholarship to Oxford in 1940 but enlisted London Irish Regt. Officer, the Parachute Regt. Killed 28 March 1943 leading against German machine-gun positions near Bizerta, Tunisia.

Leslie SPOONER: Born 1922. Central Grammar School, Birmingham. Royal Signals attached Royal West African Frontier Force and served in Nigeria, India and Burma (Arakan) with 81st (West African) Div., Recce Regt. Civil Service post-war.

Theodore STEPHANIDES: Born 1896, Bombay, India, of Greek parents. Educated India, Greece and France. Medical doctor, Paris 1929. Served World War One in Greek Artillery (Field-artillery and Howitzers) on Macedonian Front, 1917–18. RAMC 1940–5 in Western Desert, Greece, Crete and Sicily. Assistant Radiologist at Lambeth Hospital, 1946–61. Died Kilburn, London, 1983.

Gervase STEWART: Born 1920. St Catharine's College, Cambridge. Editor of *Granta* and Chairman of the Union. Pilot in the Fleet Air Arm, killed 25 August, 1941.

Douglas Arthur Manatanus STREET: Born 1915, mother, Belgian artist, father, member Air Council. Scholar Hertford College, Oxford. French Foreign Legion, extricated by Foreign Office, 1938. Commissioned 1/7 Middlesex, MMG (Medium Machine Gun) TA British Expeditionary Force, 3rd Division Dunkirk. Chief Instructor Intelligence Staff Course. Liaison with General Leclerc, Free French. GSO 1 Intelligence 8th Army. SOE Yugoslavia and Greece, liaison in Trieste. Commanded Allied Information Services under the then General Sir John Harding. Foreign Office post-war.

John Richard STRICK: Wellington and London University. London Irish Rifles, i/c Battle Patrol, twice wounded. Killed by shell at Anzio. 1944.

Sydney TAYLOR: Intelligence Corps, attached to 51st Division, posted to Syria/Iraq on field security. Liaison with French security service. Work with Bedouin tribes. Returned for Normandy invasion. Work with the Resistance groups in Holland.

Frank THOMPSON: Born 1920, Darjeeling, son of First World War poet Edward Thompson. Winchester and New College, Oxford. Royal Artillery and special duties Western Desert, Sicily. Major with GHQ Liaison (Phantom Regiment). Parachuted into Serbia to work with Bulgarian Partisan Army. Captured and executed 1943.

Terence TILLER: Born Cornwall 1916. Latymer Upper School and Jesus College, Cambridge. Lecturer in English History Fuad I University, Cairo 1939–46. Radio writer and producer BBC post-war.

Henry TREECE: Born 1912, Wednesbury, Staffs. Birmingham University. RAF Intelligence 1941–6. Editor of *Wartime Harvest*, novelist and teacher.

James WALKER: Born 1911, Manchester. Secondary school in North Wales. RAF. Playwright, novelist, critic and broadcaster.

R.N. WALKER: Born 1917, Stoke-on-Trent. RAMC, Middle East, retrained as cypher operator, Persia, Iraq, India and Burma. Commissioned India BAOR 1945. At Nuremburg trials. Post-war, teaching.

John WALLER: Born 1917, Oxford. Weymouth College and Worcester College, Oxford. Middle East 1941–6, RASC, Captain. Ministry of Information, Athens. Succeeded to Baronetcy 1954. Keats prize for Poetry, 1947.

John WARRY: Born 1916. Haileybury and Queens' College, Cambridge. 1940 Essex Regt. Intelligence Corps attached to Signals. 1945–6 Army Educational Corps. Post-war Lecturer Education Dept, Alexandria University, Cyprus. University of Libya. Senior Lecturer RMA Sandhurst. Author of books on ancient world, historical novels and short stories.

A.H. WATKINS: Lieutenant, Home Guard. *Home Guard Rhymes*, 1943.

John WEDGE: Born 1921, London. Roan, Greenwich; RNVR 1939. Telegraphist on minesweeper HMT *Norse*, officer HMS *Worcester*, *Garlies*. Post-war, Barclays Bank.

Gerry WELLS: Sherwood Rangers Yeomanry 8th Independent Armoured Brigade, North-West Europe 1944–5.

Victor WEST: London-born, taken prisoner-of-war in Crete and then spent war in German prison camps. Poems collected into *The Horses of Falaise*.

Alan WHITE: Born 1920. Lieutenant in Royal Artillery. Killed at age of 24 at Cassino, 12 May 1944. Poems collected in *Garlands and Ash*.

Lyall WILKES: Middlesex Regiment, commissioned 1941 after machine gun officer Corps Training Unit Princess Louise (Kensington) Regiment. Overseas 1942. Military Liaison (Greece). Attached to Force 133 for reconnaissance in Occupied Greece 1944 (despatches). Member of Parliament 1945–51. Circuit Judge until 1982. Three books on the art and architecture of the North East.

Darrell Sheldon WILKINSON: Born 1919. Epsom College and St Thomas's Hospital, London. Qualified 1941, Surgeon–Lieutenant, RNVR. 1942–6 mostly with SOE, Forces 1933 and NE (Greece and Crete) 67. Consultant dermatologist in Amersham, Bucks. British Council and British Medical Association tours overseas.

Charles Lancelot WIKNER: Born 1914, Hendon, E. Yorkshire. Bridlington School. Royal Signals India, January 1938. Commissioned 1941. OC Infantry Brigade Signal Section, Burma. Later Egypt, Germany and Malta. Civil Service 1961 and retired 1978.

Acknowledgments

We acknowledge the permission of Professor Thomson, of Glasgow University, to reproduce part of George Campbell Hay's 'Mochtàr is Dùghall'; from overseas, Uys Krige for 'the Taking of the Koppie' and 'Midwinter', A.D. Donker for Roy Campbell's 'Snapshot of Nairobi' and 'Heartbreak Camp', Les Cleveland for 'Cassino' and Paul Buddee, 'Relativity'.

We acknowledge the John Johnson Literary Agency for permission to use Henry Treece's 'To Certain Ladies on Going to War', David Higham Associates for three poems by John Pudney and Charles Causley, Allen & Unwin Ltd for the poems by Alun Lewis, Chatto & Windus Ltd for the poems by Norman Cameron and Terence Tiller, Jeremy Robson for the poems by Vernon Scannell, Hutchinson for the poem by Kingsley Amis, A.M. Heath for the poems of John Jarmain, The Bodley Head for the poem by David Bourne, Jonathan Cape Ltd for the poem by Henry Reed and Macmillan Ltd for the poem by Robert Conquest.

The following poets have given their written assent to the inclusion of their work in this book: Jack Bevan, Dirk Bogarde (D. Van den Bogaerde), John Buxton, Ralph Currey, Lawrence Durrell, Gavin Ewart, Roy Fuller, Bernard Gutteridge, Melville Hardiment, Quintin Hogg (Viscount Hailsham), Hamish Henderson, Michael Hamburger, E.D. Jordan, Geoffrey Matthews, Enoch Powell, Alan Ross and Alan Rook.

This book was only made possible by the selfless help of the many people who sent in manuscripts, advised the editors where to locate poetry and offered further advice and assistance in the promotion of our work. The help has come not only from Britain, but also from all the Commonwealth countries and from South Africa. In this context we must thank the BBC Overseas Service whose broadcasts of appeals for manuscripts produced such a rewarding response. In Britain the BBC Radio has also publicised our work. We thank, too, the printed media for carrying the appeal by Field Marshal Lord Carver and General Sir John Hackett for manuscripts: the Press Association, whose story was picked up by the provincials to good effect, *The Times*, *Daily Telegraph*, *Guardian*, *Daily Star*, *Times Literary Supplement*, the magazine *Yours*, and many of the service and ex-service magazines and publications.

In the collection of material we thank, too, Air Commodore Harry Probert, MBE, and the Librarians at Adastral House and at the Old War Office who researched at length on our behalf; Commander P.R. Compton-Hall, Director, The Royal Naval Submarine Museum for information on Lieutenant-Commander W. Dunkerley; The Parachute Regimental Association London Branch (Eric Richards) for sending the poem by Sapper Phil Hyatt, MM, 'The Weeping Beeches of Sonnenberg'; J.F. Oliver of the Burma Star Association for his collection from which we have taken J.F. MacGregor's 'Rice'; Ralph Hitchens, also in Burma, for handing over his copy (through Paul at the Plough, Rottingdean, where other material arrived for this book) of the SEAC anthology *Muse in Exile*; Lord Dulverton for sending Ted Beckwith's 'The Wind in the Wire'; and Group Captain Palmer for his copy of *Poetry from the Air Force*.

As in our previous anthologies we are indebted to the help and advice from staff of the Imperial War Museum; Dr Christopher Dowling, Roderick Suddaby, Phil Reed, and Clive Hughes, who helped compile the 'In Memory' page of this book. Jenny Woods at the Museum helped us to select the picture for the front cover of this book. We also thank Jonathan Barker and Jennifer Insull at the Arts Council Poetry Library.

The editors must thank the Trust's advisers, Field Marshal Lord Carver and General Sir John Hackett, not only for what they have contributed to this book but for a great deal of other support in our work.

Finally in this section of acknowledgments we must mention the help received from the Trust's Hon. Legal Adviser, Christopher Frere-Smith, in the difficult area of copyright. The reader will appreciate that after forty years it is not easy to establish in many cases where and when a poem was first published and who in law is the holder of copyright. We even had the situation of the rights in a poem being equally claimed on both sides of the Atlantic. As will be mentioned in the Bibliography it is not unusual to find a poem published in six or more publications and the fact that one of those publications has carried the poem does not mean necessarily that it is the owner of copyright.

It is standard practice to acknowledge each poem and its contributor and, where applicable, the previous publisher.

We have decided to complete the Acknowledgments in the form of a bibliography to guide the reader in the poetry of the Second World War. At the same time, we acknowledge our sources and the kind co-operation of poets, agents, publishers and Trustees. We have tried to contact all concerned and apologise for any omissions.

Our poets fall into these categories:

1 Established poets whose work has been published in anthologies and in the collected works of that poet (the poets are mainly the copyright holders).

2 Poets who submitted manuscripts to be published in our previous anthologies, *Return to Oasis* and *From Oasis into Italy*.

3 Those contributing manuscripts to be published for the first time in this anthology.

4 Both named and anonymous poets whom we cannot trace: they appeared in wartime collections with no biographical or other details to help us.

We divide the sources of previously published poems of the Second World War into the following categories:

I *Anthologies*
  a *Printed in war-time*
  b *Post-war*

  The war-time anthologies include paper-backed collections often produced by the services, not easily obtained, such as *Poems from the CMF* (Sicily), *Poems from Italy*, *Muse in Exile* (published by the SEAC Newspaper, Calcutta). *Oasis*, Cairo 1943, published by the Salamander Society, belongs to this category.

II *Works by individual poets*
  This group includes collections privately printed or in a limited edition.

III *Service and other wartime magazines*
  Today these are very difficult to locate.

The student of Second World War poems will find a considerable duplication between the various anthologies and other sources.

With the advice of Dr Gwyn Bayliss of the Imperial War Museum and Catherine Reilly (editor of *Chaos of the Night*, women's poetry and verses of the Second World War, including civilian poetry), we have drawn up a recommended list of anthologies and added a list of works by individual poets.

Anthologies 1940–46

Air Force Poetry, ed. John Pudney and Henry Treece, London, 1944.

An Anthology of War Poetry, ed. Julian Symons, London, 1943.

A Middle East Anthology, ed. Erik de Mauny and John Waller, Macmillan, 1946.

Poems from the Forces, ed. Keidrych Rhys, London, 1941.

More Poems from the Forces, ed. Keidrych Rhys, London, 1943.

Poems from India, Oxford, 1946.

Poems from Italy: Verses. . . by Members of the Eighth Army in Sicily and Italy, July 1943 – March, 1944, London, 1945.

Poetry in Wartime, ed. M.J. Tambimuttu, London, 1942.

The War Poets, ed. Oscar Williams, New York, 1945.

Post-War Anthologies

For Your Tomorrow: an anthology of poetry written by young men from English public schools who fell in the World War, 1939–1945, OUP, 1950.

GARDNER, Brian, ed., *The Terrible Rain: the war poets 1939–1945*, Eyre Methuen, 1978.

HAMILTON, Ian, ed., *The poetry of war, 1939–45*, Alan Ross Ltd., 1965.

LEHMANN, John, ed., Poems from *New Writing, 1936–1946*, John Lehmann, 1946.

Poems of the Forces, Fortune Press, 1949.

SKELTON, Robin, ed., *Poetry of the Forties*, Penguin Books, 1968.

WINTON, John, ed., *Hands to Action Stations! Naval poetry and verse from World War Two*, Bluejacket Books, 1980.

WOOLMAN, Maurice, ed., *Poems of the war years: an anthology*, Macmillan, 1948.

Return to Oasis (Middle East poems 1940–46), Shepheard-Walwyn, London, 1980. Ed. Victor Selwyn et al.

From Oasis into Italy (Middle East, North Africa, Italy and Balkans),
Shepheard–Walwyn, London, 1983. Ed. Victor Selwyn et al.

Works by Individual Poets

ALLISON, Drummond
The poems of Drummond Allison, Edited by Michael Sharp,
Whiteknights Press, 1978.
The Yellow Night: poems 1940–41–42–43, Fortune Press, 1944.

AMIS, Kingsley
Bright November: poems, Fortune Press, 1948.
Collected poems, 1944–1979, Hutchinson, 1979.

BAYLISS, John
Venus in Libra, Outposts Publications, 1977.
The White Knight, Fortune Press, 1944.

CAMERON, Norman
The Collected Poems of Norman Cameron, 1905–1953, Hogarth Press,
1957.

CAMPBELL, Roy
The Collected Poems of Roy Campbell, Bodley Head, Vol. 1, 1949,
Vol. 2, 1957.
Selected poetry, Edited by J.M. Lalley, Bodley Head, 1968.

CORBY, Herbert
Hampdens going over, Editions Poetry London, 1945.
Time in a Blue Prison, Fortune Press, 1947.

CURREY, R.N.
Indian landscape: a book of descriptive poems, Routledge, 1947.
This Other Planet, Routledge, 1945.

DOUGLAS, Keith
Alamein to Zem-Zem, Editions Poetry London, 1944. (N.B. This
includes Keith Douglas' own version of his poetry.)

DURRELL, Lawrence
Collected Poems 1931–74, Faber, 1980.

EWART, Gavin
The Collected Ewart, Hutchinson, 1980.
The New Ewart, Hutchinson, 1984.

FRASER, G.S.
Home town elegy, Editions Poetry London, 1944.
The Traveller has regrets, and other poems, Harvill Press and Editions
Poetry, 1948.

FULLER, Roy
The Middle of a War, Hogarth Press, 1942.

Collected Poems 1936–1961, London, Deutsch, 1962.
A Lost Season, Hogarth Press, 1944.

GARIOCH, Robert
Collected Poems, Carcanet Press Ltd and Macdonald, 1980.

GUTTERIDGE, Bernard
Traveller's Eye, Routledge, 1947.
Old Damson Face, London Magazine Editions, 1975.

HENDERSON, Hamish
Elegies for the dead in Cyrenaica, University of Edinburgh, 1977.

JARMAIN, John
Poems, Collins, 1945.

KEYES, Sidney
The Collected Poems of Sidney Keyes, edited by Michael Meyer, Routledge, 1945.
The Cruel Solstice, Routledge, 1943.
The Iron Laurel, Routledge, 1942.

LEWIS, Alun
Ha! Ha! Among the Trumpets: Poems in Transit, George Allen & Unwin Ltd, 1945.
Raiders' Dawn, and other poems, George Allen & Unwin Ltd, 1942.
Selected poetry and prose, with a biographical introduction by Ian Hamilton, George Allen & Unwin Ltd, 1966.

MACLEAN, Sorley
Spring Tide and Neap Time: Selected poems 1932–72, Canongate, 1977.

MANIFOLD, John
Selected Verse, Dennis Dobson, 1948.

MONAHAN, James
After Battle, Macmillan & Co. Ltd, 1948.
Far From The Land, and other poems, Macmillan, 1944.

POWELL, Enoch
Dancer's End; and, The Wedding Gift: two books of poems, Falcon Press, 1951.

PRINCE, F.T.
Collected Poems, Anvil Press and Menard Press, 1979.

PUDNEY, John
Dispersal Point, and other air poems, John Lane The Bodley Head, 1942.
For Johnny: poems of World War Two (revised ed.), Shepheard-Walwyn, 1976. (1st ed. published in 1957 by Putnam as *Collected Poems*).
Selected Poems, John Lane The Bodley Head, 1946.

ROOK, Alan
Soldiers, This Solitude, Routledge, 1942.

These are my Comrades: poems, Routledge, 1943.
We who are Fortunate, Routledge, 1943.

ROSS, Alan
Open Sea, London Magazine Editions, 1975.

SCANNELL, Vernon
Graves & Resurrections, Fortune Press, 1948.
Walking Wounded, Eyre & Spottiswoode, 1965.
Epithets of War, Eyre & Spottiswoode, 1969.
The Tiger and the Rose, Eyre & Spottiswoode, 1971.

SPENCER, Bernard
Aegean Islands, and other poems, Editions Poetry London, 1946.
Collected Poems, Alan Ross Ltd, 1965.

SPENDER, Richard
The Collected Poems of Richard Spender, Sidgwick & Jackson, 1944.
Parachute Battalion: last poems from England and Tunisia, Sidgwick & Jackson, 1943.

TREECE, Henry
The Black Seasons, Faber and Faber, 1945.
The Haunted Garden, Faber and Faber, 1947.
Invitation and Warning, Faber and Faber, 1942.

WALLER, John
Fortunate Hamlet, Fortune Press, 1941.
The Kiss of Stars, Heinemann, 1948.
The Merry Ghosts: poems, Editions Poetry London, 1946.

WEST, Victor
The Horses of Falaise: poems on the experience of a fighting soldier in World War II, Salamander Imprint, 1975.

WHITE, Alan
Garlands and ash, Fortune Press, 1947.

Other Royal Air Force poetry will be found in:

RICHARDSON, Anthony
Full Cycle, Hodder & Stoughton, 1946.

WRIGHT, James
Airman Singing, Sidgwick & Jackson, 1944.

GORDON, James
Epitaph for a Squadron, Arthur H. Stockwell, 1965.

F/O A.N.C. WEIR DFC
Verses of a Fighter Pilot, Faber and Faber, 1961.

MOGG, (Sgt) P.L.
For This Alone, Basil Blackwell, 1964.

We acknowledge that the following poems were previously published in *Return to Oasis* and *From Oasis into Italy*. (We exclude the poets in those books who had been published elsewhere: Drummond Allison, Keith Douglas, Sidney Keyes, Uys Krige, John Jarmain, Enoch Powell, John Pudney, F.T. Prince, Alan White.)

Return to Oasis

'ALMENDRO'
  Night Preceding Battle

MAX BOWDEN
  Myriad Destiny in Neat Black
  Shoes. . .

J.E. BROOKES
  Tobruk 1941

LOUIS CHALLONER
  Alternative

MOLLY CORBALLY
  Ad Astra

MICHAEL CROFT
  Leaving the Med

JOHN CROMER
  Asleep in War

D.M. DAVIN
  Cairo Cleopatra
  Grave near Sirte

ERIK de MAUNY
  News from Home

C.P.S. DENHOLM-YOUNG
  Dead German Youth

DONALD EVERETT
  Envoi

IAN FLETCHER
  Soldiers at the Base

G.S. FRASER
  An Elegy for Keith Bullen
  Egypt

BRIAN GALLIE
  To a German Airman

JOHN GAWSWORTH
  The Fallen

E.F. GOSLING
  Mechanization

HAMISH HENDERSON
  So Long

L.K. LAWLER
  Poem

CALVIN MAKABO
  Desert Conflict

J.G. MEDDEMMEN
  L.R.D.G.

N.T. MORRIS
  It's Always Mealtime

G.C. NORMAN
  Night Raid

JOHN RIMINGTON
  Danse Grotesque
  The Flap

JOHN ROPES
  Voluntary Ladies of the Town

ALF SAMSON
  Back to the Beginning

THEODORE STEPHANIDES
  Western Desert – Two Years
  After
  Duologue

R.N. WALKER
  Living and Dead

JOHN WALLER
  Convoy

JOHN WARRY
To a W.A.A.F.

DARRELL WILKINSON
Drifting at Sea

ANONYMOUS
Leave, Compassionate,
Children, Production, for the
use of

ANONYMOUS
Cairo Love Song

From Oasis into Italy

ROBIN BENN
Dalmatian Islanders

J. BEVAN
Ubique (Motto of the Royal
Artillery)

W.H. BURT
Stane Jock

H. COMPTON
On a Soldier Playing the Piano

DONALD EVERETT
Kyrenia

IAN FLETCHER
Naked Africa

ALAN FREEDMAN
August

ROBERT GARIOCH
Kriegy Ballad

TONY GOLDSMITH
The I.G. at War

ALEC GRANT
Randolph's Gethsemane

QUINTIN HOGG
Night Patrol

MICHAEL HAMBURGER
For the Dead

PETER KNEEBONE
See Naples

LAWRIE LITTLE
Sentry Duty, 7.15 a.m.

KEVIN MCHALE
Com-bloody-parisons

COLIN MCINTYRE
Motor Transport Officer

N.T. MORRIS
Sicilian Town: August 1943

M. RAWLINSON
Mediterranean Song

HENRY REED
Naming of the Parts

R.M. ROBERTS
Italian Road
Troop Train

N. ROBINSON
P.O.W. Camp, Italy

DOUGLAS STREET
Cassino Revisited

JOHN STRICK
Vineyard Reverie

N.J. TRAPNELL
Lament of a Desert Rat

JOHN WARRY
Athens – January 1945 (extract)

ANONYMOUS
The D-Day Dodgers

ANONYMOUS
Ode to a Gezira Lovely

We thank those poets who sent us manuscripts for publication: or authorised us to include their previously published poem in this book. Where the poet has been included in the list of published works on a previous page, the name has been omitted here to save duplication.

1 *1939–40*

BRIAN ALLWOOD
Ack Ack Said The Instructor

LEON ATKINS
Dunkirk

DONALD BAIN
War Poet

HUGH BARTY-KING
Horses

TOM BEAUMONT
The Colonel's Eye

WINIFRED BOILEAU
Sounds

B.G. BONNALLACK
Dunkirk (extract)

DAVID BOURNE
St. Valery – May 1940

JOHN BUXTON
The Tarn

WILLIAM CLARKE
Military Cemetery

G.E. COCKER
Nickel Raid – 1940

JACK LINDSAY
Squadding

K.W. PARKHURST
The Padre

FRANCIS SCARFE
25-Pounder

GERVASE STEWART
Parting

DOUGLAS STREET
We're gonna set fire to the Sea
Non-Walking wounded will be
 left with civilians where possible

2 *Middle East*

MARTIN BELL (per Peter Porter)
Reason for Refusal

JOCELYN BROOKE
Landscape Near Tobruk

HAMISH HENDERSON
Seven Good Germans

E.D. JORDAN (from
Phantasmagoria, Septentrio)
Maqil: I wanna go home
Western Desert: Aftermath

**SOMHAIRLE MACGILL-EAIN
(SORLEY MACLEAN)**
Heroes (Curaidhean)
An Autumn Day (Latha Foghair)

H.B. MALLALIEU
State of Readiness

WILLIAM E. MORRIS
The Captured

CHARLES SMITH
Field Hospital
Casualties

TERENCE TILLER
Lecturing to Troops
Flying to Tripoli

FRANK THOMPSON
Day's Journey

N.J. TRAPNELL
Lament of a Desert Rat

JAMES WALKER
From Portrait And Background

3 *Home Front*

STEPHANIE BATSTONE
Poem

R.P. Brett
Point of View

D. Van den Bogaerde
Steel Cathedrals

Elsie Cawser
Salvage Song

Robert L. Chaloner
Home Front: 1942

William Clarke (from *Shades of Khaki and other poems*, Harry Chambers/Peterloo Poets)
Return to Base

G. Haslett Connor
Remembrance Sonnet, 1941

M.J. Corfield
First Night In Barracks
I Didn't Believe It. . .
Morse Lesson

N.K. Cruickshank
Posting

Madge Donald
Sonnet: To Albert In A Pub on New Year's Eve

Keith Foottit
Two Pairs of Shoes

Wilfred Gibson
The Shelter (extract)
The Morass
He Took Like Easy. . .

George T. Gillespie
Promotion

John H. Goss
Lance Corporal

Grace Griffiths
Doodlebugs

Charles Hamblett
Bombs on my Town

W.J. Harvey
Maps
Portsmouth

Desmond Hawkins
Night Raid

F.A. Horn (sent by Mrs Irene Horn)
Reveille – 1943
Train Piece – 1943

Stuart Hoskins
Polish Airman

Patricia Ledward
From Air-Raid Casualties: Ashridge Hospital

Geoffrey Matthews
Nocturne
Embarkation Song

Neil McCallum
Stand-To

James Monahan
Kentish Lines in War

Kenneth Smith
A Rose By Any Other Name

David Stafford Clark
Casualty

A.H. Watkins
The Tragic mystery of Corporal Plum

4 *N. Africa, Italy & Balkans*

J.E. Brookes
Thermopylae 1941

George Campbell Hay
Bizerta
Mokhtar is Dughal (extract) (per Professor Thomson, Glasgow University)

Les Cleveland
Cassino (extract)

Erik De Mauny
Morning After Battle

Reg T. Gilchrist
Sand Fly Fever
Malta 1942

Robin Ivy
Soldiers at Capracotta.
Appennines

GWENYTH HAYES
This Italy

SEAN JENNETT
Mahoney

EDWARD LINSTEAD
On The Troop-Deck

UYS KRIGE
Midwinter

JAMES MCADAM CLARK
The Capture of Rome

SPIKE MILLIGAN
The Soldiers At Lauro

A.F. NOBLE
When The Heat Is On

HAROLD V.S. PAGE
Epitaph

LYALL WILKES
Troopship: 1942

ANONYMOUS
Ballad of Anzio

ANONYMOUS
The Highland Division's
Farewell To Sicily

5 *Air*

L.O.C. CHAVE
There Are No Frontiers in the
Sky

E. DENYER COX
Elegy

P. HEATH
We, The Bombers

THOMAS RAHILLEY HODGSON
Searchlights over Berlin

REDMOND MACDONOGH
Heil Hamburg, Forty One
Epitaph for Johnny Brown
To Germany Three Nights a
Week

ANTHONY RICHARDSON
Kit And Effects
Address To The Mother Of A
Dead Observer

ANONYMOUS
The Gremlins

6 *Sea*

LIZBETH DAVID
Air Sea Rescue
Sunday Watch (extract)

W.D. DUNKERLEY
Honour

NORMAN HAMPSON
Foreign Commission
Assault Convoy

C.A. JONES
Shipbound

JOHN MOORE – (sent by Lucile
Bell)
Carrier Off Norway

KENNETH MOULD
Night Clothing

HUGH POPHAM
Against the Lightning

J.H. SCHOFIELD
Ode To A Steam Fly
Snippet

HERBERT SMITH
Convoy 1943 (After An Attack)

JOHN WEDGE
Still No Letter
Convoy Episode

7 *Normandy to Berlin*

E.G.C. BECKWITH – (from *The
Wind in the Wire*)
Innocence (28 July 1943)
Night Bombers

MICHAEL DAVIS
Winter In Holland

MELVILLE HARDIMENT
Holed-Up Cyclops
A Man of Few Words
Poor Dead Panzer

P.A. HYATT
The Weeping Beeches of
Sonnenberg

JOHN BUXTON HILTON
Armistice
Rest On Your Arms Reversed
Belsen
Valkenswaard Cemetery

GEOFFREY HOLLOWAY
Airborne Log

JIM HOVELL
Distant Destinations
Landscape With Tanks

ROBIN IVY
S.E.P. (Surrendered Enemy
Personnel)

F.E. MACÉ
The Padre
Belson

ALEXANDER MCKEE
The Question
Maple Leaf Down

JOHN A. OTTEWELL
'Evrecy' July 1944

MICHAEL RIVIERE
Eichstatt, 1943
Oflag Night Piece, Colditz

LARRY ROWDON
Counterpoint
Divertimento

P.M.B. SAVAGE
For A Friend

DOUGLAS STREET
Love Letters of the Dead – A
Commando Intelligence
Briefing

SIDNEY TAYLOR
Collaboration?

GERRY WELLS
Jones

8 South East Asia & Pacific

TOM BEAUMONT
Range Discipline at Rawalpindi

MARTIN BELL
Three Days: The War Ends
(sent by Peter Porter)

STEVEN BRACHER
14th Army

CLIVE BRANSON
Untitled

G.A.G. BROOKE
Home thoughts from Abroad,
9th May, 1945.

PAUL BUDDEE (from *Stand To
and other war poems*)
Relativity

DOUGLAS COLE
Fragments

JOHN DURNFORD
Lying Awake At Night
Prisoner of War Mail

GEORGE T. GILLESPIE
Sleeping

L.R.V. GIBSON
Police Report

R.C.M. HOWARD
The Voyage Back

EDWARD LOWBURY
The Soldier
August 10th 1945 (from
Equator, the Mombassa Arts
Club, December 1945.)

J.F. MCGREGOR (Burma Star
Association, J.F. Oliver)
Rice

W.A. MURRAY
The Desolate Market

EUGENE D. MORGAN
A Prisoner Dies. . . .

VERNON POWELL
Mr. and Mrs. Mosquite

ROGER ROTHWELL
A Prayer For Food
Another Prayer For Food

JOHN SIBLY
I Shall Come Limping Back To You

IVOR ROBERTS-JONES
Battalion H.Q. Burma

JOHN CHARLES SHARP
The Night-Walker's Complaint

LESLIE SPOONER
Burma: Reflections

JOHN SMITH
Private Mathy's Teeth

G. STEWART-PETER
Organisation: GHQ Delhi

C.L. WILKNER
The General
The Charger

ANONYMOUS
Lines To The Censor

ANONYMOUS
Jungle Night 15 June '45

Index of Poets